Innovative Education and Training for Care Professionals

of related interest

Handbook of Theory for Practice Teachers in Social Work
Edited by Joyce Lishman
ISBN 1 85302 098 2 pb

The Changing Role of Social Care
Edited by Bob Hudson
ISBN 1 85302 752 9

Practice Teaching – Changing Social Work
Edited by Hilary Lawson
ISBN 1 85302 478 3 pb

Competence in Social Work Practice
Edited by Kieran O'Hagan
ISBN 1 85302 332 9 pb

The Essential Groupworker
Teaching and Learning Creative Groupwork
Mark Doel and Catherine Sawdon
ISBN 1 85302 823 1

Learning and Teaching in Social Work
Towards Reflective Practice
Edited by Margaret Yelloly and Mary Henkel
ISBN 1 85302 237 3 pb

The Working of Social Work
Edited by Juliet Cheetham and Mansoor Kazi
ISBN 1 85302 498 8 pb

Negotiation for Health and Social Service Professionals
Keith Fletcher
ISBN 1 85302 549 6 pb

Observation and its Application to Social Work
Rather Like Breathing
Edited by Karen Tanner and Pat Le Riche
ISBN 1 85302 623 9 pb

Social Workers, the Community and Social Interaction
Intervention and the Sociology of Welfare
John Offer
ISBN 1 85302 731 6 pb

Innovative Education and Training for Care Professionals

A Providers' Guide

Edited by Rachel Pierce and Jenny Weinstein

Jessica Kingsley Publishers
London and Philadelphia

First published in the United Kingdom in 2000 by
Jessica Kingsley Publishers Ltd,
116 Pentonville Road, London
N1 9JB, England
and
325 Chestnut Street,
Philadelphia PA 19106, USA.

www.jkp.com

© Copyright 2000 Jessica Kingsley Publishers

Library of Congress Cataloging in Publication Data
Innovative education and training for care professionals : a provider's guide / edited by Rachel Pierce and Jenny Weinstein.
      p.   cm
Includes bibliographical references and index.
ISBN 1 85302 613 1 (alk. paper)
    1. Social work education -- Great Britain. 2. Social work education. 3. Human services personnel--Training of--Great Britain. 4. Human services personnel--Training of. 5. Human services personnel--In-service training--Great Britain. 6. Human services personnel--In-service training. I. Pierce, Rachel, 1933–   II. Weinstein, Jenny, 1947–
HV11.8.G7I56   1999   99-41652
361.3'071'041--dc21   CIP

British Library Cataloguing in Publication Data
Innovative education and training for care professionals : a provider's guide
    1. Social service – Great Britain 2. Social workers – Training of – Great Britain
3. Social work education – Great Britain
I. Pierce, Rachel II. Weinstein, Jenny
361.3'2'0941

ISBN 1 85302 613 1

Printed and Bound in Great Britain by
Athenaeum Press, Gateshead, Tyne and Wear

Contents

CHAPTER I

The Changing Context of Professional Education

Rachel Pierce and Jenny Weinstein

Introduction

This book is a collection of individual accounts addressing different aspects of education and training for care professionals. All the authors draw from their learning, teaching, research and practice. Within a shared commitment, there has been no attempt to prescribe a particular 'line'. It would probably, however, be fair to say that all the contributors share the editors' distaste for the commercialization of welfare and the right-wing backlash which has scapegoated social work, and to a lesser extent other care professions.

Some authors set out their proposals for innovative education and training in the context of a critical overview, while others argue their position through the presentation of more detailed case studies. All seek to enhance the providers' active role in developing innovative education and training and the involvement in this role, of all parties – tutors, practitioners, users, assessors and students.

While most of the authors draw their material primarily from social work, connections are made with, and the implications drawn for, other care professional training. This chapter dwells almost exclusively on key developments in social work education, particularly on the role of the Central Council for Education and Training in Social Work (CCETSW), its achievements and shortcomings. However, the issues will undoubtedly resonate and provide a useful basis for comparison for other care professions.

In order to understand the challenges presented to professional social work education, and to place the achievements described in this book in context, it is necessary to consider the rapid changes to which social work was subject during the last decades of the twentieth century. Aldridge (1996 p.182) asks 'If a profession is so tenacious, why can it not be more successful?' This book sets out to demonstrate both tenacity and success. By the time it is published, General Social Care and Social Services Councils will be established: first and foremost, to safeguard the interests of service users; second, to ensure high standards and an improved image for social work and social work education.

The role of social work in society has always been controversial and ambiguous. Parton (1995 p.4) suggests that these upheavals 'reflect much wider and fundamental changes in the state, the economy and society more generally.' Dominelli (1996 p.153) goes further by saying that 'social work is changing in response to major societal shifts – the globalisation of the economy, the internationalisation of the nation state and the fragmentation of society into isolated individuals and groups'.

The impact of these worldwide phenomena is affecting all the welfare professions, not just social work. Doctors, nurses, therapists and teachers are also finding that the shifts of emphasis in their roles, from delivery of direct care to fundholding, purchasing, budgeting and managing, have caused conflict, demoralization and identity problems. These developments in the field have inevitably led to controversies about the content and delivery of professional education (Jackson and Preston-Shoot 1996; RCGP 1994; Watkins, Drury and Preddy 1992; Webb 1992).

Social work is a complex generic term for which Payne (1996) identifies five separate contexts: its underlying concepts and theories; its roles and responsibilities for implementing a range of laws and social policies; its organizational contexts; occupational groupings; and forms of education. At the turn of the millennium, social work and all its different contexts are in the midst of transformation.

New legislation, the breaking down of barriers between health and social care and the diminishing role of local authority social services departments as direct service providers have led to significant changes in the roles and responsibilities of social workers. Recruitment to social work and other care professional training, which had dropped following the devaluing of the public sector that occurred during the Thatcher years, was further reduced with the introduction of tuition fees in 1998. The replacement of CCETSW by a combination of National Training Organizations and General Social Care and Social Services Councils will have a significant impact on occupational groupings and forms of education.

At this critical time it is important to learn from good practice; to seek to understand why things developed the way they did, appraising strengths and weaknesses, in order to provide a sound analysis on which to shape new arrangements. It is also a good moment to review and restate with clarity and confidence the fundamental values of social work, which were continually challenged and undermined during the 1980s and 1990s.

We have tried to pull out enduring issues, debates, principles and values that will remain relevant within the changing environment. The themes that recur throughout the book include: the transition to more user-centred services and user involvement in education and training; the integration of anti-racist and anti-discriminatory practice into the delivery of services and education; the need to improve interprofessional collaboration; the importance of learning and assessment in the workplace as well as in the university; the bridging of gaps between theory and practice; the relationships between pre-qualifying, qualifying and continuing education; the link between generic training and competence in practice specialisms; and the need for care professionals to be more research minded, continually reflecting on and evaluating their practice to make it more evidenced based and in line with quality standards.

In order to set the scene, our introduction aims to provide a brief reminder about the historical context of social work education.

Developments in Social Work Education

There has never been a truly halcyon period for social work education, never certainty, mirroring the ambiguous role of social work in society and its response to changing needs. The brief historical references instanced below resonate with contemporary issues. They locate the historical involvement in social work education and training of employers, educationalists, professional associations, training bodies, government departments; all with legitimate interest in professional training, but seeking to have power over it, at times, to the detriment of other interests. The voices of users have been largely missing, until the present, along with sound evidence from researched-based practice.

It was employers – Charles Locke and the Charity Organisation Society (COS) – who led the way, from the Society's inception in 1869, in providing social work education, mainly casework (Richmond 1917), for its voluntary and paid workers (Marshall 1975; Mowat 1961). The COS also campaigned for the introduction of social work training in the universities and had a major influence on the curricula adopted by the LSE and the other university social science departments that followed. There were, however, early concerns in academia about the vocational nature of such courses and they rapidly became more academic (Hartsthorn 1982). The professional associations, such as the Hospital Almoner's Council (1906), responded by setting up their own supplementary courses outside the universities providing specialized training for their own client groups.

The growing doubts about the precise role of the universities and the increase in training schemes outside them, were probably incentives for the formation of the Joint Universities Council (JUC) for Social Studies in 1918, with its Social Work Education Committee (SWEC) from 1950 (Hartsthorn 1982). The JUC was advisory and after World War II provided a channel of communication between the universities and the various bodies responsible for specialist training – the various professional associations, the Ministry of Health and the Home Office. With the post-war welfare state legislation, government departments and their training boards played an increasingly powerful role, which was exerted through their direct funding of training and of students.

Eileen Younghusband was, however, to articulate growing professional concerns in her report in 1947: 'The conclusion of any general survey of preparation for social work seems to be that the situation has got out of hand. Academic freedom, coupled with the rich luxuriance of professional training bodies, has led to something approaching chaos' (Younghusband 1951, para 309; Hartsthorn 1982 p.2). She saw the university social science courses as 'of good academic standing, but weak on the practical side', while the professional courses emphasized practical experience, but made no significant contribution to the general body of knowledge, nor did they 'continue the students' education in basic principles' (Younghusband 1951, para 195; Hartsthorn 1982, p.4).

Her ideas bore fruit, with support from the JUC, the professional associations and the government training bodies, culminating in the first generic case-work course experiment at the LSE, from 1954 (Hartsthorn 1982). This was to become the dominant pattern of postgraduate social work training, very much in the North American tradition. There is also evidence (Hartsthorn 1982) that although recognition was given to the need for specialization, the United Nations Social Commission believed that the emphasis should be on generic basic training. So Britain's move to the generic pattern as the basis of postgraduate social work education was in line with wider international trends.

Another cornerstone was laid when the Younghusband Report into local authority health and welfare services (Ministry of Health 1959) identified a plethora of specialist services and less than a hundred social workers with a recognized qualification. Training was seen as the key to change and two-year, non-graduate courses for older students were initiated in colleges of higher and further education, outside the universities. This development – a revolution at the time – led to colleges producing more qualified social workers than the universities within ten years.

Sinfield (1970) argues that the influence of psychiatry and psychoanalysis on social work, following from the American influence and often referred to as the 'psychoanalytic deluge', was responsible for neutralizing the profession's social conscience. This conscience, always present in the other main influence on social work in the UK – the settlement movement – was soon, however, to be restored. The rediscovery of poverty in the 1960s, the growing influence of sociology on social work education and new developments such as the sociology of deviance all contributed to a broader theoretical grounding. Understanding how class and poverty affected life chances gained momentum from the earlier emphasis on individual pathology.

For some, the 1960s period of generic training, when social work still meant case work, is perceived as an idealized era of social work education and of the establishment of social work as a profession, or at least a semi-profession. It had found a knowledge base, not just for social diagnosis but also for intervention and treatment. This new-found professional confidence was to be influential in the Seebohm committee rec-ommendations to establish unified social services departments (HMSO 1968); in the campaign by social workers for their implementation; in the establishment of the British Association of Social Workers (BASW); and in the co-ordination of all social work training under the auspices of the Central Council for Education and Training in Social Work (CCETSW).

Central Council for Education and Training in Social Work (CCETSW)

Introduction

From its foundation in 1971, CCETSW attempted to bring together professional, academic, employment and government interests and to reconcile their sometimes conflicting concerns. It is not surprising that this was an uphill battle and, retrospectively, a virtually impossible task.

From its inception CCETSW was government funded, but initially a Council of elected representatives guaranteed its status as an independent statutory body, with the duty to promote training in social work, to approve courses and with powers to conduct examinations and to carry out research into matters relevant to training. However, from 1983 onwards, government gradually constrained its independent status by reducing the number of Council members and by directly appointing them.

The Council was berated from all sides and could never please everyone. Some colleagues believed that if social work training continued to focus on case work and counselling skills (Yelloly and Henkel 1995), or on the sociological and political causes of hardship (Novak 1995), that the changes in the social work role and the new systems of service delivery would somehow disappear. CCETSW was directly blamed by some for the introduction of the market into social services (Jones 1997). On the other hand, the Conservative government accused the Council of putting political correctness before the needs of the service (Bottomley 1994). It is to CCETSW's credit that social work training managed to adapt to the new forms of service delivery and the changing context of higher education (HE), while social work values remained enshrined in social work training requirements at all levels.

In preparation for the new social services departments that were established in the early 1970s, CCETSW's first task was to bring together a plethora of different generic and specialist social work training courses into one generic qualification. In 1971 it approved the Certificate of Qualification in Social Work (CQSW), which was higher education based, lasting one or two years, depending on whether candidates held a relevant degree. CCETSW's next task was to bring together the training and qualifications for those working in residential care, in day care and community work. In 1976 it approved the Certificate in Social Service (CSS) – a two-year, in-service education and training programme, which was offered at further education (FE) level.

In spite of its dubious academic status, the CSS proved to be a popular model of training which successfully pioneered effective co-operation between agencies and education institutions, initiated modular patterns of education and training and produced satisfied customers in the form of employers and certificate holders. In contrast, many students who had been trained on more academically rigorous CQSW courses, felt themselves unprepared and deskilled very shortly after arriving in their first jobs.

Campaign for three-year training

Consultations with educational, professional and employment interests about the future of these two qualifications were initiated in late 1981. It was not until 1987 that proposals were eventually presented to government (CCETSW 1987), for a three-year Qualifying Diploma in Social Work (QDSW), comprising a two-year generic foundation and a third year of 'special emphasis'. (This model mirrored project 2000 in nursing which provides an 18-month generic foundation followed by an 18-month specialist training). The proposed QDSW combined the most successful elements of CSS:

- partnership with agencies
- opportunity to concentrate on a particular service user group
- flexible access via opportunities for employment and part-time routes

with the key strengths of CQSW:

- a generic social work qualification
- firm roots within higher education to ensure the acquisition of knowledge at an appropriately critical and analytical level
- rigorous assessment systems and processes linking professional and academic qualifications.

At the core of the QDSW proposals was a 'Statement of Minimum Requirements of the Social Worker at the Point of Qualification' (CCETSW 1988). This was the first attempt by a statutory body to bring together the key interests (professional, academic and employment) to focus on and gain agreement to the knowledge, values and skill requirements for a professional qualification. All endorsed the outcome, formally and in writing. It is significant to note that service users were missing from the key interests involved. Their crucial role in social work education was not recognized at all then, and indeed is only gradually being recognized and taken forward now (see Hastings, Chapter 6).

By 1988 CCETSW was coming under ever tighter budgetary and policy control exercised by government. The essential reforms that CCETSW and all its constituents had agreed on were rejected as 'too expensive'. Government refused to lengthen social work training to three years, to raise the social work qualification to a graduate level award, to the standard of all other caring professions and to European standards. It is salutary to reflect on the impact of the government's decision and that decisions of such importance should be made by government and not by the profession.

The introduction of DipSW

Instead, a two-year Diploma in Social Work (DipSW) was introduced (CCETSW 1989), with many of the key features described above. However, in a two-year programme it was inevitable that the qualification would fail to meet the high expectations which had been raised during the consultations.

Could CCETSW and the social work interests have done more to avert this catastrophic decision? With hindsight, there may have been too much emphasis on the need for three-year training, rather than on the need for a graduate academic level award and research-minded practitioners, to achieve the desired improvement in social work standards. Damaging professional and academic consequences remain. These have been set out elsewhere (Michael Sieff Foundation 1995) and more recently (the JUC/SWEC response to the DipSW Consultation 1999). They include:

1. The lack of adequate time:
   - for preparation for the complexities of the social work task and the depth of analysis required
   - for acquiring the breadth and complexity of the knowledge base to inform decision making
   - to develop the skills of critical appraisal and critical thinking.

2. The status of the qualification, its lack of comparability with other health care professionals (Chapter 13)

3. The international and particularly the European implications for the interchange of qualifications (Chapters 2 and 3)

4. The knock-on effect for the academic levels of the Post-Qualifying Award in Social Work (PQSW) and the Advanced Award in Social Work (AASW).

To amplify this final point, the current situation is anomalous with the two-year DipSW being offered at DipHE, Bachelor and Masters levels. If the DipSW was at minimum graduate level, the post-qualifying award in social work (PQSW) could be at minimum Masters level and the Advanced Award (AASW) at the pre-requisite level for a PhD dissertation. This would provide the incentive for promoting doctorate social work research and a stimulus to the enhancement of social work as a knowledge, research-led practice discipline in the universities (Pierce 1998).

Anti-racism

During the 1980s the black community found a voice to protest about the racist nature of social services provision (Dominelli 1996). A particular concern was the child-care system where black children were over-represented but which was run almost entirely by white people (Ahmed, Cheetham and Small 1986). The importance of bringing black people into the profession at all levels began to be recognized and equal opportunities policies were introduced into social services departments in inner city areas and into some colleges.

The requirements of the new DipSW reflected changes in legislation and service delivery and incorporated knowledge, skills and values which, for the first time, were described in terms of learning outcomes. One of the most radical and controversial components was a specific statement on the nature of individual and institutional racism (CCETSW 1991, Annex 5). It is significant, in retrospect, that this statement for which CCETSW was so severely criticized was fully justified by the Stephen Lawrence Inquiry

(HMSO 1999) and the term *institutional racism* is at last being recognized and understood.

With hindsight it is not surprising that, at the time, mainly white educators and trainers found it difficult to implement the new anti-racist requirements. Relevant literature and training workshops were only just beginning to raise awareness before social work was pilloried for political correctness by the media and by government. This difficult period culminated in DH prematurely requiring a review of the DipSW in 1994 and seriously setting back social work's anti-racist development work. Aymer in Chapter 8 reflects on the background and proposes ways of taking this vital work forward.

Continuum of education and training

CCETSW had made some early, but not very successful, attempts to address the training needs of the wider social services workforce and the post-qualifying training needs of social workers. Its range of certificates, mainly in-service courses for the largely untrained workforce in social care, had made little inroads. When it became clear that only a major employment-based initiative could succeed, the Council saw the potential of the competence-based vocational revolution. CCETSW became a member of the Care Sector Consortium, the lead body for vocational qualifications in care, from its inception in 1987 and was accredited by the National Council for Vocational Qualifications as an awarding body. CCETSW's early post-qualifying studies (from 1980) had also only a minimal take-up in the universities, so the need for an employment linked scheme for qualified social workers was, likewise, recognized and in 1990 CETSW approved the Framework for Continuing Professional Development (CCETSW 1990).

In the past there was no clear educational progression for social care staff; it had been difficult for care workers to become qualified social workers. This changed when CCETSW recognized and promoted vocational qualifications in care at level 3 as an entry point to the DipSW from which social workers could then proceed, on a progressive continuum, to post-qualifying and/or advanced awards.

Government's premature review of the DipSW

By the beginning of the 1990s most local authorities had reorganized into specialist departments providing either services for children and families or services for adults. Newly qualified social workers were expected to pick up a caseload of child protection cases or to act as competent care managers. Employers said that the new DipSW still did not prepare social workers for practice. The government said it was 'too political'. In the meantime, some universities found it too prescriptive and insufficiently theoretical. The debate about whether there should be a more specialist or a more generic approach to the qualification continued in all quarters with strong lobbies for specialist qualifications for residential child care and (from the Home Office) for probation training.

At the same time, competence-based education and training (Mansfield and Mitchell 1996) was making strong headway. Lead industry bodies and consultants using functional analysis methodology were involved in developing national occupational standards as the basis for assessment of competence in the workplace. There was a missionary zeal among the proponents who saw the future in terms of the vocational qualifications framework – as the one overriding framework – to which education could contribute the underpinning knowledge base. These enthusiasts envisaged the same process for higher professional levels, thus bypassing or supplanting the academic framework. It was in this context that CCETSW was required by government to review the DipSW.

In many ways social work education and training was in advance of these developments. CCETSW had already led the way in bringing together educational, employment and professional interests and, since 1989, had required higher education institutions (HEIs) to work together in partnership with social service agencies in providing the DipSW.

CCETSW has been criticized for tempering – ahead of other professions – with the moves towards competence-based qualifications (see Dominelli, Chapter 2). Certainly, there were legitimate concerns about the lack of sufficient emphasis on research and critical thinking. On the other hand, the interests of service users and the demands of employment interests had to be taken into account. Pragmatically, it was clear that the competency movement was here to stay, at least for the foreseeable future. Many professions, resistant to the NVQ framework, have subsequently recognized that the competence approach – appropriately transformed at the professional level – can make a contribution to education and training. It can demystify professional practice and clarify what service users can expect from professionals.

Thus, closely scrutinized by government, the revised DipSW requirements, based on rapidly developed draft national occupational standards, sought to bridge the professional, academic and vocational frameworks. Despite misunderstandings of academics at the time, a 'telephone directory' of performance criteria was avoided and the revised requirements of the DipSW (CCETSW 1995) were rationalized as six core competences with a specified knowledge base and a statement of values. CCETSW's definition described competence in social work as 'practice founded on values, carried out in a skilled manner and informed by knowledge, critical analysis and reflection' (CCETSW 1995, p.17; 1996, p.17). It is this definition which also underpins the post-qualifying awards in social work (CCETSW 1990, 1997).

Despite many continuing criticisms of this approach (Horder 1998), it also has its defenders (Gonczi 1994; O'Hagan 1997; Winter and Maisch 1996). The 1999 consultations on the DipSW and PQ, the evolving work of the national training organizations (NTOs) and the plans for the general social care/service councils (GSCC and GSSC), suggest that qualifications based on outcome standards, expressible as occupational standards, are the direction of the future.

The 'politically correct' language with respect to anti-racism, so hated by the right wing, was modified with much pain and anger from committed anti-racists in the field of social work education and practice. The wording changed from *demonstrating ways … to combat racism … through antiracist practice* (CCETSW 1989, p.16) to *demonstrate action to counter … racism … using strategies appropriate to role and context* (CCETSW 1995, p.18). The statement about institutional racism was lost. Nevertheless, the assessment requirements were strengthened from the aspirational intentions of Paper 30 (CCETSW 1989, p.24) to the clear requirements of the revised DipSW (CCETSW 1995, p.48) that social work values had to be demonstrated in the student's evidence of all six competences.

The revised DipSW sought, yet again, to meet the educational grounds for a generic professional qualification and the very real practice grounds for students to develop competence in particular areas of practice. While the six competences, underpinning knowledge and values were non-negotiable, they could be demonstrated by students following either general or particular pathways through the diploma. Pathway guidance was incorporated for probation training (Pierce 1996) and produced later for a range of aspects including child care/residential child care and adult services.

CCETSW's 1994–5 DipSW review strategy and methodology are recounted elsewhere by Doherty and Pierce (1999) and Pierce (1996) who argue that its bold move to work in partnership with the Occupational Standards Council, and to adopt an incorporative strategy achieved a number of significant aims:

- At a time of uncertainty for the future of social work, it achieved continued employment support for the DipSW as the professional qualification for a career in social work and kept the DipSW firmly rooted in higher education, thereby continuing to bridge professional and academic frameworks.

- It secured the DipSW as part of the progressive continuum of qualifications for social work and social care, thus also bridging the vocational framework.

- By bringing professional, academic and vocational frameworks together and focusing on learning outcomes, it increased opportunities for flexibility, for different routes to the required standards, and for recognition of prior learning, whether in college or the workplace (see Croton, Chapter 12 and Baldwin and Ennis, Chapter 14). It thus increased opportunities for qualifying, post-qualifying, and potentially inter-professional learning and assessment.

While acknowledging these strengths, there were also problems with the strategy. It was unfortunate that government's premature demand for a review of the DipSW meant that it was not possible to undertake it in association with other care professional training bodies. This could have enhanced collaborative working inter-professionally and demonstrated the value, already recognized by the other professional training bodies, of a graduate level professional qualification.

Although it was important to win employers' support for social work training, CCETSW's preoccupation with this meant that insufficient priority was given to the importance of academic standards and of research for achieving professional standards. The transformation of institutional arrangements, resulting in complex bureaucratic DipSW partnerships and PQ consortia, was made by CCETSW without sufficient regard for the consequences. In retrospect, a simpler approach with joint arrangements for the qualifying and post-qualifying levels may have been more successful (Chapters 3 and 5 discuss the pros and cons of partnership arrangements).

Structure of the Book

Our aim in this opening chapter has been to extract continuing themes and analyse failures and successes and to encourage all interested parties to influence the new, post-CCETSW arrangements so that the highest standards of qualifications, education and training in social work and social care can be assured.

Chapter 2 begins with an overview of the international scene. Dominelli addresses the impact of globalization on social work practice. She sets out the implications for social work education, the challenge to raise it above its current parochial focus, to integrate international perspectives, to develop international exchanges and practice placements and to harmonize qualifications. The chapter emphasizes two recurring themes of the book:

that human rights and involvement of users must be at the centre of social work education.

Rowlings in Chapter 3 continues the broad canvas as she considers European comparisons of social work education. She then analyses the relationships between social work education, social work practice and the essential contribution of HE. The chapter reflects critically on partnership requirements, the demands on resources and the problems of quality assuring practice placements.

Cheetham in Chapter 4 endorses the contribution of research to social work education as she addresses the profession's long-standing research deficit and social work education's failure to produce research-minded practitioners. Most importantly, she sets out practical ways of guiding providers to incorporate research and involve users in research.

Kemp, Chapter 5, provides a very positive view of collaboration in a reflective case study of a college and agency DipSW partnership that has worked really well. She analyses why and looks ahead to the inclusion of users in its future development.

Chapter 6 is seminal. Hastings sets out with clarity and conviction that services will not be appropriate for users until care professionals really understand the essential qualities of respect for users, based on equality. This will be achieved when users participate fully in the design, teaching, assessment and evaluation of training courses. Hastings helpfully addresses many of the problems user involvement is said to pose for providers.

Wilkes, in Chapter 7, takes up the theme. Quality assurance systems are here; but, rather than being subject to them, professionals should have a responsibility for their own closer involvement and for the representation of the users of their services. Wilkes demonstrates opportunities for this management-derived process to be used to monitor and improve the quality of social work education when its participants – tutors and students – become active in the process.

Aymer in Chapter 8 reviews the background to anti-racist training in social work and analyses the problems it has faced in a hostile environment. She shares her own experience as a social work tutor over many years and recommends successful strategies for teaching and developing anti-racist and anti-discriminatory practice in the college or workplace.

In Chapter 9, a case study of one DipSW programme, Weinstein analyses the procedures adopted for selecting students onto the programme and compares them with other care professional programmes at the same university. In his investigation of high failure rates, he identifies the vulnerability of non-traditional students and the importance of providing adequate support systems to retain them through to successful completion.

Doel in Chapter 10 analyses innovations in practice teaching and learning. He charts the progress from an implicit to an explicit practice curriculum and from implicit to explicit criteria for assessment of competence to practice. He illustrates his guidance with useful case examples and looks forward to increased involvement of users in the teaching and assessment of students.

Preston-Shoot in Chapter 11 sets out to demolish some of the intellectual and psychological barriers that have previously characterized the relationship between social work and the law. He outlines a tripartite definition of social work law on which an academic curriculum can be based. He illustrates his text with practical guidance for providers, including case examples and scenarios.

In Chapter 12 Croton argues that the assessment of professional competence – taking account of its impact on public credibility, professional status and job reservation – requires clear structures and explicit criteria, which are valid and reliable. She provides guidance on all the essential elements, whether college or workbased, which must be subject to independent and external scrutiny. Her messages for the future are: the need to involve service users in assessment; and to develop credible and workable arrangements for inter-professional learning and assessment.

Chapter 13 takes up the inter-professional challenge. Lowe and Weinstein review progress in inter-professional collaboration in educational and practice settings. They analyse the barriers that can impede joint working and propose key strategies to overcome them. The chapter advocates attention to 'training the trainers' and emphasizes an approach that involves users at all stages and provides students with specific competences – knowledge, skills and values – for collaborative practice.

The book concludes with Chapter 14 on lifelong learning for care professionals. Baldwin and Ennis see lifelong learning as a necessary response to the growing pressures of globalization and the need for a better trained, more highly skilled and flexible workforce – the issues raised by Dominelli in Chapter 2. Experience of continuing change in the field of social care, exemplified throughout the book, demonstrates the need for continuing professional development, the need to underpin improvements in the quality of services through lifelong learning. Baldwin and Ennis identify priorities for moving from vision to reality.

Future Agenda

Together, the messages of this book provide an agenda for the twenty-first century. We urge that any future regulatory bodies with responsibility for social work education should represent all the interests – of service users, academics, employers, practitioners and students – and not be dominated by any one interested party, particularly government.

We urge that qualifying training be at graduate level, accessed by those with relevant experience and academic qualifications or potential, or by progression with relevant VQs. This should be followed by an important first year of protected employment and appraisal, prior to registration with the GSCC and GSSC. All qualifying workers should then progress towards a Masters level post-qualifying award, some should progress further to an advanced award, of whom some should then register for PhD research and dissertations. Workers of all levels should be involved in lifelong learning. These various stages of training and qualifications will, we hope, provide the time and opportunities to address the continuing generic and specialism requirements for competent practice.

The innovations discussed in this book – educational models of practice learning, research-minded preparation for practice, rigorous assessment of professional competence etc. – could together significantly improve education and training, but only if users are involved at the centre of its provision. Providers must also continue to give their commitment to anti-racist and anti-discriminatory practice, to the preparation of students for competent reflective practice and high standards of service delivery. All those involved – tutors, practice teachers, assessors, students, users, as well as managers and the new regulatory councils – will need to be actively engaged in quality assuring the provision and achieving successful opportunities and outcomes for students and service users.

This agenda for the twenty-first century continues to endorse the need for competence in the law and for the services of each national jurisdiction, and the need for competence in each of the individual care professions. However, we hope that the early years of the twenty-first century will see education and training established within an inter-professional context to achieve collaborative practice, and within an international context to achieve international recognition, harmonization and interchange of each profession's qualifications.

References

Ahmed, S., Cheetham, J. and Small, J. (1986) *Social Work with Black Children and their Families*. London: Batsford.

Aldridge, M. (1996) 'Dragged to market: being a profession in the postmodern world'. *British Journal of Social Work 26*, 177–194.

Bottomley, V. (1994) 'National core curriculum for social work training'. *Conservative Party News 137/94*, 26 February. London: Conservative Central Office.

CCETSW (1987) *Care for Tomorrow: The Case for Reform of Education and Training for Social Workers and other Care Staff.* London: CCETSW.

CCETSW (1988) *Statement of Minimum Requirements of the Social Worker at the Point of Qualification,* Paper 20.9. London: CCETSW.

CCETSW (1989) *DipSW Rules and Requirements for Social Work,* Paper 30. London: CCETSW.

CCETSW (1990) *The Requirements for Post Qualifying Education and Training in the Personal Social Services,* Paper 31. London: CCETSW.

CCETSW (1991) *DipSW Rules and Requirements for Social Work,* Paper 30, 2nd edn. London: CCETSW.

CCETSW (1995) *Assuring Quality in the Diploma in Social Work – 1 Rules and Requirements for the DipSW.* London: CCETSW.

CCETSW (1996) *Assuring Quality in the Diploma in Social Work – 1 Rules and Requirements for the DipSW,* Second Revision. London: CCETSW.

CCETSW (1997) *Assuring Quality for Post Qualifying Education and Training – 1.* London: CCETSW.

Doherty, G. and Pierce, R. (1999) 'Professional capability: a case study bridging vocational, academic and professional frameworks'. In D. O'Reilly, L. Cunningham and S. Lester (eds) *Developing the Capable Practioner.* London: Kogan Page.

Dominelli, L. (1996) 'Deprofessionalizing social work: anti-oppressive practice, competencies and postmodernism'. *British Journal of Social Work 26,* 153–175.

Gonczi, A. (1994) 'Competency based assessment in the professions in Australia'. *Assessment in Education 1,* 1, 27–44.

Hartsthorn, A.E. (1982) *Milestone in Education for Social Work: The Carnegie Experiment 1954–1958.* London: Carnegie United Kingdom Trust.

HMSO (1968) *Report of the Committee on Local Authority and Allied Personal Social Services (Seebohm Report),* Cm 3703. London: HMSO.

HMSO (1999) *The Stephen Lawrence Inquiry (Macpherson Report),* Cm 4262. London: HMSO.

Horder, W. (1998) 'Competence(s) without tears?' *Social Work Education 17,* 1,

Jackson, S. and Preston-Shoot, M. (eds) (1996) *Educating Social Workers in a Changing Policy Context.* London: Whiting and Birch.

Jones, C. (1997) 'The case against CCETSW'. *Issues in Social Work Education 17,* 1, 53–64.

JUC/SWEC (1999) *Response to JM Consulting Ltd: Review of the Content of the DipSW.* London: JUC/SWEC.

Mansfield, B. and Mitchell, L. (1996) *Towards a Competent Workforce.* London: Gower.

Marshall, T.H. (1975) *Social Policy in the Twentieth Century.* London: Hutchinson.

Michael Sieff Foundation (1995) *Towards Three Year Social Work Training: The Case for Change.* Surrey: Michael Sieff Foundation.

Ministry of Health (1959) *Report of the Working Party on Social Workers in the Local Authority Health and Welfare Services (Younghusband Report).* London: HMSO.

Mowat, C.L. (1961) *The Charity Organisation Society 1869–1913, Its Ideas and Work.* London: Methuen.

Novak, T. (1995) 'Thinking about a new social work curriculum'. *Social Work Education 14*, 4, 4–10.

O'Hagan, K. (ed) (1996) *Competence in Social Work Practice.* London: Jessica Kingsley Publishers.

Parton, N. (ed) (1995) *Social Theory, Social Change and Social Work.* London: Routledge.

Payne, M. (1996) *What is Professional Social Work?* Birmingham: Venture Press.

Pierce, R. (1996) 'Social work education under attack: the present and future of social work and probation education'. *Issues in Social Work Education 16*, 1, 64–76.

Pierce, R. (1998) 'Promoting student and practitioner demand for social work research findings'. *Issues in Social Work Education 18*, 2, 3–24.

RCGP (1994) *Re-evaluating General Practice.* London: Royal College of General Practitioners.

Richmond, M. (1917) *Social Diagnosis.* New York: Russell Sage Foundation.

Sinfield, A. (1970) 'Which way for social work?' In Fabian Society (ed) *The Fifth Social Service: A Critical Analysis of the Seebohm Proposals.* London: Fabian Society.

Watkins, J., Drury, L. and Preddy, D. (1992) *From Evolution to Revolution: The Pressures on Professional Life in the 1990s.* Bristol: University of Bristol in conjunction with Clerical Investment Group.

Webb, D. (1992) 'Competences, contracts and cadres: common themes in the social control of nurse and social work education'. *Journal of Interprofessional Care 6*, 3, 223–230.

Winter, R. and Maisch, M. (1996) *Professional Competence and Higher Education: The Accreditation of Social Services Experience and Training (ASSET) Programme.* London: Falmer Press.

Yelloly, M. and Henkel, M. (1995) *Learning and Teaching in Social Work: Towards Reflective Practice.* London: Jessica Kingsley Publishers.

Younghusband, E. (1951) *Social Work in Britain: A Supplementary Report on the Employment and Training of Social Workers.* Dunfermline: Carnegie United Kingdom Trust.

CHAPTER 2

International Comparisons in Social Work

Lena Dominelli

Introduction

Social work is undergoing a period of rapid change throughout the world. This change has been brought about through factors both external and internal to the profession. The external ones include forces such as the growth of the new social movements, the spread of new computer-based technology, the impact of a global economy on all areas of social life, the restructuring of the welfare state, and the different roles for social work within a market-driven economy. These forces have an international dimension, but they also operate in specific ways at the local level. The internal factors have focused on the changing nature of the profession as it struggles to raise its status, seeks to modernize itself and responds to increased managerial control over its activities.

Although there is a profession and a discipline called social work which is recognized worldwide, the meaning of this label varies according to national jurisdiction. Even organizations such as the International Association of Schools of Social Work (IASSW), which is the professional body for social work educators across the globe, has difficulty providing one description of the profession which applies everywhere. Similar difficulties have beset the International Federation of Social Workers (IFSW).

In this chapter I examine some of the trends that have affected the development of social work. I highlight those that are evident in the international domain and consider some of the responses which practitioners and educators have made in dealing with the profound changes occurring in social work education and practice in many parts of the globe. I also suggest that social work needs to become more rooted in human rights if it is to acquire greater legitimacy as an internationally relevant discipline.

Defining Social Work Internationally

With respect to definitions, there are difficulties in using language in ways that assume that words do not carry existing relations within them. The failure to secure neutrality need not be problematic in all cases. However, in certain situations, this problem is critical, even though the solution is not easy to find. The meanings attributed to the terms 'black people', 'indigenous people', 'race' and 'clients' are examples of where it does matter. These words are hotly contested and socially constructed. I use them in quotes to indicate their contested and heterogeneous nature.

The definition of what constitutes social work can vary considerably across different regions of the globe. Yet no directory has tracked these in a systematic manner. The International Association of Schools of Social Work (IASSW) has created a Commission on the World Census to undertake this task. It is expected to report on the subject at its Congress in Montreal in the year 2000. Meanwhile, it is recognized that different countries in Europe emphasize different elements within a social profession loosely defined as social work. For example, social pedagogy is a strong feature of German social work while 'animation' (an innovative educational approach) is prevalent in France. In other regions of the globe, for example, in parts of Latin America, conscientization movements (teaching people to understand the impact of power relations on life chances of different groups) are strong. In Zimbabwe, social development is a common approach to the social problems encountered there. In other countries, the 'indigenization movements' – the attempts of peoples to move away from western models of social work associated with colonialism – are gaining ground, for example, the Maori approach in New Zealand, the 'aboriginal model' in Australia, the First Nations perspectives in Canada and the Asian family model in Malaysia and Singapore.

Despite their differences, there are certain characteristics which these models share and which make the social work label an appropriate one to apply to them. Each is concerned with improving the well-being of their target groups and dealing with personal issues by locating the individual within his or her social situation. Moreover, by working in holistic ways, the practitioners elaborating these models seek to mediate the tensions that exist between the individual's definition of his or her needs and the resources available for meeting them, regardless of whether these are publicly supplied or privately purchased.

Additionally, in redefining social work, 'indigenous' movements have brought in some new questions for western-trained social work educators and practitioners to consider. One was to identify the importance of spirituality and holistic approaches to the intervention process. A second was to highlight the significance of the total institutional context within which social work practice occurs for both practitioner and 'client'. A third was to argue for the return of the individual to his or her own self-defined community base. This includes considering members of the extended family as parties with a legitimate interest in the work undertaken by social workers with any given person. They have also challenged the monolithic sway of the state and the legislative framework within which practitioners operate by demanding that their own specific cultural practices and views of the world provide the basis for social work interventions.

The attempts by different peoples throughout the world to create more locality relevant models of social work are exciting developments and stand to challenge the cultural hegemony accorded in the literature to clinical casework models formulated in the USA. Because they emphasize the unity between the individual, society and the environment, these alternative approaches may bring a new meaning to established social work tenets such as 'working with the person in their social environment'. The innovations inspired by these 'indigenization movements' are likely to become highly influential in the next century.

Moreover, their impact will be widespread. I expect their concerns to be relevant even in western countries where the dominant ideology leads people to consider themselves immune from such developments. I take this stance because 'indigenous' and 'black peoples' have successfully created their own unique forms of social work practice and theories. Some of these have already made major contributions to the rethinking of social work in western countries. For example, the Maori innovation of the family group conference has spread from New Zealand to England, Sweden and Canada as a particularly useful approach to working with children and families. The Latin American concepts of conscientization and emancipatory social work (enabling people to take control over their own lives) have grabbed the imagination of those looking at empowering social work in the UK, New Zealand, Australia and Canada. This is additional to their major challenge to white social workers – to take seriously the implementation of ethnically sensitive and anti-racist social work (see Aymer, Chapter 8). Moreover, many propositions emanating from these 'indigenous' models will be picked up by minority ethnic peoples of diverse origins within the metropolitan countries of the west. Additionally, members within the majority populations will become aware of the significance of the propositions in the 'indigenous' models as these will speak to the voids left by a society driven by market considerations rooted in profitability, consumerism and the commodification of interpersonal relations. Thus, they will draw on these tenets for further inspiration in dealing with their own difficulties.

While the differences between the 'indigenous' approaches and the more traditional ones have become more visible and acknowledged, their commonalities are less apparent. However, similarities do exist. Otherwise, social workers would not be able to talk to each other across geographical boundaries at international conferences and through the Internet without hopelessly confusing each other. These commonalities appear at the conceptual level, in the value base and around practice skills. Each of these may be examined systematically in great detail although I do not have the space to do so here. Conceptually, social workers can relate to one another according to the work they do with different 'client' groups, for example, older people, or through their emphasis on similar types of social problems such as child abuse and neglect.

A shared value base is evident in social workers' commitment to securing social justice for marginalized groups. Social workers can also identify common elements within general practice skills. Yet, when it comes down to action in a given case, their specific interventions are guided by different cultural traditions, authorized by different kinds of legislation and conducted in different languages. When one moves away from discussions pitched at fairly abstract levels such as working with individuals, groups and communities, it becomes clear that practitioners often draw on different methods. Thus, claims to commonalities must be examined with caution to identify their specific content and context. Commonalities and differences seem to go together in a dialectical interaction that specifies the commonalities in our differences and the differences in our commonalities.

Other points of similarity pivot around the social legitimacy that the profession draws from society in order to justify its existence and the location of social work within the institutions of civil society. When placed within their specific contexts, these general characteristics enable social workers to talk about the care and control dilemmas they face in their work with 'clients' and to know they are able to share these concerns with a range of practitioners in other countries. At the same time, they may discover that their authority to intervene stems from very different sources – legislation in some western countries, religious authority in some eastern countries. Thus, there are differences embedded within their shared characteristics. Additionally, the features that locate social work within the interstices of the state make it a political activity that can attract hostile reactions from those in charge of both local and national governments and the populations they serve. Social work education's emphasis on the specifics of the profession, its deconstruction of the meaning of professionalism and its examination of the skills required from its personnel in the light of the definition of its status and place in society, are responses to the political nature of its position.

The different approaches taken in social work practice also enable its adherents simultaneously to focus on different issues or even the same ones by different means. This allows for the diversity that can be found in social work. It is far from being a monotone discipline. For example, social workers addressing the needs of a poor lone parent woman following social development models in Africa will focus on the alleviation of poverty and the creation of community-based resources in a way that an American, using a clinical casework approach, would not. This is not to say that social workers, usually called community workers in the USA, do not deal with poverty, but they tend to work outside the mainstream social work remit so their activities would be conducted on different terms. This would set different constraints within which each is able to operate. One other interesting difference in this situation is the greater remove from the local state experienced by an American community worker than would be the case for a social development worker in Zimbabwe, even though both may be working with poor people.

Another different feature is that the organization of social work and its positioning vis-à-vis the welfare state is dependent on the political system that prevails in any particular country. In some countries, for example, Sweden, social work is clearly an integral part of the welfare state. Its social workers tend to be employed by the state. In the USA, many social workers are self-employed. In some countries in Latin America social workers attached to churches have played a key role in organizing liberation movements aimed at tackling poverty. In New Zealand Maori social workers are held accountable to their *whanau* (kinship group) which gives them the legitimacy to intervene in their communities. Yet, they are operating within the confines of a welfare state which is being rapidly privatized. Ironically, privatization has offered Maori people some opportunities to develop provision that would otherwise not have been available to them. It has enabled them to create services they can fund through their own initiatives rather than rely on state sources. The global variety is greater than is evident in my analysis, but in a single chapter I can only highlight a few instances. Nonetheless, in looking at social work through an international focus, it is clear that the profession can lay claim to both commonalities and differences as its identifying features. A more systematic examination of these characteristics in the near future is certainly necessary.

Internationalizing Forces in Social Work

Globalization and the privatization of the welfare state in those countries where it exists, for example, western European states, Canada, New Zealand and Australia, have been crucial in subjecting social work to internationalizing forces. These include the growth of private companies in what used to be public sector domains, the requirement that people make (some) direct payment for the services they use, the importation of market-oriented management systems of control over practitioners, the accountability of professional labour and a changing service ethic. Many of the private companies entering the social work arena are multinational corporations with a prime interest in making a profit rather than responding to the needs of clients who have few resources with which to pay for the services they require. In short, social work has become part of a commodity exchange process in which those that pay get what is available.

Those who are unable to pay for the services they need are expected to obtain them from either the voluntary sector or from a residual welfare state. These solutions are inadequate in the context of societies that espouse democratic tenets and citizenship rights. The strong emphasis on means testing associated with the residual welfare state carries with it stigmatization. The very act of having recourse to such provision is taken as an indication of inadequacy and serves further to exclude and marginalize the claimants. In the voluntary sector, even if services are provided without stigma or demand for payment, there is a limit to the numbers that can be covered by these means. For the resources coming into this sector have tight boundaries of eligibility drawn around them. Moreover, the availability of charitable provision enables the state to proceed for some time without having to confront awkward ethical questions about its moral responsibility to provide for those in need. Nonetheless, globalization and privatization have meant that the issues associated with commodifying need have cropped up in one form or another in different countries.

The privatization of the welfare state has also submitted service provision to the imperatives of market discipline (Dominelli and Hoogvelt 1996). This has affected how services are organized and the conditions under which social workers perform their duties. One outcome of market-driven approaches to the social services is the 'Taylorization' of the professional labour process. 'Taylorization' is a term derived from the organization of workers under mass production techniques in factories. Taylor was a management theorist who believed that tasks should be broken down into their component parts and assigned to particular workers. In social work, the repertoire of functional analysis has been used to facilitate the division of complex professional activities into their simpler constituent elements. The outcome is the formulation of competencies that define the particular activity associated with a specific role. The break-up of tasks which this analysis produces is expressed in ways that ignore process and the interconnections between one of its parts and the others. Consequently, both services and working practices have become quantified, i.e. made measurable. In short, they have been commodified. As a result of the loss of a holistic approach to the intervention, the 'Taylorization' process contributes to the deprofessionalization of social work (Dominelli 1996). These practices have also increased the forms of managerial control that can be exercised to hold practitioners more accountable for their use of resources and time.

Managerial concerns to measure the effectiveness of social workers' interventions and the efficient use of resources have therefore increased the popularity of competence based approaches in defining and measuring the tasks for which a particular social worker is responsible. Their use in measuring performance has also made them invaluable for the purposes of conducting appraisal and promotion procedures. The prominence of 'Taylorist' methods in a service profession has led to concerns being expressed about the deprofessionalization of social work practice. The deskilling of practitioners is accompanied by a lowering of the standards used in skills evaluation and in compiling the intellectual content of social work courses as competence-based training in the workplace takes over a university-based education (Dominelli 1996). Although these developments are very evident in the recent removal of probation training from universities in England, social work educators in other countries, for example, New Zealand, are experiencing similar pressures. Several provincial governments in Canada have also recently begun to consider the value of competence based approaches for social work in their jurisdictions.

The social work profession has also been required to respond more closely to the agenda for practice set by employers who support competence-based approaches. Employers' concerns with the ability of social workers to take on the practicalities of practice on a day-to-day basis have resulted in management undertaking tighter procedural control of social workers' activities. The desire for greater accountability has been particularly strong in difficult areas such as child welfare where risk assessments, for example, are becoming highly bureaucratized instruments of intervention. These may not necessarily protect a child from being harmed, but in the event of media scrutiny they facilitate an agency's defensive claims to have followed procedures. Hence, the emphasis on procedures is now finding favour in countries that had previously ignored them, for example, the risk assessment schedule adopted after the Gove Inquiry in Canada.

The impact of globalization and privatization on the role of the voluntary sector, whether in the national or global arenas, also has aspects to consider in the international context. These are related to the fiscal powers and the organizational spread of some voluntary agencies. Some of the largest international non-governmental organizations (NGOs), for example, the Red Cross, Age Concern and Oxfam, are linked to the social work sphere in the work they do. Many of these NGOs are involved in providing humanitarian aid relief to refugees and civilian victims in war zones or assisting in the development of local agricultural and industrial projects. Thus, they play a major role in the organization of welfare services during times of trauma such as war and civil conflicts, and in the modernization process through which many industrializing countries are being integrated into the global market system.

Some of these NGOs have budgets that exceed the funds under the control of the host governments in the local areas where they work. This can give them enormous powers for which they are not held democratically accountable (Deacon *et al.* 1997). Funding bodies may scrutinize their ledgers and the outcomes of their interventions, but local people at the receiving end of their ministrations do not have an automatic say in the planning or delivery of the services made available by them. Consequently, social workers engaged within such NGOs are not able to endorse the realization of the universal human rights held by their 'clients' or ensure that self-determination occurs. This is a gap in proceedings which empowering forms of social work seek to fill by advocating the involvement of local people in the decision-making processes of NGOs.

Furthermore, the administration of NGO activities relies on extensive global networks that require servicing and maintenance if they are to realize the organizational objectives and tasks set for them by funders. Development aid going into NGO coffers for distribution on the ground in countries other than those where their headquarters are based may not all find its way there. Paying for an administrative superstructure means that a sizeable portion of the income acquired by charities is expended in keeping the infrastructure going rather than on direct services. Moreover, funding can also be dependent on international institutions such as the International Monetary Fund and the World Bank where the criteria for funding are guided more by corporate interests of profitability than 'helping' considerations.

NGOs may find, therefore, that their money comes with certain strings attached. The constraints these carry are usually more in keeping with business ethics than being concerned with needs-led services (Deacon *et al.* 1997). Globalization is also raising questions about the 'voluntary' nature of many large 'voluntary' bodies. In order to be funded to do their work, these organizations have to be run like businesses, engage in corporate management techniques and be adept at fundraising. All of these tasks require professional skills and a high level of proficiency if the work at hand is to be done well. Acquiring personnel who can meet these requirements may be beyond the means of small neighbourhoods based voluntary agencies. Well-resourced, professional 'voluntary' bodies with international connections are in a different league from these small-time players.

Some social work issues are international by their nature. They are the concern of all social workers because they cannot be dealt with solely by social workers located within one country. This is because they involve the movement of vulnerable people from one part of the globe to another, whether by legitimate means or not. One illustration is the international trade in women and children for the purposes of sexual exploitation; another is fostering or adoption across national boundaries. Parental abductions of children can also have international dimensions if the abducting parent removes the children to a domicile in another nation state. Activities of this nature require social workers to work together across national boundaries if they are to respond adequately to the clients' needs. Practitioners working in these areas need to understand the legal frameworks, cultural traditions and working practices of all the countries involved in order to intervene effectively in these situations.

Moreover, there are no easy practice solutions to the complicated issues raised in these circumstances. For example, in disputed custody cases, international agreements covering child abductions do not apply everywhere because not all countries in the world have signed up to them. These complexities become apparent if, for example, a European woman marries a North African man, gets divorced and is given custody of their children in Europe. She will find that if her former husband takes the children to live in his country of origin without her consent the options available to her to secure their return are few. On a less controversial level, most countries in the United Nations (UN) have signed the Convention on the Rights of the Child. But in many countries it is difficult to enforce its provisions, which are aimed at improving the quality of life for children.

Poverty is an acknowledged major deterrent to children's ability to grow and develop to their full potential. Yet, although the world has the technology to eradicate poverty, those holding political and economic power have failed to tackle it. Moreover, under the current international regime, the observance of UN conventions that have children's interests at heart cannot be effectively enforced. Children are therefore deprived of the resources they need and to which they are legally entitled. The issue is one which social workers can make their own because they have first-hand evidence of the damage caused to the world's children. Their knowledge of the day-to-day realities faced by children can be profiled on a global basis and can be accompanied with demands for the realization of current children's human rights legislation. In such a campaign many countries, including some of the world's richest, can be exposed as having a shameful record.

With regard to commonalities in the value base, the concern with social justice as a legitimate part of the social work agenda has become more widespread in recent years. This has been particularly evident where the new social movements involving indigenous peoples, women and disabled people have directed their energies at questioning the inappropriate services delivered by social workers to oppressed groups and have created alternative provision based on their own definitions of their needs. The demands of claimants from these movements have caused social workers to become involved in addressing the injustices ('isms'), which can be perpetrated through their own practice and set out the terrain for improving their responses (see Hastings, Chapter 6). In some western countries their doing so has set the scene for considerable controversy and debate about the lost neutrality of the profession and its entry into the forbidden territory of political activism. But through such actions, social justice as a priority for social workers stands as a counterbalance to the agenda being set by neo-conservatives. The debate about social work priorities has been particularly heated in the UK, USA and New Zealand, where neo-conservatives have a stranglehold over communications in the mass media.

The spread of the main preoccupations of neo-conservative groups through the endorsement of neo-liberal economic policies at national level has also given social workers a number of common problems in different countries. Some of these revolve around the creation of 'moral panics' which target particular client groups. Single parent women, young offenders and older people are at the forefront of these attacks. People within these categories are facing a climate that seeks to de-legitimize their expectations of welfare assistance from the public purse as of right. For lone mothers, particularly those in England, Canada, the USA and New Zealand, this has meant the application of 'workfare' – the requirement to work or undertake training in order to receive benefits.

This policy has reduced these women's ability to raise their children, an important task they may wish to undertake themselves, rather than passing it on to others. Such treatment calls up the question of which groups in society are deemed to have the 'right' to a family life. The impact of these initiatives on children have yet to be adequately assessed by social workers in both general and specific terms. This becomes an item to be used in constructing a research agenda for social work in the future. In the meantime, social workers committed to social justice have a duty to question the wisdom of punitive approaches to those who are seeking to do the right thing by their children.

The creation of a 'moral panic' around young offenders has also resulted in draconian measures being enacted in relation to youth justice. Punishment has become the order of the day. Additionally, demands that the age for being taken to adult courts be lowered are gaining popular support in both Europe and North America (Schissel 1997). These moves have been prompted by media orchestration around the myth of 'dangerous' youths, hooked into a life of crime, who hold society in contempt. Such negative images have been created around rare examples of young people murdering other young people, for example, the killing of James Bulger in England, or Sharon Dean in the USA. These kinds of events have served to shift public support away from the rehabilitation of young offenders within the community towards a punishment model aimed at separating them off from society by incarcerating them in 'tough' institutions. This attitude towards youth enables society to ignore the reciprocity in its relationships with its members. The duties of individuals to act within certain accepted boundaries require some responsibility on the part of society to ensure that there is within it a respectable place for them individually and collectively. In short, excluded people have rights and duties which only make sense in the context of society's responsibility to make them feel included and to open up opportunities through which they can achieve this status.

The 'moral panic' around elders is being formulated on different grounds – their cost to society. Older people in both Europe and North America are being depicted as an unacceptable burden that society is being unfairly asked to carry. The lack of welfare resources is cited as a reason for this state of affairs, but the facts are that the public purse provides only a small amount of the direct care required for elders. Their families are the main providers, even in places with substantial welfare states such as Britain and the Nordic countries. This depiction of older people also ignores the fact that many of them have contributed to their care through payment of taxes or insurance premiums. Similar characterizations of older people are beginning to surface in some Third World countries undergoing industrialization as young women move away from home into the waged labour force. With their departure, the unpaid pool of those with the time to care for older people has diminished.

At the conceptual level, these 'moral panics' have 'othered' those with claims to social assistance (Dominelli 1997). Through the 'othering' process, those promoting these 'moral panics' have dehumanized groups of people and turned them into 'objects' that are superfluous to a well-ordered society. As a result, those groups of people who have come under attack have been denied the rights of citizenship and participation in the broader social realm. Official attempts aimed at drawing these groups into leading more socially acceptable lives through 'workfare' initiatives are unlikely to succeed. By equipping them primarily to take low-paid or part-time jobs, this approach leaves them at the margins. At best it locks them into employment opportunities which do not allow them easily to access mainstream resources including welfare benefits such as health care and pensions through the private market or, at worst, it raises expectations which cannot be fulfilled. Thus, people who have already been excluded from mainstream society are pushed further into its periphery.

These 'moral panics' also serve to divide claimants into new 'deserving' and 'undeserving' groups, that is, they fragment the so-called 'underclass'. This division is also useful in ensuring that the rationing of welfare resources can be conducted on a seemingly rational or justifiable basis. Additionally, curtailing the number of claimants who are entitled to access social provision is easier to undertake in the present context because it has successfully commodified need.

The commodification of need and the assigning of a price tag to it are important dimensions of globalization. But the issue goes beyond the focus on need. Persons are also becoming commodities in the global economy. As capital moves from country to country in order to reduce labour and production costs and increase profits, people become dispensable parts of the machinery. One person's labour in one locality can be substituted easily by another in a different place. Thus, flexibility in production and service delivery becomes both a cause of and a response to the workers' loss of control over the labour process. In short, they become alienated cogs in an indifferent wheel that continues to spin round. Multinational firms can constantly move production and service delivery from one location to another with minimal disruption to profit margins. The securement of public subsidies in the form of grants and tax holidays acts as major incentives attracting companies to a particular terrain. The public funds for these allocations are usually transfers made possible by cutting back on state welfare budgets. Thus, reductions in public expenditure for welfare provision facilitate the transfer of money from the public to the private sector. In the process, society's most vulnerable groups suffer, including those who have been vilified through 'moral panics'. These transfers, which typify the neo-liberal project in countries such as Canada, Britain, the USA and New Zealand, can be deemed a hidden welfare system benefiting private corporations.

Issues for Social Work Practice

As social work agencies join the computer highway, exchanges of information between practitioners can occur more readily than they do now. However, matters of confidentiality, 'client' access to computerized records and 'client' control over information held about them, remain issues to be addressed within the international arena. The internationalization of social work also raises questions about what forms of practice can be considered as falling within the social work remit. At the moment, there are areas of overlap and competition between various elements of what can be called the 'caring' or 'social' professions. These are especially acute in provision delivered by both the health service and social services, particularly at the level of community.

Delineating professional boundaries requires a detailed interrogation of the models of service delivery each uses in practice. Social workers have been reluctant to engage in such exercises, while other professions have been busy extending their borders (see Lowe and Weinstein, Chapter 13). Territorial moves of this nature have been particularly evident in undermining the divisions between health and social services in Canada, the UK and USA as a result of initiatives dealing with the care of older people. Social work practitioners and educators have few resources for promoting an examination of the advantages and disadvantages of these developments in terms of the actual services received by the community. Hence, most of them remain wedded to their locality based analyses or practices and will engage little with the international dimensions that answering these questions will require. Governments, on the other hand, have sent policymakers and practitioners to other countries to investigate their policy and practice initiatives, to learn from the mistakes made in those countries and to apply their learning at home.

Official endeavours in this respect have not always carried the endorsement of practitioners based in the home country. For example, probation officers and their professional associations spoke against the 'boot camps' for young offenders imported into the UK from the USA by Michael Howard when he was Home Secretary. But he proceeded with his plans regardless. Similar trends have been evident in the growth of private prisons for adult offenders in the England.

The importation of initiatives of this type has resulted in some degree of convergence becoming apparent in countries which have shared experiences. For example, the models of private practice and case management, developed largely in the USA, have been adapted for use in countries with different traditions, particularly those with a welfare state undergoing privatization such as New Zealand, Sweden, Canada and the UK. There has also been considerable international activity in work with refugees in the former Yugoslavia. In this illustration, foreign experts, particularly those with counselling and psychiatric skills, went to war-torn countries to practise their skills. The extent to which local sensitivities have been taken on board in such situations has yet to be systematically ascertained through research. A similar comment can be made with regards to western support for social work in the People's Republic of China.

Issues Raised for Social Work Education

Understanding the forces of globalization has implications for social work education and training (Midgley 1997). To begin with, there is a need to theorize global developments if the unique realms of knowledge applicable to social work are to be extended and the identity of the profession is to be maintained in the future. Social work educators have the responsibility to advance the profession's knowledge base in this area and to incorporate the resultant theories into their teaching programmes. Besides theorizing practice, tracking the impact of globalization on practice itself is also important. Social work practice is being redefined by the spread of multinational firms into countries once outside their remit. The contract culture is affecting the way the welfare state functions and is determining the opportunities which are available for social workers to practise both within and outside its ambit. A number of changes in the ways that social services are delivered are likely to have profound repercussions for the profession. These include: the growing possibilities of self-employment in the form of working freelance as a private practitioner who sells his or her services; of becoming an organizer of resources that have been contracted out by the state; or of being involved in direct service provision in the voluntary sector. Describing, tracking and understanding these developments on a global basis are crucial tasks for academics and practitioners to undertake.

Social work courses have been slow to consider such issues as part of the 'normal' curriculum that is taught to students. Part of the reason for this is that social work is, in many ways, a parochial discipline rooted in the locality where it is practised. Often, because their legal framework does not extend to other countries, it is difficult for social workers to work across national divisions. This makes intervention problematic when one of the parties in a transaction resides within their particular jurisdiction while the other(s) do(es) not. The international legislation that exists to facilitate interventions in such cases is inadequate.

For social work educators, the internationalization of the curriculum requires more than the description of different social work systems or models of intervention in use in various societies and the pasting of these between the covers of a single text. A major task will be the development of tools to facilitate comparative analyses. When highlighting features held in common, these instruments must not lose sight of the unique aspects of social work in the different countries. Comparative analyses also require social work educators to be able to explain these similarities and differences in such a way as to heighten understanding of the benefits and disadvantages of any particular system both in its country of origin and when it is transposed overseas.

The use of computer technology has become increasingly significant in facilitating the development of fast and cheap communication links between social workers across the globe. In the educational spheres, there is already a series of internationally based networks which have been set up to exchange course curricula, publish materials for computer assisted learning and distance learning programmes to promote modes of delivery using these new mediums. These trends are likely to be accentuated in the future as rapid modes of communication become harnessed to international exchanges of teaching materials and research.

Globalization also requires a flexible and mobile workforce. Within social work, those wishing to respond to this aspect of globalization will seek international exchanges in both academic courses and practice placements as individuals attempt to make themselves more relevant to the global movement of labour from one country to another.

In this context, harmonization and the recognition of qualifications across frontiers become significant parts of the professional infrastructure. There have been attempts to address the issues of transferable skills and the recognition of academic awards at both national and regional levels. These efforts have usually been based on an individual presenting for recognition before the relevant national association. Useful as this approach has been, it is time consuming and wasteful when many individuals with similar qualifications ask for their credentials to be accepted. In this kind of situation, a response is needed that takes the academic awards as the basis for international recognition. Transferability of skills, a wider recognition of academic credits and mechanisms for the accreditation of prior learning become important ingredients in making this happen. Countries in the European Union (EU), Canada, the USA and Mexico have sought to make this an important aspect of their foreign policies by funding various programmes and experimental projects.

The EU has issued directives to encourage the harmonization of professional qualifications which have sought to govern the conditions under which mutual recognition could occur. The EU has also promoted and funded exchanges of academics and students to enable them to explore the problems encountered in recognizing each other's educational approaches and find solutions to the difficulties that have arisen between them. For example, the ERASMUS (now SOCRATES) and TEMPUS programmes have been crucial in encouraging exchanges in the European context.

The results achieved thus far are somewhat mixed. Institutions of higher education have been jealously guarding both their curriculum materials and awards. Thus, mutual recognition of teaching and assessment materials has been possible primarily when the institutions of higher learning concerned have strictly controlled the process. International systems of credit rating courses have also been developed, although their take-up to date has not been universal. Yet some system for securing recognition of academic and practice qualifications across borders is essential in a world that is rapidly shrinking and in which labour mobility is becoming commonplace.

One of the problems with the approach of people trained in one country being given permission, via recognition, to practise in another, is the danger of certain models of social work being imposed abroad, whether or not they are relevant to the new environment. Such practices can be experienced as exploitative of local peoples or as cultural or educational imperialism. They do little to support those at the receiving end in responding appropriately to local agendas. As a way of proceeding, this was particularly problematic in the early days of US and western European initiatives in eastern Europe.

Assumptions about the lack of social work experience in these countries guided western attempts to help eastern Europeans develop the necessary infrastructure for social work education and personal social services. These responses ignored the fact that there had been a history of social work experience in these countries before and after the Communist period. Despite formal state denials under the former Communist regimes, forms of assistance which were recognizably social work were being conducted among needy people. However, these were often undertaken under the aegis of women based in local communities or, occasionally, religious groups. Both carried on with their work regardless of the lack of official acknowledgement from the state's ruling elite.

Conclusions

International forces are at large in social work. They are helping to shape the profession and lead it in new directions. Some are more evident than others and some are also more desirable. The impact of each of these forces on social work education and practice needs to be tracked and systematically analysed for its record in supporting individual and community well being. Moreover, given the need for social mobility and the advent of multinational firms in the practice arena, it is crucial that social work practitioners of the future are able to operate within an international context and take up those opportunities for mobility which are on offer. For this, they need training that integrates international perspectives into the social work curriculum which they study and provides possibilities for academic staff, students and practitioners to undertake exchanges, including practice placements, in other countries. They should also be enabled to participate fully in the drive towards the development of mechanisms to facilitate the harmonization and recognition of different qualifications and awards worldwide.

Such exchanges will also lead to a bringing together of teaching materials in ways that make them both international and locally relevant. In a context where the Internet and distance learning packages are being promoted as ways of transcending the time and space limitations of traditional teaching, it is crucial that multimedia teaching materials are developed in ways which acknowledge the specificity of locality as well as the commonalities between countries. Otherwise, these materials will provide the setting within which a new imperialism of the mind can be readily conducted. Developments of the colonizing kind must be avoided for their impact on practice will be most keenly felt by the 'client' who is usually excluded from the discussions which produce these curriculum materials and the innovative forms of practice based upon them. Putting the observance of human rights at their centre will be one way in which the interests of 'clients' can be sustained. Another is by involving them in their creation and delivery in the first place (see Chapter 8). Both actions will enable social workers to pay homage to values that unite their commitment to enhancing people's well-being in empowering ways. Moreover, these values have resonance on a global basis.

References

Deacon, B., Hulse, M. and Stubbs, P. (1997) *Global Social Policy: International Organisations and the Future of Welfare*. London: Sage.

Dominelli, L. (1996) 'Deprofessionalising social work: competences, equal opportunities and postmodernism'. *British Journal of Social Work 26*, 2, 153–175.

Dominelli, L. (1997) *Sociology for Social Work*. London: Macmillan.

Dominelli, L. and Hoogvelt, A. (1996) 'The technocratisation of social work'. *Critical Social Policy*, April, 45–62.

Midgley, J. (1997) *Social Welfare in Global Context*. London: Sage.

Schissel, B. (1997) *Blaming Children: Youth Crime, Moral Panics and the Politics of Hate*. Halifax: Fernwood Publishing.

CHAPTER 3

Social Work Education and Higher Education

Mind the Gap

Cherry Rowlings

In the past decade in particular, there has been much innovation within social work education and this chapter considers the changing structures for qualifying and post-qualifying education and how these connect with the higher education sector within which most professional education is located. The term 'higher education' incorporates provision outside universities, albeit that some is formally linked into degree programmes. However, for the purposes of this chapter the focus is on the university environment and the 'place' of social work education within universities, which have themselves been subject to major change with regard to funding, expansion in student numbers and the growth of new degree programmes. A further dimension is explored, namely the 'place' of higher education and how far innovation has challenged or consolidated the higher education base of professional programmes.

To be writing this chapter in 1999 is a very different experience than would have been the case if there had been no change of government in 1997. This is not to say that New Labour has a view of social work, social work education or higher education that is so different from that of its Conservative predecessors. The confirmation of Conservative policy to withdraw social work from the arena of criminal justice in England and Wales and the changes in funding of higher education are ready examples of continuity. New Labour's support for greater devolution to Scotland (Rowlings 1998) and to Wales and the ensuing positive response to the referenda on a Scottish Parliament and a Welsh Assembly will have major implications for social work, for higher education and also, thereby, for social work education. The peace process in Northern Ireland has also held out hopes that, as in all areas of Northern Ireland society, social work and social work education can develop without the constraints imposed for so long by 'The Troubles'.

Constitutional change has introduced a new dynamic or allowed latent ones to achieve prominence. The Welsh Assembly and the Scottish Parliament are assuming responsibility for social work and for education. Later in this chapter the possible significance of this will be considered.

The 'gap' referred to in the chapter title is borrowed from the view that social work education's relationship to its two constituents – social work on the one hand, higher education on the other – is characterized by distance rather than integration. Hence the gap, expressed, albeit sometimes rather crudely, between theory and practice, between the academic and the professional (or, even more, the vocational), and between education and training. It is usually perceived in negative terms and gives rise to a good deal of debate and often anxiety. However, the injunction to 'mind' the gap is significant because of the various meanings that the verb 'to mind' can convey (New Collins Concise Dictionary 1982): one is 'to pay attention to; to heed'; another, 'to be cautious or careful about'; while a third is 'to be concerned about; be troubled about'. A fourth meaning, 'to make certain', and a fifth, 'to have charge of', are also pertinent. Singly or in multiples and more or less explicitly, these meanings can be found in most if not all discussions about social work education. With the current emphasis on the gap as a cause for concern (and therefore to be closed), rather than as something that can stimulate questions or offer protection from unhelpful extremes, conformity rather than creativity may be the guiding influence on the continuing development of social work education.

In this chapter 'social work education' is used as a shorthand for recognized programmes of study, practice and assessment which might be full time, part time, delivered on or off campus and leading to professional (qualifying or post-qualifying) awards. The focus is on social work education within higher education: its place within that sector and its relationship to it. However, social work education cannot, by definition, be isolated from social work. Its origins were in practice, in the recognition that the activities which constitute what we now call social work can be analysed, understood and, literally, practised and that this would improve effectiveness. The relationship to and with social work therefore permeates the chapter.

Initially, there is an overview of social work education within Europe to provide a comparative perspective. This is followed by a consideration of the state of social work education in the UK and then of issues concerning higher education that impact upon it. Finally, a discussion of the implications of constitutional reform and of the quinquennial review of CCETSW

(Department of Health 1997) precedes a return to the starting point of 'minding the gap'.

Social Work Education and Higher Education in Europe

A survey of 21 countries (Brauns and Kramer 1986) showed that by the mid-1980s throughout Europe qualifying education was located within the higher education sector. The same would be true for the late 1990s if a larger survey were undertaken to include the countries in central and eastern Europe. Given the very different national histories of social work education, this could be regarded as positive evidence of strength. At the very least, it demonstrates a consensus about the minimum educational attainment necessary to fulfil the responsibilities of a qualified social worker. At most, it implies that social work can be studied, researched and developed as a discipline, that it can be theorized and can both produce and be the product of scholarship. To be a social worker requires more than an apprenticeship, more than learning simply by doing.

However, in their introduction to the survey, Brauns and Kramer were struck by the diversity and incoherence of what they saw. Their initial impression was that, 'social work education has reconstructed the Tower of Babel, this time as a ramshackle post-war low-rise sprawling over most of Europe' (1986, p.5). Their language seems rather harsh, but it is worth unpicking what they had to say.

An immediate response is that the extent of difference was (is) to be expected. It links into the nature of social work itself. Whether one takes a historical view within a particular country or a contemporary one across several, it is very clear that the boundaries and remit of social work are socially constructed and thus lack an enduring or consistent definition. Social workers, as Howe (1996, p.77) has said, 'work-the-*social*' – the space between the individual and the state (Donzelot 1979) – and social work stands, often uneasily in what is a highly contested space.

The way in which the social is conceptualized, structured and maintained is far from static. Social work must needs be flexible – even though this will bring what Harris (1997, p.437) describes as 'a certain lack of precision and an embarrassing degree of definitional elusiveness', even though this imprecision has arguably contributed to the vulnerability of social work as a profession (Rowlings 1997).

So if European social work contains something of the ramshackle, with different job titles and boundaries, social work education is unlikely to be otherwise. Taking an overview, one sees a range of higher education locations. Finland, Slovenia and Ireland, for example, train social workers through degree programmes located in universities (with the exception of

Finland's Swedish School). The university base and the uniformity is unusual, though it is increasing, as in the newly introduced programmes in Estonia and Lithuania and the 'affiliation' of social work education to universities (Spain and Italy). Countries such as the UK, Sweden (Hort and McMurphy 1997) and Poland (Les 1997) have mixed arrangements, part in universities and part in other higher education institutions, though not always leading to a degree. A far more common location for social work education is outside universities. In France, Denmark and Norway, for example, schools of social work are separately constituted institutions.

The absence of a university base has implications for the development of social work as a discipline, for it restricts the pursuit of research. Higher level studies may instead have to be undertaken within the disciplines of sociology, psychology or education. Nationally and internationally, this diminishes the profile of social work as an area of study and of professional practice. At a time of the redefinition of welfare in the industrially developed countries, professional territories are less secure and professional groups will maintain their usefulness 'not only by the relevance of their current expertise but also by their political influence and the entrepreneurial talent of their members' (Eraut 1994, p.166). If social work is academically subordinate to other disciplines, it is not well placed to demonstrate what it has to offer in the face of competition from those which are more established such as psychology and law.

The 'low-rise' nature of social work education is not, however, only about its location mostly outside universities. Where there has been affiliation of schools of social work to universities or alignment of the educational institution to the standards and procedures of universities, qualified social workers have not featured prominently among the academic staff as they have not held the requisite higher degree. The teaching of social work theory and practice has commonly been undertaken by associate or sessional staff, often women, thereby further relegating the professional to the margins of the institution. In these circumstances, (male) social scientists rather than (female) social workers have the primary roles in social work education.

The existence in the UK of a much higher number of professionally qualified senior academics, of a history of postgraduate degrees in social work and of staff groups that are mostly, if not completely, qualified marks it out from much of the rest of Europe. But it has to be said that these achievements have been possible because UK universities have in the past had a more tolerant attitude towards the necessity of a doctoral degree for appointment to academic posts. With increasing importance attached to research productivity, professional experience must now, in a growing number of institutions, be accompanied by academic qualifications at a higher level.

The place of social work education in the higher education sector in Europe is therefore far from uniform and the professional element in particular is not securely positioned in a number of countries. Of significance for the next section of this chapter is a further difference noted by Brauns and Kramer (1986), namely the extent to which the educational institution has autonomy over social work education. There is clearly wide variation in the amount of control that is exercised over the institution and the way that this is done (through legislation, through guidance, at the national level or devolved to regions). They place the UK at the 'centralized' end of the spectrum with a system that (p.37) 'gives employing agencies a degree of influence which many Europeans would view as untoward'. They could also have included central government, for CCETSW's status as a non-departmental public body, dependent on government for its funding and with its Council members appointed by government (See Pierce and Weinstein, Chapter 1), is a major influence on the way it operates. Interestingly, Brauns and Kramer also note that, despite this centralization and involvement by employers, the criticisms that are made of social work education in the UK are not dissimilar from those voiced by employers in Germany, which they would place at the opposite, decentralized end of the spectrum. This needs to be remembered, for it suggests that trust in social work education depends on more than the establishment of a particular set of institutional arrangements.

Social Work Education in the UK

It is probably no exaggeration to say that social work education in the UK is currently experiencing major turbulence which is likely to continue over the next few years in the light of pending (though as yet uncertain) changes. This is in marked contrast to the confidence in social work education and the value of the social sciences as the basis of practice which were a feature of its early and middle years. In Chapter 1 Pierce and Weinstein trace the early years of social work training pioneered first by the Charity Organisation Society and then the London School of Economics. Younghusband (1978, p.86) describes the 'tremendous training effort of the 1960s' which was promoted in universities and later polytechnics for (fieldwork) child care officers.

But the last ten years or so have seen a very different climate. Social work education has been subject to criticisms of lack of relevance, over-academicization and a tendency to be unduly influenced, if not ruled, by ideology. Employers, who were the most vocal critics, blamed social work education for failing to equip students to 'do the job' of a qualified worker, seemingly oblivious to the fact that roughly 50 per cent of social work education consists of agency based practice and is thus substantially in their hands.

It has to be said that social work education is not alone in this position. The education of teachers has been similarly described and, like social work education, has been subject to significant reorganization of the way it is delivered. The scepticism about professional education should also be placed in the current context of a general questioning of the nature and the validity of the expertise of the professional and the power that the professions possess. Eraut (1994, p.5) captures this well in his suggestion that 'whereas previously the State sought to protect its citizens from the unqualified practitioners, it now seeks to protect them from the qualified'. The debates at the time of writing this chapter on how social work should be regulated and the role of central government in regulation make Eraut's point highly relevant for contemporary social work.

Social work education is bound to be vulnerable in a climate of decreasing trust in the professions and in the educational processes that have sustained them. Both its relative newness and its less than secure position within higher education exacerbate the problem. But, more seriously, social work is a contentious and politically sensitive undertaking, subject to competing tensions and forces. The 'vastness and vagueness of the social work task' (Goldberg and Warburton 1979), and the absence so far in the UK of a systematic linkage of qualification to specific tasks, has made it difficult to define with confidence exactly what people were being educated for. The 'definitional elusiveness' noted earlier by Harris (1997, p.37) has proved 'embarrassing' in times of challenge. Notwithstanding the definition of the DipSW as a higher education qualification (CCETSW 1989), the multiplicity of routes to the DipSW and the variety of institutions at which it is offered may be interpreted as an uncertainty about how and where social work education should 'really' be provided.

This is venturing into sensitive territory. Diversity and proliferation have been associated with wider access to social work education and 'access' has rightly been one of the aims of the recent history. To raise questions about whether the several ways of becoming a qualified social worker need re-examining is likely to be met with accusations of elitism (a term that has bedevilled the intellectual development of social work) and of flying in the face of government policies to increase participation in higher education. Pragmatists, too, would no doubt see the benefits of a diverse qualifying system with diverse sources of funding.

Problematic though it is for social work educators to face the question of where social work education should 'really' be located, it is increasingly necessary for them (us) to do so, not least because government departments have begun to ask the very same (Department of Health 1997). However, it is not just a question of whether there are too many institutions providing social work education but what kind(s) of institution should do so and what kind(s) of programme there should be. How important are a research base and research activity? Where might social work education fit and be funded to fit in a reorganized world of universities divided mainly into research institutions, mainly teaching or a mixture of both? How sustainable is public confidence in a qualifying system that incorporates such diverse educational experiences as an employment-based route and a full-time, college-based route and regards both as equally fitting for the DipSW? How secure can the DipSW be when its very flexibility (that double-edged sword again) can be as much a sign almost of 'anything will do' as of a robustness that can be adapted to different circumstances?

Within social work, the debate illustrates the uncertain attitude to social work education from within the profession. There is a rejection of the relevance of the academic to social work practice and therefore a wish to restrict the influence of higher education upon the way qualifications are gained. The reasons are diverse. Some are about fears of becoming removed from the users of social work service, of becoming 'professionalized' with all the negatives associated with the professions: that they are essentially self-serving and self-protecting, the reinforcers of inequality by the act of setting themselves apart as 'experts'. Not unrelated to this is a second reason for rejecting the academic: that social work needs the heart more than the head. In this understanding of social work, feelings rather than thoughts are important, intuition rather than analysis, common sense rather than theory. Feelings and intuition, of course, are the stereotypical characteristics of women, and social work has always been primarily women's work (except when it becomes management), thus allowing these two factors to feed into each other. Third, and this comes from a different direction, the academic is resisted by those who would wish social work to be brought under tighter control. In a climate of managerialism and a preoccupying fear of risk taking, compliance to guidelines and procedures is highly regarded rather than the use of imagination and a questioning of established ways of working or thinking. From this perspective, the academic encourages disturbance, for disturbance is the product of the higher education culture of dispute, debate and exploration of the alternative.

The DipSW itself, as an educational programme, attracted fundamental criticism in addition to that of a misguided flexibility. The introduction of a competency-based approach to professional education and the requirement of 'partnership' by educational institutions with agencies have been seen as diminishing the integrity of social work education and fuelling the anti-intellectualism that has been a feature of social work in the UK (Dominelli, Chapter 2; Jones 1996; Parton 1996). The tighter regulation has been interpreted as an attack on higher education, especially the universities (Webb 1996), and as a reflection of attempts within agencies to reduce social work to itemized activities that are susceptible to managerial control.

In many ways, though, if threats to social work education are to be seen, it is the arrangements approved by CCETSW for post-qualifying awards (CCETSW 1990) that provide the better example. The competency approach here was, from the outset, more explicit and arguably even less appropriate at the higher levels of functioning that post-qualifying work required. Structures for professional approval of taught programmes and assessment of candidates through a portfolio route were located outside the higher education system. Indeed, the very existence of a portfolio route, with no requirement for study on any kind of formal course, infers a limited relevance of higher education to the attainment of post-qualifying awards. It is the workplace that is intended to be the major location of learning and assessment, especially for the lower of the two post qualifying awards which it was hoped almost all social workers would gain. True, the awards have been aligned with academic levels. But they are outside academic institutions and separate from an academic framework and this conveys a very particular message. Comparison with the membership examination of the royal colleges and chartered institutes does not hold up to close scrutiny, given the very different academic base upon which they are founded and the very different professional ethos which they represent.

Both the DipSW and the post-qualifying arrangements were the products of a set of political, economic and educational circumstances prevailing at their time – a time generally not good for social work or social work education. Some of the criticisms directed at them are open to accusations of overstatement and exaggeration. For example, while there may be justifiable concerns about the appropriateness of a competency-based approach to qualifying and post-qualifying awards, it must also be acknowledged that in neither case has this been applied in the full sense of what a strict competency approach involves. There must also be questions of social work educators about the ways they (we) have implemented the regulations, and whether unnecessary timidity on the one hand or undue zeal on the other have brought additional problems. Furthermore, we do not fully know what the new DipSW and PQ requirements have protected social work education from, though the dangers of what they have exposed it to have been well chronicled.

Recognition of all these caveats, however, still leaves social work education rather uneasily placed between the workplace and higher education. This has been accentuated by the findings of research undertaken by Triseliotis and Marsh (1996) which have rumbled around discussions about social work education. This is the first major study of the outcome of social work education (which in itself shows what an under-researched area this is). Because of this and the size of its sample of newly qualified staff, it is a significant piece of work, albeit that the data rely heavily on experience of a qualification (CQSW) that no longer exists. The study contains messages for social work education and for the way agencies manage newly qualified staff.

Three points in respect of social work education illustrate the contradictions in the research findings. First, within the sample, almost one half were there not for the purpose of education but in order to do what was necessary to gain the qualification and thereby be assured of future employment or promotion. With the subsequent reduction in the number of employee secondments, this rejection of learning may well now be less, but in the context of the study it is highly significant and a further indication of the way social workers regard social work education. Second, although respondents were critical of insufficient time spent on social work and social science teaching, they were against the idea of extending training to include more time in the educational institution. Finally, despite the time spent on practice placements, many respondents said they had been unprepared for actually working as a social worker.

It is easy to plunder the Marsh and Triseliotis study to extract evidence to support whatever argument one wishes to promote. A more productive approach is to ask how far and in what ways would a replication of their study today yield similar results and what is necessary to maximize the benefits of social work education. This would properly acknowledge the 'snapshot' nature of the study and use its findings to promote debate on what would facilitate better education. In this debate it is important to remember that, taking an international perspective, UK social workers are undereducated at the qualifying level, spending too little time on a rather narrow academic agenda (a link into Jones's 1996 point about the way in which social work education has 'plundered' the social sciences).

However, the idea that some of the difficulties in social work education might in fact stem from there being too little of it has not carried widespread support in the UK and, as a result, changes have only been considered within the 'given' of a two-year qualification. There are signs in 1999, that in Scotland at least the two years is finally being seriously questioned, but the nature of any extension is far from certain and is guaranteed to be strongly contested. In the qualifying process, as we have already seen, social work education as a higher education activity is not secure.

The Higher Education Context

Despite this insecurity, social work education contributes undoubted benefits to higher education. The good employment record of social work students helps to demonstrate the relevance of university education to the needs of the employment market. In universities where social work education has been part of social science degrees, the presence of professional training has at times helped to sustain other academic programmes. Less tangible is the influence that social work education can have upon the functioning of the university. Parsloe (1996, p.124) suggests that social work academics bring an 'understanding of process' which can facilitate the progress of university business. To this can be added a heightened awareness of the significance of gender and ethnicity, of the power relationship between staff and students and of equal opportunities in selection, assessment and appeals procedures. This is not to say that social work academics have a monopoly in these areas, especially now with the increased emphasis on quality assurance within higher education generally. But attention to the structures and processes of education has had a centrality within social work education, in part due to development work by CCETSW, which has not, in the past, generally been the case in the wider institution. Historically, though, the development of social work education within higher education has not been without critics from within the sector. This section considers how higher education has viewed social work education and how developments within higher education, as much as within social work education, have a significance for the future.

Although social work education in the UK began and experienced its initial expansion within universities, this development was not welcomed by all academics. The hope was that location in universities would 'help to transform vocational courses from technical know-how to professional education' (Younghusband 1978, vol 2, p.26). However, it took some time to establish that 'professional' training rather than simply a degree or postgraduate diploma in the social sciences was needed for the job. Although progress was slower in Scotland, the introduction in England of new child care legislation in 1963 and 1969 helped to maintain the drive towards professional training and prompted the development, at the request of employers, for non-graduate programmes in the then polytechnics and for part-time programmes for existing staff. 'As time went on', Younghusband (1978 p.83) says, 'almost every type of course had been started that would attract candidates. Naturally this led to swaying battles about quantity and quality and differing views as to whether the one letter of recognition [in child care] guaranteed an acceptable minimum standard of achievement.' Her words have a familiar ring over twenty years later. On a much smaller scale, psychiatric social workers and medical social workers established their training within universities and probation training, after an initial uncertainty as to whether a specialist training was to be preferred, eventually passed to selected (generalist) higher education institutions.

Through a variety of routes, therefore, social work education became established in higher education and, with the recognition of polytechnics as 'new' universities, is now substantially within the university sector. How well it 'fits' here remains an issue, in part because of the nature of the endeavour but increasingly because of changes taking place within higher education.

Universities have a long tradition of educating for the professions (law and medicine are two examples). Social work's own ambivalence, not to say at times hostility, to a higher education base can undermine social work education within higher education, especially in the more traditional universities.

In any form of professional education, there will be a tension between it and its university base (Eraut 1994). The intellectual tradition of universities values the explicit, the scientific, the discipline-based theory. Knowledge is pursued for its own sake, through patient scholarship and the challenging of presently accepted ideas and theory. The current climate outside universities that knowledge 'is overwhelmingly for use' (Henkel 1995, p.67) and must be relevant to the employment market is bringing its own influence to bear but the essence of the tradition remains. Professional education, on the other hand, has a knowledge base that is often implicit, coming out of practice. Theory may well be drawn from different disciplines insofar as they inform the professional task, while professional theory may be poorly articulated and expressed as much through practice.

In Erant's (1994) elaboration of the differences between what he refers to as the academic environment and the clinical environment, he notes that timescales, too, are in tension. Whereas the academic encourages debate and the pursuit of argument in detail, and therefore over time, the clinical requires rapid decision making and action, often in unexpected and volatile situations. An interest in what constitutes 'professional' as opposed to academic knowledge was behind Schön's (1983) study of 'how professionals think in action'. This is especially important for social work education since, unlike some other forms of education for the professions (e.g. law or accountancy), it incorporates assessed practice within the academic programme. Schön's work has gained a considerable following within social work education. However, the tension between the academic and the professional (and therefore between higher education and social work education) remains, emanating from two very different intellectual traditions, one of which is established whereas the other is still in the process of struggling for wider recognition.

With its attention to professional practice, therefore, social work education can be viewed as on the margins of academic activity. This position has arguably been accentuated by the way in which the practice element has been structured within DipSW regulations, effectively making it no longer 'of' the institution.

Universities have a contractual relationship with the student registered with them. Failure to provide a proper quality of educational experience can result in legal challenge. Any structures or processes that the universities do not control have the potential to weaken their ability to fulfil the responsibility that they alone hold for the programmes they run (which brings a certain hollowness to notions of 'partnership'). Within social work, this responsibility includes practice placements – an integral part of the programme yet one where universities are unable to ensure standardization and have infinitely less power over whom to accept as practice teachers than they have over the appointment of all other staff who teach social workers. Whereas nurse educators assess the suitability of clinical areas for the placement of student nurses and identified teaching hospitals provide the practice base for medical students, the academic institution has almost no part in the practice placements of social work students. From the perspective of universities, this is a risky situation and it contributes to the anxiety and activity that placement finding arouses. Equally worrying, though, is that this separation of the academic from the practice conveys the message that the development of practice really belongs outside higher education. If this is the case, universities might ask with some justification why, to put it rather crudely, they should continue to bother and be bothered about the practice element in social work education when they have so little part to play in it.

Such questions acquire greater strength when a set of other higher education issues are addressed. First, social work education is a high cost activity. The costs of the placement element and of partnership activity assume more significance when universities are faced with year on year cuts in funding. Efficiency savings (i.e. teaching more students with fewer resources) are less possible, given that economies of scale are more difficult with a small student group. The professional curriculum has to be covered by teaching large groups which, though part of a social work education tradition elsewhere as in Germany, is not rooted in the UK. The costs of social work education have therefore become more exposed and, to at least some universities, the benefits may be less evident.

In one very important area, it is the opportunity costs which are probably more worrying. Those universities that intend to maintain and increase a research profile require a level of research activity and output that will enhance their position in the regular research assessment exercise (RAE). The RAE poses problems for professional programmes where academic staff are required to continue with some clinical practice and/or to be involved with the practice of students. At the time of writing, clinical academics in medicine have raised their very real concerns that RAE requirements, as they currently stand, are incompatible with their clinical responsibilities. The seriousness of this for social work has already been evidenced by the decision of the LSE to end its long association with qualifying social work education. Not only is the development of a research base held back, but a low grade in the RAE significantly reduces funding to the educational institution and pushes it in the direction of replacing the lost research element of its income with higher student numbers and a worsening staff: student ratio. Even if social work education were prepared to move in this direction, its ability to do so is severely curtailed by factors such as placement availability and the tradition of small group teaching.

This section has so far dealt with the 'known' elements of the higher education context and social work education's place in it. The changing pattern of funding, whereby students contribute to their fees and finance themselves by loans rather than the student grant, is a major 'unknown' for the institution as well as for social work education. Social work attracts older, so-called 'mature' students, often as a result of a career change or a late entry into higher education. Will the funding changes result in a decrease in numbers or will the near certainty of employment after training (providing that remains) help to attract recruits? If it does and student numbers elsewhere become less secure, might social work education be seen to bring more benefit to the institution? The questions are no less pertinent for the funding of graduates who qualify through postgraduate programmes. Without payment of their fees and a bursary, would they continue to train? If this protected money continues, on what basis do graduates receive public support whereas other social work students do not?

The politics and funding of higher education therefore become as important as the politics of social work and social work education for the future of qualifying and post-qualifying programmes. Social work educators have probably in the past looked more to outside agencies ('the field') than to higher education colleagues in other disciplines when building relationships and alliances, but we are learning, sometimes painfully, that we cannot afford to be aloof from our institutional base.

Facing the Future

Minding the gap

One of the certainties of the future of social work education in the UK is that it will exist without CCETSW and it is difficult to predict whether its absence will make social work education more or less secure. For what was a routine quinquennial review, conducted according to the format for all non-departmental public bodies, the report (Department of Health 1997) on CCETSW identified some far-reaching questions. Some followed from government policy to establish national training organizations (NTOs) and from a commitment to set up a regulatory body for social work which will take the form of general councils in the different countries.

The outcome is that in a post-CCETSW world there will be no single forum within which the vocational, the qualifying and the post-qualifying can be debated and decided upon; no one organization in which education and training concerns are the prime agenda. Whatever the criticisms of CCETSW for the way it has undertaken its work and for the extent to which Council has been dominated by the concerns of government and employers (Pierce and Weinstein Chapter 1), CCETSW has been in the position of 'holding the ring' for the education of the social work workforce. In the more fragmented system of the future, there is no body to perform this function, unless national training organizations and general councils come together in their respective countries, and we do not know what the implications of this will be. Social work education may have more arenas for making itself heard, but its voice may be weakened because it lacks a consolidated organizational base. If this happens, the danger is that it will be less able to manage its place within higher education or to safeguard itself as a professional rather than a technical training.

Another certainty for the future of social work education is that a new diversity will emerge as the responsibility for higher education and for social work devolves to the Welsh and Northern Ireland Assemblies and the Scottish Parliament. We can expect developments that reflect more directly the concerns of individual countries rather than UK uniformity. Already, we have the situation whereby social work is differently defined in Northern Ireland and Scotland, which have maintained the DipSW as the qualification for probation and criminal justice social work, whereas England and Wales have established a new specialist qualification. It remains to be seen whether there will be reciprocal recognition of qualifications or whether some kind of 'conversion' training will be required to cross national boundaries. An even more fundamental divergence (in UK but not in international terms) will follow if Scotland moves to a three-year qualification, while elsewhere in the

UK, the two-year qualification remains. Gaps of a different nature from those already considered in this chapter may therefore have to be managed in the future.

But the gaps that currently affect social work education will continue to be significant in the post-devolution, post-CCETSW world. If there have been Cassandra-like qualities to this chapter, it is because social work education does not feel secure throughout the UK. The gap between social work education and its social work constituency is one to be troubled about, not just because of the insecurity this promotes within social work education (but not, interestingly, within social work) but because the closing of the gap is seen to lie in giving higher prominence to the workplace. The criticism is that social work education does not 'fit' people for the job, not that the job or the employing organization might themselves be 'unfit' in certain respects (as in the way newly qualified staff are often unsupported in the year following qualification).

A more productive approach would be to pay attention to the gap for what it might tell us of the 'fitness' of both social work education and of social work organizations. In this approach, the gap has a value, even though it is necessary to take care how it is negotiated. The gap offers protection. Without it, professional programmes could become too abstract and hypothetical or too limited to the technical and the short term needs of employment. In social work practice terms, this would show itself in workers unable to use their learning in practice or unable to function without checklists and according to predefined situational responses. Increasingly, social workers are operating in circumstances that require engagement with complexity and the unpredictable, balancing the risks of one course of action against those of another. None of this is new to social work but its recognition is within government guidance, not as in the past mainly in textbooks. If workers are to be equipped to handle the complexity, qualifying and post-qualifying experiences need the level of intellectual ability that is the product of the discipline of higher education learning. They also need practice experience which matches the intellectual rigour, where 'why' is as important as 'how' and where, to quote Eraut (1994 p.71) they acquire 'the disposition to theorise' and (p.90) 'bring their knowledge under greater critical control'. Both the present length of the DipSW and the organizational distancing of the practice component from the higher education base make the attainment of this level of practice consciousness an extremely difficult if not impossible task. But without it, practice will be too limited by personal experience and too dependent on individual assumptions that have not been subjected to a wider professional scrutiny.

The direction of this argument is to make for a stronger academic presence in placement experience. An alternative view is to take the present separation (or gap) to its full conclusion and to use the academic experience as the foundation for practice but not to integrate the two. The academic experience might well include case discussion, role plays, observation exercises and the like but sustained practice experience in agencies would come after academic assessment and conceivably could have no academic involvement – a kind of portfolio route to the qualifying award. This might in fact be a more honest arrangement than we currently have and would enable social work education to fit more easily within its own employing institutions. Although such an arrangement flies in the face of the concurrent theory–practice nature of social work education, this is not sufficient reason to reject it out of hand. Indeed, the ensuing debate might clarify at least some of the expectations both of social work education and of what its higher education base can contribute.

But what of the gap between social work education and higher education? This, too, is one to be troubled about. Research motivated institutions can see qualifying education as at best marginal and at worst antithetical to their prime agenda. For the sector as a whole, though, education for the professions is an important part of the task and an important part of income; and over time professional requirements have been accommodated within the academic institution. This is to the advantage of social work education but, in size and status, social work education is less significant than a number of other professional programmes and it needs higher education more than the other way around. Social work education is now having to pay more heed to the gap between its activities and those of the educational institution. The narrowing of this particular gap should be to the benefit of social work, as it will bring a clearer articulation of the professional and of the development of theory from practice instead of the traditional view of theory leading to practice. But this will be realized only if some gap is maintained, sufficient for the knowledge that is expressed in practice to be respected in its own right.

To conclude, it is important not to overlook the fifth meaning of 'to mind' that was cited at the beginning, namely 'to have charge of'. This applies both to social work education itself – who is or should be in control of it? – and to definitions of what is a tolerable lack of fit between it and its two constituent parts – social work practice and higher education. This has been the theme of the CCETSW years. It is apparent in the follow-up to the quinquennial review and will be carried forward into devolved political structures and the dispersal of CCETSW's responsibilities to different organizations. Social work education will need to be an active participant in the negotiations for future arrangements, exploiting the 'multiple marginalities' (Henkel 1995, p.81) that are a characteristic of the position it occupies in relation to social work and to higher education. Otherwise there is a very real danger that there will be no gaps to mind, for uniformity will have been imposed.

References

Brauns, H.J. and Kramer, D. (1986) *Social Work Education in Europe.* Frankfurt/Main: Eigenvarleg des Deutschen vereins fur Öffentliche und private Fürsorge.

CCETSW (1990) *The Requirements for Post Qualifying Education and Training in the Personal Social Services,* Paper 31. London: CCETSW.

Collins (1982) *New Collins Concise English Dictionary.* Glasgow: Collins.

Department of Health (1997) *Review of the Functions of the Central Council for Education and Training in Social Work.* London: DoH.

Donzelot, J. (1979) *The Policing of Families.* London: Routledge.

Eraut, M. (1994) *Developing Professional Knowledge and Competence.* London: Falmer Press.

Goldberg, E. and Warburton, W. (1979) *Ends and Means in Social Work.* London: Allen and Unwin.

Harris, R. (1997) 'Internationalizing social work: some themes and issues'. In N. Mayadas, T. Watts and D. Elliott (eds) *International Handbook on Social Work Theory and Practice.* Westport: Greenwood Press.

Henkel, M. (1995) 'Conceptions of knowledge and social work education'. In M. Yelloly and M. Henkel (eds) *Learning and Teaching in Social Work.* London: Jessica Kingsley Publishers.

Hort, S. and McMurphy, S. (1997) 'Sweden'. In N. Mayadas, T. Watts and D. Elliott (eds) *International Handbook on Social Work Theory and Practice.* Westport: Greenwood Press.

Howe, D. (1996) 'Surface and depth in social work practice'. In N. Parton (ed) *Social Theory, Social Change and Social Work.* London: Routledge.

Jones, C. (1996) 'Anti-intellectualism and the peculiarities of British social work education'. In N. Parton (ed) *Social Theory, Social Change and Social Work.* London: Routledge.

Les, E. (1997) 'Poland'. In N. Mayadas, T. Watts and D. Elliot (eds) *The International Handbook on Social Work Theory and Practice.* Westport: Greenwood Press.

Marsh, P. and Triseliotis, J. (1996) *Ready to Practice?* Aldershot: Avebury.

Parsloe, P. (1996) 'Managing for reflective learning'. In N. Gould and I. Taylor (eds) *Reflective Learning for Social Work.* Aldershot: Arena.

Parton, N. (1996) 'Social work, risk and "the blaming system".' In N. Parton (ed) *Social Theory, Social Change and Social Work.* London: Routledge.

Rowlings, C. (1997) 'Europe'. In N. Mayades, T. Watts and D. Elliott (eds) *International Handbook on Social Work Theory and Practice.* Westport: Greenwood Press.

Rowlings, C. (1998) 'Interesting times: a comment on the 1997 review of CCETSW'. *Social Work Education 17,* 2, 241–243.

Schön, D. (1983) *The Reflective Practitioner.* London: Temple Smith.

Triseliotis, J. and Marsh, P. (1996) *Readiness to Practice.* Edinburgh: Scottish Office Central Research Unit.

Webb, D. (1996) 'Regulation for radicals: the state, CCETSW and the academy'. In N. Parton (ed) *Social Theory, Social Change and Social Work.* London: Routledge.

Younghusband, E. (1978) *Social Work in Britain, 1950–1975,* vols 1 and 2. London: Allen and Unwin.

CHAPTER 4

The Importance of Research in the Education of Care Professionals

Juliet Cheetham

What does research conjure up for most care professionals. What are its purposes and activities. Who is involved in it? These are the first questions to be explored about the place of research in education and training programmes. Typical private responses might be 'research is alright in theory but does not have any bearing in the hectic round of my daily responsibilities'; 'research is for academics, not for people in the real world'. There are also more confidant doubters, like the director of social work who cheerily remarked: 'Research is very important, very important indeed, but then I have never come across a single thing in social work, which was affected by it!' In the classroom, research might be described as 'an academic activity', 'a scholarly inquiry', 'the systematic collection and evaluation of data'.

Practical Purposes of Research

None of these brief descriptions is likely to be particularly appealing for care professionals at the outset of their education and training when, typically, they are intent on acquiring practical knowledge and skills. However, an important argument of this chapter is that research is extremely practical. This becomes evident when its major purposes are understood. In social work and social care these are:

- to illuminate the etiology of social and personal problems, including the impact of social problems on individual citizens, families and communities …

- to determine the impact of social work …

- to influence policy and practice. (Cheetham 1997, p.298)

Research should therefore support the rational foundation of social work and social care and steer them towards effective outcomes.

This conception of research as extremely practical may be hard to sustain if it is seen as an esoteric activity largely carried out by academics. The Oxford English Dictionary's inclusive definition usefully challenges such a perception and underlines the relevance of research to social work. Research here is:

- the act of searching
- a search or investigation directed to the discovering of some facts by careful consideration or study of the subject
- a course of critical and scientific inquiry.

According to this definition, research would include a critical exploration of social and individual problems ('the act of searching … careful consideration or study of the subject') as well as specific empirical studies and review and synthesis of existing knowledge ('critical and scientific inquiry'). A research-minded person can therefore be expected to be inquisitive, to observe, to question, record, analyse and weigh evidence; all activities which are at the heart of the practice of thoughtful care professionals.

Understanding social problems

If this is accepted then research must be seen as being central to the knowledge on which care professionals seek to understand the society in which they work and the individual and social problems that are the focus of their responsibilities. Such a disciplined approach is essential given the complex knowledge base of social work, which is:

> diffuse, diverse and inclusive. It places the issue, problem or person at the centre of investigation and tries to understand events through available knowledge … someone who offends is not defined exclusively or primarily in terms of the offense, but as a person in a social context within which the offense occurred … behaviour is better understood in the context of an interplay of different social science perspectives, unified in the vision of the social worker. (Fisher 1998 p.93)

The essential point is that this kind of knowledge is interdisciplinary, a simple truth which can be difficult to sustain in the hurly-burly world of care professionals. It is difficult because the time for complex analysis may be strictly limited (although the huge emphasis given to assessment in some situations can demand such exploration), but also because the practicalities of service delivery often require a rather single-minded focus. This is excellent when such a focus has been tailored to fit with what can feasibly be tackled by social work and social care, but it can be disastrous if the essential complexity of a problem has been disregarded (Smith 1995; Stewart, Smith and Stewart 1994). For example, cognitive behavioural help for offenders that focuses on behaviour conducive to criminal activity and which is combined with help with pressing practical problems can be effective compared with less focused approaches (McGuire 1995). An effective probation service can therefore expect to have a modest impact on recidivism but the total amount and type of crime in society are associated with age, opportunity, policing and the influences of the family, schools, communities and even the business cycle (Field 1990; Smith 1995). At an individual level social work can have little or no influence on any of these factors.

Mental illness is another subject that can be surrounded with sloppy thinking, sometimes compounded by hostility to the assumed simplifications of a 'medical model', which allegedly rejects social influences in favour of physiology. The reality is that while there is no complete understanding of the causation of serious mental illness such as schizophrenia and severe depression, it is known that both drug therapies and forms of social care and support can be beneficial (Goldberg and Huxley 1992). Studies of women's depression have also identified social influences and life events that exacerbate or protect from illness (Brown and Harris 1978). Knowledge of such research is an essential foundation for social work with individuals and the planning of care programmes.

Other examples of uncritical or uninformed thinking about social issues can be found in the gloomy contemporary political and media discourse about the state of our nations and citizenry and therefore about the dire consequences of social problems, usually simplistically defined. In such analyses, divorce, family breakdown and single parenthood can be seen as permanent, undifferentiated, pathological states and not, as is more often the reality of the matter, as transitional periods of great stress which can be survived and coped with through a combination of personal initiative, support and practical help and the passage of time (Rutter and Smith 1995). Crude links may also be made between many of the ills of modern society – poverty, low educational attainment, a variety of deviant behaviour – and specific groups, sometimes racial minorities but, most recently, an unreal entity called 'the underclass'.

Care professionals are not immune from such ruminations and their increasingly brief and 'targeted' contacts with those people whose depth of distress and disadvantage makes them eligible for help may reinforce such perceptions. These are not just wrong but dangerous because they encourage stereotyped thinking, fear and pessimism about the possibility of change; this diminishes human experience and practical research-based interventions.

The first essential practical use of research as a 'search or critical consideration' is to challenge broad social analyses by questioning their theoretical and evidential basis. For example, what is driving this account? Is there a political or ideological motive? What supporting evidence is being used? Is this anecdotal or systematically collected; local or more broadly based; covering what time period, social groups and classes? Are age, gender and ethnicity taken into account, together with any relevant conflicting perspectives? How is quantitative information presented? The following simple examples are often part of scaremongering or thoughtless analysis. An observation that group y is twice as likely as group x to be involved in offending is more or less significant depending on the proportion in group y; if this is 10 per cent then 5 per cent of group x is involved. Majorities can range from 51 to 99 per cent; and the statement that three-quarters of an unhappy or disruptive group of people come from broken homes (a concept which itself requires unpicking) does not mean that this will be the destination of three-quarters of people with such backgrounds. Indeed, a recent review of studies of children in these circumstances confirms their adjustment and successful coping (Rodgers and Pryor 1998).

The point here is not to expect perfect and comprehensive studies but to be critical about the contributions and limitations of their data. Large, representative population studies can yield important information, for example, about the education, income, work experience, accommodation and so on which allow comparisons between men and women, social classes, age groups and localities. This is important contextual information for planning social work services. Smaller studies can provide information about opinions and experiences, which throw light on the reactions of different groups to problems and hardship. Such studies can illuminate apparently illogical or damaging behaviour. This was an important contribution of Graham's (1993) study of women's smoking. She found that although poor and stressed mothers were well aware of the dangers of smoking, and felt they should not do it, they found in this activity at least temporary relief from stress – a brief occasion which gave them something for themselves – in lives dominated by anxiety and responsibility for others. Such research can enlarge understanding and suggest a focus for help.

Generalized accounts of social problems must also be subjected to some exploration of the weight they give to individual responsibility and capacity to determine events and to the influence of life chances. For example, the capacity of disabled people for independent living can be greatly improved by social environments that encourage employment for them, access to buildings, suitable transport and an adequate income. The frequent absence of all this is the context for the social model of disability in which discrimination against disabled people creates or greatly exacerbates the disadvantage of their physical handicap. The extent to which a social model of disability prevails crucially influences the services and support provided (Morris 1993). Yet more inquiry is needed because disability is a heterogeneous phenomenon; the experiences of parents caring for a handicapped child are very different from the caring roles that may slowly increase and eventually engulf an elderly person looking after a spouse with dementia.

It should not be necessary in social work and social care to have to argue for such research-based thinking but some contemporary preoccupations can be undermining. In part this may be a consequence of a focus on practice competencies. This can (but should not) encourage the belief that the essence of social work and social care is the acquisition of specified skills to deal with discrete problems with defined structures. In this working world – which does not accord with the realities of daily social work and social care – understanding of causation and context is not necessary. The social sciences therefore have little or no contribution, a view which from time to time has been aired by government bodies and local authority managers.

Happily there are now signs that such blinkered analysis holds less sway in government, an encouragement for those responsible for education and training to be similarly inclusive. For example, the government's consultative paper *Our Healthier Nation* (Department of Health 1998) reviews the complex causes of ill health and their interaction and discusses how social and economic factors, environment, lifestyle and access to services can be included in strategies to improve health; strategies which are variously the responsibility of government, local authorities, communities and individuals. There is much here that is relevant for care professionals. The government's Social Exclusion Unit adopts a similarly inclusive and multi-disciplinary approach, describing social exclusion, in its explanatory leaflet, as 'a shorthand label for what can happen when individuals or areas suffer from a combination of linked problems such as unemployment, poor skills, low incomes, poor housing, high crime environments, bad health and family breakdown'. The best practice for promoting solutions is strongly research based. Even closer to social work the *Communities that Care* (Joseph Rowntree Foundation 1997) programmes designed to build safer neighbourhoods and to promote the development and achievement of young people are based on international research on risk and prevention and on high quality local studies which identify the areas' strengths and problems.

Understanding individuals' problems

While care professionals may agree at a general level that a broad understanding of social structures and problems is relevant to their activities, their most pressing concerns are with the individuals, groups and communities with which they work. What practical help can research be in these contexts? An important first caution is that since research deals with collectivities there can be no certainty that findings concerning a group will be relevant to a particular individual. This is why care professionals place (or should place) so much importance on learning about individual perspectives – in our various jargons – 'the user's view', or 'starting where the client is'; hence the importance attached to 'social diagnosis' in the early twentieth century and to assessment today. In a small way each such exploration is an act of research. However, the practical contribution of the research of others is that it can alert people to relevant matters not immediately on an individual's agenda. For example, a bereaved person may not know about the stages of grief and the changes in the intensity of the feelings of loss which research has revealed. People who begin to care for an elderly or disabled relative may not be aware of the particular needs and support that studies of carers have shown to be particularly important (Twigg and Atkin 1995).

Research can also make sense of apparently contradictory or upsetting behaviour, as Graham's (1993) study of smoking shows. Parents' and children's reactions to visiting and contact in foster or residential care provide another example and demonstrate the importance of helping people to manage their distress in the interests of sustained and important family contact (Aldgate and Simmonds 1988; Triseliotis, Sellick and Short 1995).

There are also many illuminating accounts, often autobiographical, of the perspectives and experiences of people who are regarded as being well beyond the bounds of social acceptability (Parker 1963, 1971, 1972, 1974; Sereny 1998), or of those who have not traditionally had a voice (Atkinson and Williams 1990).

Limitations of Research and Alternative Strategies

In short, research helps care professionals not to listen in ignorance. It can therefore enhance their empathy and the helpfulness of their responses, but it cannot always be called in aid. Care professionals can confront new situations about which very little is known. Examples include working with the first victims of HIV/AIDS and my own activities as a social worker in the 1950s with the then immigrant communities in south London. There were then no contemporary studies to help us understand the background, expectations and experiences of immigrants and the racial discrimination faced by West

Indians and Asians. There were therefore two possible strategies. The first was to admit ignorance and to ask individuals about their experiences, to recognize them as expert witnesses. This was an honest approach which today, when partnership with service users is more on the agenda, would be more expected and commonplace.

The second strategy was to try and generalize from research on related matters – in this case on the experience of migration. This attempt to transfer learning is important when there are extreme pressures on the time available for education and training. Although it is now enthusiastically espoused, there are some risks which the experience of work with West Indian mothers in the 1950s illustrates. At that time many came to work or train to improve their own and their families' life chances. They expected therefore to be able to arrange care for their children. Today this would be understood and some practical support, or at least information, might be given. In the 1950s crude understandings of the effects of maternal deprivation prevailed and the regular separation of young children from their parents, even for a few hours a day, was widely regarded by care professionals as detrimental. Day care was scarce and reserved only for parents with serious problems. To their stunned amazement these West Indian mothers' requests for help with the care of their pre-school children were refused, sometimes with garbled accounts of the bad effects such arrangements would have on their children. What went wrong in this attempt to transfer knowledge from research?

First, there was in social work an insufficiently critical consumption of Bowlby's (1953) and others' accounts of maternal deprivation. Findings from studies of very young children reared in institutions, or suddenly removed as evacuees from everything familiar, were generalized to children spending a few hours a day away from their parents. The effects on women's and children's lives of such continued close encounters were disregarded until the critiques of feminist writers began to be widely read (Friedan 1971; Greer 1971; Oakley 1972). By that time too, accessible and authoritative critiques of maternal deprivation theories were available (Rutter 1972).

The second failure in this resort to research was to give too little credence to the messages being given over and over again by sensible and ambitious women intent on doing the best for their families. The assumption was that they were wrong or misguided. There was no weighing of evidence from research carried out in very special circumstances with the experiences of women who had lived in families where work had always been a necessity and priority. This is therefore a good example of a contested theory – of which there are many surrounding social care, not least because its activities are often intimately connected with the moralities of individual, family and state responsibility. Although today there is much clearer evidence of the effects – for good and ill – of day care for children and of the implications of too much and too little work for parents, there can still be fierce debates about what is right for mothers to do; fathers tend to be invisible. Encouragement for single mothers to work is now government policy and in this context the outcomes for parents and children will need careful independent scrutiny.

There is one important research footnote to all this. The West Indian mothers who asked for help with child care were not deterred by refusals of help or their rationale. They simply sought child care elsewhere, often in the least regulated and most unsatisfactory quarters – unregistered childminders and private foster parents. Social workers were aware of this and the serious harm that could sometimes ensue, but at individual and office level it seemed too difficult to make the connections between refusals to help with requests for child care and the dreadful alternatives which were sometimes the consequence. The evidence of fostering and childminding was gathered by Holman (1973) and Jackson (1979) respectively, but it was still many years before positive policies and practice could ameliorate some of the worst experiences of this kind of care. It is worth thinking what contemporary examples there may be of this misapplication of research and the failure to respond to care professionals' accumulating knowledge of the unintended consequences of their policy and practice.

Understanding the Impact of Practice

The second highly practical reason for research is its contribution to the identification of helpful processes and effective practice. This is an extremely challenging agenda if the goal is to pursue practice, which can irrefutably be shown to be effective.

An important first question is to consider what kind of evidence can count as worthwhile support for a particular intervention. Possibilities include users' opinions, measures of improved well-being or of decreased problems or disruptive behaviour and professional opinion (if backed up with serious argument and systematic observation). Any of these is better than nothing; some are more credible than others; none provides conclusive proof of effectiveness; all can provoke thoughtful reflection.

There is now a large amount of evaluative research and inquiry of many different kinds. This includes the extensive research programmes in research centres such as the Personal Social Services Research Centre at the universities of Kent and Manchester and the London School of Economics, the National Institute of Social Work, the Centre for Evidence-Based Social Services at Exeter University, the Social Work Research Centre at the University of Stirling and the Social Work Research and Development Unit at the University of York. This research is funded by government, research councils and charities, and especially the Joseph Rowntree Foundation with its focus on research to help the development of policy and practice and its active dissemination programme designed to be of immediate use for professionals. The Department of Health programmes of research which can extend over many years, exploring responses to evolving problems of social work and social care, are also usefully drawn together to distill their implications for practice. Examples include the research on child protection (Dartington Social Research Unit 1995) and *Looking After Children* materials developed to help identify the problems, potential and progress of children who are the responsibility of local authorities (Ward 1995).

Also relevant are the quality assurance arrangements of social care agencies which use a variety of means to determine services' adherence to standards and users' reactions to services received. The purpose of such reviews is to help ensure standards of practice which, ideally, are known to be effective and acceptable to users but, in the absence of this information, which conform to professionals' understanding of best practice.

Debate, however, abounds in the social work research field about the validity of various types of comparative studies. The growing importance attached to evidence (or knowledge) based practice, initially in the health field, now more widely in the social work arena, has led to calls by some researchers for an acknowledgment of a hierarchy of valid methodology (Macdonald 1997). Macdonald and Sheldon (1998) argue that 'Random Control Trials (RCTs) offer maximum attributive confidence in the relationship between intervention and the outcome(s).' The case is made by Macdonald (Oakley and Roberts 1996) for random control trials to be accepted as the 'gold-standard' experimental method, although their cost and the realities of social work mean that not all evaluations can be undertaken in this way. Nevertheless, in her view, alternative approaches to evaluation should be designed and interpreted in ways that address concerns about lack of rigour. After RCTs, in the absence of experimental control of *who* is exposed to *what*, *where* and *when*, Macdonald acknowledges the value of *quasi-experimental studies* to maximize external validity by careful attention to the process of data collection, control for sources of internal validity and to maximize external validity. Next, although *pre-experimental research designs* have no random allocation and no pre-intervention matching of groups, she accepts there are examples which feature a range of clients in different circumstances and produce similar outcomes, where some degree of attributive confidence can be commanded (Oakley and Roberts 1996).

In order to ensure that the learning from research is immediately available to care professionals and educators, Oakley and Roberts (1996) have recommended the establishment of a database of evaluations, similar to that being developed under the aegis of the Cochrane Collaboration for medical interventions.

Outcomes for Individuals

Studies of the impact of services have to focus on outcomes, either analyses of what was delivered in relation to what was identified as needed or desirable, or of changing measures of users' circumstances and experiences. These might include, for example, their degree of dependence, their ability to manage important aspects of daily life, degrees of distress or well-being or, most ambitiously, their quality of life. The key questions may not always be whether positive changes were achieved. For example, when help is offered to very elderly people with degenerative illnesses, it is more realistic to determine whether a stable state has been maintained or whether deterioration has been delayed more than might otherwise have been expected.

There are many such measures which have been established as reliable, valid and user friendly and some may be included in routine assessments of need, especially in community care. They have an important place in recording change (or its absence) over time. Experience shows that service users can find it helpful to be involved in giving this information and observing changes. Experience also shows that care professionals often object to using these research instruments, complaining about their imperfections and intrusiveness. No research instrument is perfect, but many have now been widely used with positive results. Without such measures, there can be no systematic assessment of changes in users' circumstances, experience and lives. A training priority may therefore be to help care professionals learn how to incorporate these standardized measures into their ongoing work.

Studies using these measures of outcome can record whether there was any change during intervention. This is an important first question, but a positive answer is not enough to justify the assumption that the help was effective. Such a judgement requires a series of other questions, some of which are difficult to answer for technical research reasons. First, how long were positive changes maintained after help ceased? For example, can parents who have been helped to respond to their child's difficult behaviour – in ways which reduce the likelihood of violent or abusive responses – sustain this newly learnt behaviour without continued support? Similarly can people who have learnt techniques of reducing a damaging intake of alcohol keep using these without regular supervision?

Harder, but just as important, are questions about the comparative impact of different kinds of help, or none at all. Responses to these questions require studies which compare the outcomes of different forms of help given to groups with the same characteristics and problems. What, for example, are the differences in outcomes for low income mothers who have to manage very difficult children, who receive either a programme of social activities and personal counselling, a series of sessions on the management of difficult behaviour or nothing?

These comparative studies require similar (preferably identical) groups who receive different services. A more reliable way of identifying impact is to compare two different kinds of help (or help and no help) and then randomly assign people, with their informed consent, to one or other intervention. It can be difficult, sometimes for political reasons, to offer no help, but this is a necessary strategy if attempts are to be made to determine whether the help offered was instrumental in achieving change or whether there were other factors: the passage of time; support from friends and family; an important life event.

Another practitioner and agency friendly method, so far too little used in Britain, is single case design (Kazi 1998; Kazi and Wilson 1996; *Research on Social Work Practice* 1995; Sheldon 1984). Briefly, this helps practitioners and users to trace in a systematic fashion any changes which follow intervention. A baseline measure is taken, for example, of the number of temper tantrums a child has a day, or a person's ability to perform certain practical tasks like cooking a simple meal. Then, after help designed to tackle these issues, the measures are taken again to record whether change followed help. Users and practitioners often find it a useful aid to identifying problems to be tackled, the help to be given and the progress made. If more elaborate designs are used which involve stopping help and seeing if there is a return to the original baseline, or at least a deterioration, with further progress after help is started again, then some tentative judgements can be made about the causal relationship between intervention and change.

Single case design is one relatively simple method whereby practitioners can undertake their own research. There is also a growing body of experience of other kinds of practitioner research, using a range of methods and designs, whereby practitioners can carry out small studies of direct relevance to their agencies (Cheetham and Kazi 1998; Connor 1993; Everitt and Hardiker 1996; Fuller and Petch 1995). As well as giving useful insights into a range of practice matters, such research also sharpens practitioners' understanding of the scope and limitations of research. It is a major method of promoting research-minded practice.

Sharing Research Information with Service Users

Ideally care professionals should be able and willing to discuss frankly with the people they try to help the knowledge basis of the services provided. This is possible when research has yielded information about the outcomes for service users or at least about their reactions to help received. For example, older people considering residential care should know that since research has shown people's overwhelming preference for single rooms, then homes should take this into account in their actual and planned provision. It could also be helpful for prospective residents to know that key workers for individual residents are required by most inspecting authorities, although the evidence that they can provide the special and continuous attention expected is shaky. Residents' wish for key workers is also not established. They are the product of professionals' beliefs about good practice and therefore require further systematic inquiry. Residents and their families may therefore want to explore the role key workers are expected to play.

In the happy but quite rare cases when it is known that a special kind of help (properly carried out) is likely to have positive results, for example, task-centred social work or cognitive behaviour therapy (CBT), this can be explained. What is known about users' reactions to social work services, for example, when parents take part in child protection conferences, can also be frankly explored (Thoburn, Lewis and Shemmings 1995). With newer or unresearched ways of working, or when a series of interventions is required, an honest approach to practice would include reference to their rationale and justification: for example, that x seems the best or only thing to do in the circumstances, that it is what the user wants or prefers, that there is some suggestion from other people's experience that a particular approach could be helpful.

Most practice is a long way from such honest sharing of information, but the advantages it offers are not just integrity in a professional relationship but the routine discipline of having to make explicit the thinking behind what we do. A useful start could be made by encouraging such exploration as part of the supervision of students and qualified care professionals. In addition to the positive developmental influence this could have, it would give some pause for thought and reconsideration when a new intervention is being pursued with ignorant enthusiasm. An obvious example was the use of pin-down procedures in children's homes. This had no research basis, no reasonable theory, but a major unpleasant impact on the lives and liberty of residents.

Users, their Views and Contribution

Considerable importance, rightly, has been attached to users' perspectives on their needs, priorities, the services they receive and the people who help them. There is now a substantial literature on users' views, with the UK being seen as a leader in this kind of research. Beresford and Croft (1997) argue that most of this has provided information for professionals, with users playing little or no part in influencing the ends and means of the research. There is much to be developed here which is beyond the scope of this chapter but usefully explored by Beresford and Wallcroft (1997), Evans and Fisher (1998), Bowes (1996) and by Hastings in Chapter 6 of this book. It is however, extremely important to take seriously what users tell us about social work and social care. There are, for example, key messages about workers' attributes and ways of working which users over and over again emphasize as priorities. These are things which individual workers, supervisors and educators could aspire to and monitor. They include reliability, openness, honesty, attentive listening, the ability to clarify and agree problems with clients, warmth and genuineness (Howe 1993; Sinclair 1992). Other studies, worryingly, have shown users to find many workers unable or unwilling to deliver practical help, although these same users have appreciated the relationships they have had with their workers (Sainsbury, Nixon and Phillips 1982).

A number of key studies have highlighted the way in which institutional racism has consistently disadvantaged black service users. Discrimination against black elders has been well documented. Norman (1985) describes the 'triple jeopardy' of being black, being old and living in a second homeland. Patel (1990, p.7) lists a number of studies which demonstrate a low take-up of services by black and Asian elders, explained to the researchers by professionals on the basis that 'they look after their own'. With respect to mental illness, it has been generally acknowledged that British born Afro-Caribbeans are more likely than white Britons to be diagnosed as suffering from schizophrenia and less likely to be diagnosed as suffering from depression (Littlewood and Lipsedge 1989). On the other hand, there is a comparatively low take-up of preventive community-based services by ethnic minority families who either do not know about them or do not find that they meet their specific needs.

Despite these critical responses, many studies of users' reactions to services (in health, education, social work and the commercial arena) report quite high levels of satisfaction (Gutek 1978). How should we react to this and avoid complacency? Key questions concern the studies' aims and methods. For example, how many choices were offered in questionnaires?

Faced with 'very satisfied', 'quite satisfied' and 'not satisfied' a pretty critical but not totally dissatisfied user will probably opt for 'quite satisfied'; but without further explanation, what does this mean? If people have come to expect long waiting times, bureaucratic responses and minimal services or feel that, for various reasons, they have few rights to help, then a response expressing modified satisfaction may just indicate that things were no worse than expected. This might be comforting news in the short term but it does not help longer term reform and change. There needs to be some written or spoken elaboration of the context of fairly bland responses. A useful step in this direction can be to ask respondents to indicate two or three things they would like changed.

User-led research is a growing movement, especially in the field of mental health. Ryan, Lindley and Faulkener (1998, p.16) explain that: 'Users have their own definitions of what they mean by research which often deviate considerably from the traditional approaches ... Often, a primary consideration of user researchers is to explore the subjective experience of being mentally ill or receiving services.' User-led research in mental health has challenged traditional approaches to service delivery and highlighted the need for 24–hour, community-based alternatives to emergency admission to hospital and wider access to counselling and self-help strategies.

Despite the complexities, it is inconceivable that users' views should not be a priority in attempts to explore the acceptability and impact of a service. This is a mark of integrity and partnership. As Hastings explains in Chapter 6, it is helpful for such explorations to start early in care professionals' careers. Useful beginnings can be made during placements (Baird 1991; Shardlow and Doel 1996).

A Research Focus on Services

By no means all evaluative research can identify personal outcomes for users; the focus is often on services – their purpose, the ways they are delivered and to whom. There are important policy and management reasons for such investigations. These may be a necessary first step before individual outcomes can be explored because it is clearly essential to know who is getting what and why before there can be any systematic study of impact. This service-based research has an important contribution to make to agencies' pursuit of informed and transparent practice. It may well identify unintended consequences and large gaps between objectives and their realization. Important examples affecting national policy are the studies by Gibbons, Conroy and Bell (1995) of child protection procedures. These, very briefly, identified large amounts of time and effort given to enquiries about the possible registration of children on child protection registers. However, little significant help was provided in response to the major problems of poverty, child management and family relationships found by these enquiries and which were clearly relevant to the good care of children. Support for children in need is now meant to have a higher profile than investigation of alleged abuse.

In work with offenders there have been several important studies which have identified the risk of offering help early within a tariff system of penalties when further offences, even quite minor ones, can mean a swift progression from welfare interventions to those which are explicitly restrictive or punitive. These studies have helped shape policies within social work and probation which offer help early for offenders but outside the formal penalty systems of adult or juvenile courts. The tying of help to such penalties is therefore reserved for those with substantial histories of offending or who have committed serious crimes.

Other more local examples of service based evaluative research have explored the low uptake of assessments by carers following the Carers (Recognition and Services) Act 1995. These have identified significant resistance, for example: the reluctance of relatives to perceive themselves as carers; their alienation from the language of social work bureaucracy ('would you like me to do an assessment of your needs?' is not an appealing invitation); community care workers' beliefs that they 'do all this already' (even if carers are unaware of these attentions); combined with fears of being proactive lest they raise expectations that cannot be met. (Twigg and Atkin 1995). Such studies have helped community care workers be clearer about the purposes of carers' assessments, be more positive and user friendly in the ways these are offered, including giving people leaflets to help them think about their caring roles and what problems and help they might wish to discuss.

Ideals, Reality and Progress

The principal argument so far has been that research, interpreted broadly, is an essential and highly practical means of understanding the context of social work and social care, the problems with which care professionals are involved and effective means of help. To achieve this understanding many different research approaches will be needed. None is perfect and each must be judged according to its fitness to examine the questions posed and the extent to which these are illuminated. Care professionals have to use many different kinds of evidence. Their professionalism and integrity demand that they are critical of the quality of this evidence and alive to whether it can show that something is irrefutably the case or simply suggest that it might be so.

Sadly, this argument about the centrality and practicality of research in social work and social care is not widely accepted. Students may be extremely eclectic in their selection of theories to help their understanding, picking those they like the sound of without further critical appraisal; or they may be exposed to lecturers' and supervisors' equally uncritical favourite theories (Sheldon 1986). They may also complain that college-based education seems irrelevant to practice; that research is badly taught and that neither is referred to on placements or in the first year of practice (Marsh and Triseliotis 1996; Waterhouse 1987). Added to this is the limited time care professional students, practitioners and supervisors have to read and the absence of systematic, comprehensive programmes of post-qualifying education and training which could regularly update knowledge and skills. There are complaints too about huge book lists and about inaccessible research findings.

It is a tall order to change all this but here are some suggested first steps. First, all care professionals – students, practitioners, supervisors and managers – must question themselves and each other about the basis for their understanding of a particular situation and their preferred means of help. Routine questions should be: 'What's the evidence for this? How was it gathered? How far can it be relied upon? What else do we need to know? How can we find out about this?' This research-minded approach should be an established and ordinary part of learning and practice. It is a fatal mistake to isolate research to a particular (usually small) slot in the curriculum and treat it largely as a review of research methods. Research in its different manifestations has to be a central, ever-present component of learning and practice. This requires a literate approach, that is a willingness to consult, critically, published work. With increasingly sophisticated social science and social work research (Cheetham and Deakin 1997) this literature is substantial and growing. However, a useful first step is to start with a major companion text, such as the Blackwell's *Companions to Social Policy* (Alcock, Erskine and May (1998) and to *Social Work* (Davies 1997). These have short authoritative articles on most of the major matters of concern to care professionals, with suggestions for key further reading. There are also several accessible research-based and practitioner focused texts which briefly and usefully draw together relevant evidence. These include the Barnardo's 'What Works' series of publications on child protection, (Macdonald, forthcoming; Macdonald and Roberts 1995) and other aspects of child care; the Joseph Rowntree Foundation 'Findings' summaries for each of its very large programme of practice and policy research which has special relevance to community care and user involvement with people with physical disabilities, learning disabilities or with mental health problems. These are distributed to all course leaders in social work education, to directors of local authority social work and social service departments and to some voluntary organisations. Pierce (1996) has usefully discussed how these summaries can be used in social work education and training.

It would be comforting, but a lie, to imply that the pursuit of research minded practice is easy, or that it provides a foolproof panacea. On the contrary, it is challenging hard work, often opening doors to further inquiry, confirming complexity and heightening uncertainty. Despite all this, indeed perhaps because of it, research is one essential foundation for help and care, bringing together experience, thought and systematic analysis with the intention that the best possible services are offered. Research should cast a light, at times bright, at times flickering, on the struggles and suffering which confront us, on what we do and think and on what we read, including every chapter in this book.

References

Alcock, P., Erskine, A. and May, M. (eds) (1998) *The Student Companion to Social Policy.* Oxford: Blackwell.

Aldgate, J. and Simmonds, J. (eds) (1988) *Direct Work with Children – A Guide for Practitioners.* London: Batsford.

Atkinson, D. and Williams, F. (eds) (1990) *Know Me As I Am: An Anthology of Prose, Poetry and Art by People with Learning Difficulties.* London: Hodder and Stoughton.

Baird, P. (1991) 'The proof of the pudding: a study of client views of practice competence'. *Issues in Social Work Education 10*, 1 and 2, 24–41.

Beresford, P. and Croft, S. (1997) 'Service users' perspectives'. In M. Davies (ed) *The Blackwell Companion to Social Work.* Oxford: Blackwell.

Beresford, P. and Wallcroft, J. (1997) 'Psychiatric system survivors and emancipatory research issues, overlaps and differences'. In C. Barnes and G. Mercer (eds) *Doing Disability Research.* Leeds: Disability Press.

Bowes, A.M. (1996) 'Evaluation as empowerment: reflections on action research with Asian women'. *Sociological Research on Line 1*, 1, http: // www.socresonline.org.uk

Bowlby, J. (1953) *Child Care and the Growth of Love.* Harmondsworth: Penguin.

Brown, G.W. and Harris, T.H. (1978) *The Social Origins of Depression.* London: Tavistock.

Cheetham, J. (1997) 'The research perspective'. In M. Davies (ed) *The Blackwell Companion to Social Work.* Oxford: Blackwell.

Cheetham, J. and Deakin, N. (1997) 'Research note: assessing the assessment: some reflections on the 1996 Higher Education Funding Council Research Assessment Exercise'. *British Journal of Social Work 27*, 435–442.

Cheetham, J. and Kazi, M. (eds) (1998) *The Working of Social Work.* London: Jessica Kingsley Publishers.

Connor, A. (1993) *Monitoring and Evaluation Made Easy.* London: HMSO.

Dartington Social Research Unit (1995) *Child Protection and Child Abuse: Messages from Research.* London: HMSO.

Davies, M. (1997) *The Blackwell Companion to Social Work.* Oxford: Blackwell.

Department of Health (1998) *Our Healthier Nation.* London: HMSO.

Evans, M. and Fisher, M. (1998) 'Collaborative evaluation with service users'. In I. Shaw and J. Lishman (eds) *Evaluation and Social Work Practice.* London: Sage.

Everitt, A. and Hardiker, P. (1996) *Evaluating for Good Practice.* Basingstoke: Macmillan.

Field, S. (1990) *Trends in Crime and their Interpretation.* London: HMSO.

Fisher, M. (1998) 'Social work research, social work knowledge and the research assessment exercise'. In B. Broad (ed) *The Politics of Social Work Research and Evaluation.* Birmingham: Venture Press.

Friedan, B. (1971) *The Feminine Mystique.* London: Victor Gollancz.

Fuller, R. and Petch, A. (1995) *Practitioner Research: The Reflective Social Worker.* Buckingham: Open University Press.

Gibbons, J., Conroy, S. and Bell, C. (1995) *Operating the Child Protection System.* London: HMSO.

Goldberg, D.P. and Huxley, P.J. (1992) *Common Mental Disorder: A Biosocial Model.* London: Routledge.

Graham, H. (1993) *When Life's a Drag: Women, Smoking and Disadvantage.* London: HMSO.

Greer, G. (1971) *The Female Eunuch.* London: Paladin.

Gutek, B. (1978) 'Strategies for studying client satisfaction'. *Journal of Social Issues 34,* 44–56.

Holman, R. (1973) *Trading in Children.* London: Routledge.

Howe, D. (1993) *On Being a Client.* London: Sage.

Jackson, B. (1979) *Childminder.* London: Routledge.

Joseph Rowntree Foundation (1997) *Communities that Care.* York: Joseph Rowntree Foundation.

Kazi, M. (1998) *Single Case Designs and Social Work.* Aldershot: Ashgate.

Kazi, M. and Wilson, J. (1996) 'Applying single case evaluation in social work'. *British Journal of Social Work 26,* 699–717.

Littlewood, R. and Lipsedge, M. (1989) *Aliens and Alienists, Ethnic Minorities and Psychiatry,* 2nd edn. London: Unwin Hyman.

Macdonald, G. (forthcoming) *What Works in Child Protection?* Barkingside: Barnardos.

Macdonald, G. (1997) 'Social work research: the state we're in'. *Journal of Interprofessional Care 11,* 1, 57–65.

Macdonald, G. and Roberts, H. (1995) *What Works in the Early Years? Effective Interventions for Children and their Families in Health, Social Welfare, Education and Child Protection.* Barkingside: Barnardos.

Macdonald, G. and Sheldon, B. (1998) 'Changing one's mind: the final frontier?' *Issues in Social Work Education 18,* 1, 3–25.

McGuire, J. (1995) *What Works: Reducing Offending.* Chichester: Wiley.

Marsh, P. and Triseliotis, J. (1996) *Ready to Practise?* Aldershot: Avebury.

Morris, J. (1993) *Independent Lives? Community Care and Disabled People.* Basingstoke: Macmillan.

Norman, A. (1985) *Triple Jeopady: Growing Old in a Second Homeland.* London: Centre for Policy on Ageing.

Oakley, A. (1972) *Sex, Gender and Society.* London: Temple Smith.

Oakley, A. and Roberts, H. (eds) (1996) *Evaluating Social Interventions.* Barkingside: Barnados.

OUP (1983) *Oxford English Dictionary (Shorter).* Oxford: Oxford University Press.

Parker, T. (1963) *The Unknown Citizen.* Harmondsworth: Penguin.

Parker, T. (1971) *The Twisting Lane: Some Sex Offenders.* London: Paladin.

Parker, T. (1972) *In No Man's Land: Some Unmarried Mothers.* London: Paladin.

Parker, T. (1974) *The Courage of his Convictions.* London: Paladin.

Patel, N. (1990) *A Race Against Time – Social Services Provision to Black Elders.* London: Runnymede Trust.

Pierce, R. (1996) *Social Care Research into Practice.* York: Joseph Rowntree Foundation.

Research on Social Work Practice (1995) (Special Issue: *Practical Applications of Single System Designs*) *4,* 3.

Rodgers, B. and Pryor, J. (1998) *Divorce and Separation: The Outcomes for Children.* York: Joseph Rowntree Foundation.

Rutter, M. (1972) *Maternal Deprivation Reassessed.* Harmondsworth: Penguin.

Rutter, M. and Smith, D. (1995) *Psycho Social Disturbances in Young People: Time Trends and their Causes.* Chichester: Wiley.

Ryan, P., Lindley, P. and Faulkner, A. (1998) *Research Matters: User Focussed Research.* Sutton, Surrey: Community Care Magazine.

Sainsbury, E., Nixon, S. and Phillips, D. (1982) *Social Work in Focus.* London: Routledge and Kegan Paul.

Sereny, G. (1998) *Cries Unheard.* Basingstoke: Macmillan.

Shardlow, S. and Doel, M. (1996) *Practice Learning and Teaching, BASW.* London: Macmillan.

Sheldon, B. (1984) 'Single case evaluation: review and prospects'. In J. Lishman (ed) *Evaluation.* London: Jessica Kingsley Publishers.

Sheldon, B. (1986) 'Social work effectiveness experiments: review and implications'. *British Journal of Social Work 16,* 223–242.

Sinclair, I. (1992) 'Social work research: its relevance to social work and social work education'. *Issues in Social Work Education 11,* 2, 65–80.

Smith, D. (1995) *Criminology for Social Work.* Basingstoke: Macmillan.

Stewart, J., Smith, D. and Stewart, G. (1994) *Understanding Offending Behaviour.* Brighton: Pavillion.

Thoburn, J., Lewis, A. and Shemmings, D. (1995) *Paternalism or Partnership? Family Involvement in the Child Protection Process.* London: HMSO.

Triseliotis, J., Sellcick, C. and Short, R. (1995) *Foster Care: Theory and Practice.* London: Batsford.

Twigg, J. and Atkin, K. (1995) 'Carers and services: factors mediating service provision'. *Journal of Social Policy 24,* part 1, 5–30.

Ward, H. (1995) *Looking After Children: Research into Practice.* London, HMSO.

Waterhouse, L. (1987) 'The relationship between theory and practice, Social work training'. *Issues in Social Work Education 7,* 3–19.

CHAPTER 5

Partnership in the Provision of Education and Training

Elizabeth Kemp

Introduction

The nature of collaboration between an agency and an institute of higher education is the key theme running through this chapter. On the one hand, the remarkable commitment of West Sussex Social Services Department (SSD) to resourcing partnership in education and training will be elaborated below. Its organizational culture is perhaps best illustrated by its participation in the graduation of DipSW students. The Director of Social Services attends the Institute's ceremony, at which a prize from the Social Services Committee is awarded. This symbolizes the personal and structural commitment of the agency to the DipSW partnership. On the other hand, working within an institute of higher education, the School of Social Studies enjoys a culture where the value and academic credibility of vocational courses have been a founding principle. Indeed, until it was recently shortened to two sentences summarizing its core values, the West Sussex Institute's 1991 Mission Statement included: 'To educate, to train and to develop further the continuing education of ... social workers and to provide educational support and training for these professional people'.

At the time of writing (1998) it is nine years since the planning for the West Sussex Diploma in Social Work/Diploma in Higher Education (DipSW) began. Having already undergone one major review and one revalidation, the programme is about to embark on a semesterized structure as a BA (Hons) Social Work Studies/Diploma in Social Work with a significant part-time, employment-based route.

Almost all the students in the first intake were secondees from West Sussex SSD, whereas now seconded students are a rare breed. Until summer 1997, college and placement were concurrent, in line with the programme's views on reflective and adult learning. Following the ruling by the Department for

Education and Employment, which restricted grants for students on all those programmes it deemed sandwich courses, the West Sussex DipSW decided to block most of its college input. It has not yet been possible to assess the impact of this restructuring or of the 1999 introduction of fees for students. At this watershed, it is appropriate to record and reflect on the partnership between West Sussex SSD and Chichester Institute of Higher Education (the Institute), which has been sufficiently robust to manage these changes and to develop a clear strategy to guide the programme into the new millennium.

Collaboration in Social Work Education

In 1989 the Central Council for Education and Training in Social Work (CCETSW) required social work agencies and educational establishments to collaborate in the provision of the DipSW. This was a reaffirmation of its belief that too many social work courses were remote from practice and that collaboration between agencies and colleges in a subject that required practice placements would improve students' learning. All parties were to be involved in initial decision making and monitoring with periodic opportunities to influence the programme's policies and practices (CCETSW 1989). The current structural organization for the delivery of the DipSW must ensure 'clear, well-managed collaborative arrangements between programme providers who will include at least one educational institution and one social services agency' (CCETSW 1995, p.14). Such collaboration paralleled governmental support for workplace training which was intended to be cheaper than college-based courses and to increase the power of employers as prospective purchasers of the eventual product (Jack 1995).

In West Sussex the DipSW was built on a long history of collaboration between West Sussex SSD and the Institute, which had jointly contributed towards the Sussex Certificate in Social Service (CSS) and a variety of in-service courses (West Sussex Diploma in Social Work 1990). Thus, collaboration was part of the culture from which this DipSW emerged and was never experienced as being externally imposed.

Collaboration between Organizations

While CCETSW has continued to talk of collaboration, many involved in social work education have discussed the process in terms of partnership. The distinction made by Beresford and Trevillion (1995, p.11) is that collaboration is a generic term for 'the various forms of working together', whereas partnership 'is rooted in the concept of participation'. As such, the term 'partnership' is often falsely used by those who have failed to anticipate 'conflict and inequalities of power and control' (Morris 1993, quoted in Beresford and Trevillion 1995 p.11).

As the arena within which two organizations meet, any collaborative venture can become a battleground. Much of the tension around partnership in education and training has been reflected in discussions of the tension between academy and agency and mirrored in the supposed dichotomy between theory and practice and between the competent and the reflective practitioner. Drawing on Bogo and Vayda (1987), Rumgay (1988, p.336) 'sees agency and academy as having separate primary objectives'. Academy's purpose is to educate for practice and to contribute to the building of knowledge, so it respects, values and rewards staff for research, scholarship and teaching. By contrast, agency's purpose is to provide services for those in need, so it respects, values and rewards staff for delivering effective and efficient services.

Webb (1996, p.182) expresses this more aggressively. While acknowledging that education makes compromises with the dominant forces in society, he also claims that it 'wrenches the heart out of the cherished and taken-for-granted, as it inspects and interrogates'. He contrasts this with training which 'cannot be bothered with these questions of deep structure. It looks rather to the observationally verifiable. It suspends consideration of the existentially or epistemologically troubling' (Webb 1996).

The Reflective Practitioner

While the West Sussex DipSW is clearly a collaboration between agency and academy, operationally it is a partnership between two elements of these wider organizations, namely the training section of West Sussex SSD and the School of Social Studies in the Institute. The two departments are united by an underpinning commitment to adult learning and a common vision of the newly qualified social worker. The current influence of functional analysis and the assessment of competence in the DipSW is reflected in the preference of some employers for 'doers not thinkers' (Jones 1996, p.209). However, someone who did without thinking would not meet the core competence of 'Assess and Plan' (CCETSW 1995). They would be unable to differentiate between similar yet different situations or to make effective use of even the most modest budget. They would lack the analytical skills that characterize the holder of a diploma in higher education. Lacking imagination, they would be unable to deal with social, legal and technical change and incapable of thinking the unthinkable, as is required when faced with any paradigm shift. Only the most short sighted of agencies is likely to value such a practitioner.

Reflection has been a key process in the West Sussex DipSW since its inception. For Thompson (1995) reflective practice 'unites theory and practice within the same framework, without presenting either as being ... superior to the other' (p.75). Taylor (1996) reaches a similar conclusion. Building on Cannan (1994), she rejects the narrowly defined, reductionist approach to competence that focuses on discrete observable behaviours, denies the importance of the process of learning and creativity and neglects the need to integrate skills and apply knowledge. The view of the West Sussex DipSW is that 'the process of regular reflection on practice is considered essential' if one is 'to develop and to continue to develop as a competent practitioner' (West Sussex Diploma in Social Work 1990, p.11; West Sussex Diploma in Social Work 1996, p.10). Thus the shared, explicit vision of the newly qualified social worker as competent and reflective is one which unites agency and academy in the West Sussex DipSW. However, there are other significant bonds.

The Collaborative Team

All agency staff and key academic staff are qualified, experienced social workers, committed to strengthening their common profession. A universal step towards professional status is the establishment of a practice qualification that is also academically validated. Social work educators, like social workers, are employed by and perform activities sanctioned by the state while also aiming to enhance human and social welfare (Jones 1996). Partnership in social work education provides an opportunity for agency and academy to support one another in working towards this common goal.

All this is not to suggest that relationships within the West Sussex DipSW have been utopian. There have been shifts in the personal relationships that have brought the partnership to life. After eight years only two people with major roles remain from the CSS, one on each side of the partnership. Originally the DipSW was the sole business for the five staff on each side of the partnership so it received their undiluted attention and working relationships became very close. Now both partners have diversified, to increase their chances of survival. For example, agency staff are now involved in the provision of national vocational qualifications (NVQs) and post-qualifying training, while Institute lecturers, some of whom are now responsible for other programmes, must all give a higher profile to research. Over-diversification might eventually put the DipSW partnership at risk of not receiving sufficient priority from anyone.

This dilution generated tension within the partnership. When it was addressed, nominated representatives with delegated decision-making powers were appointed to deal with some aspects of DipSW business. These representatives include immediate colleagues of every member of the staff team, so that input and feedback are as straightforward as possible. In addition to the business meetings, all staff are still expected to set time aside for 'DipSW development' sessions, when the focus has often involved developing staff learning and interpersonal relationships. Where process issues have been uppermost, an external facilitator has sometimes been involved.

Hence a situation exists where neither side of the partnership has to lose for the other to meet its key objective. As Handy (1993) observes, this is a situation more likely to be found in good sports teams than in formal organizations. These bonds sustain both partners and unite them when faced by tensions or potentially destructive forces, be they internal or external to the programme (Payne 1994).

A Team Spanning Two Organizations

Having described the team that constitutes and delivers the DipSW partnership, it is useful to consider how it operates at the interface between two large organizations. The two key people strategically responsible for the West Sussex DipSW and who manage their respective staff teams are the Deputy Training and Development Manager for West Sussex SSD and the Head of the School of Social Studies in the Institute. The status of these two senior staff reflects the standing of the partnership and affords a voice and a degree of protection in these times of rapid and turbulent organizational change. Beyond this, there is no hierarchical structure within the team. The programme co-ordinator, a member of the Institute staff, has an operational, organizational and administrative role with no managerial or supervisory function. Module leadership is an operational, organizational and administrative role. It is held by staff from whichever side of the partnership is ultimately responsible for the assessment of that module. Staff within module teams allocate module leadership among themselves, depending on their own workloads. This flat structure promotes direct communication. It is especially important that module leaders are able to make operational decisions, with their module teams, and negotiate with other module leaders about developments to enhance the quality of the students' experience.

A team that operates at the interface between two organizations requires internal strength. Some of the professional bonds uniting the team have already been explored above. Organizationally, since the West Sussex consortium contains only two parties, the team is relatively small. From 1990 to 1998 the staff team grew from ten to fourteen. Its size is now at the upper limit for effective interpersonal communication within a working group (Brown 1992; Preston-Shoot 1993). At this point it is still possible for people to communicate and know one another as whole people, not just in their professional and organizational roles. This brings an immediacy and intimacy to the team that would not be possible if working relationships were more formally structured as is required in larger teams.

The Host Organizations

Nevertheless, if a partnership is to be fruitful, it is not sufficient for small sub-units of organizations to be united in a common task 'for partnership will only thrive in an organisational policy context that supports and promotes it' (Braye and Preston-Shoot 1993). As Payne (1994) has demonstrated, partnership may contain elements of the 'romantic ideal' of the sort that is associated with the historical view of the establishment of a business partnership in English law or with the European concept of marriage. In marriage and in the early stages of a business partnership, when the romantic ideal still flourishes, ideas about unconditional mutual trust and about ties of friendship or love will thrive. However, uncritical romantic expectations of another are likely to lead to disappointment and possibly pain.

Past experiences from the Sussex CSS pointed to the advisability of a written agreement. CCETSW required that all DipSW programmes produce a formal written undertaking on all aspects of collaboration. In West Sussex this was supplemented by a *Memorandum of Co-operation* that recognized the legal complexities of the partnership and provided more secure arrangements than had existed for the CSS. For example, if either partner wished to withdraw, a minimum of two years' notice was stipulated and adequate arrangements were required to enable students to complete their studies (West Sussex Diploma in Social Work 1990; West Sussex Diploma in Social Work 1996). Payne might see this as some form of prenuptial contract in a second marriage that enabled the organizations involved to progress from a damaging experience to a new and clearer partnership.

The co-operative education and training culture in West Sussex and the Institute's commitment to professional and vocational training have also proved a healthy environment for other developments, which in turn have strengthened the DipSW partnership. The units that compose West Sussex SSD's post-qualifying year are jointly validated by the Sussex and Surrey Post-Qualifying Consortium and the Institute, so they can contribute towards the Post-Qualifying Social Work Award and the BA in Social Work Studies. One of the many in-house programmes available to West Sussex SSD staff is the NVQ offered at level 4 in Care. This will form a significant part of the portfolio for students seeking admission into level 2 of the DipSW via an accreditation of prior learning (APL) route. A critical mass has now been achieved. Networks exist across the organizations so that pump-priming activities and cultural adjustments are no longer required when considering whether future developments would benefit from partnership.

Trust, Resources and Roles

Jackson and Preston-Shoot (1996) are concerned at the failure to address a major reason for establishing partnerships in social work education, namely the chronic national shortage of practice placements. In order to ensure that all students are provided with placements to meet their learning needs and with a practice teacher who is qualified or in training, the West Sussex DipSW has consistently restricted its annual intake to 36 students. This figure is the maximum number for whom West Sussex SSD consider they can provide and support quality placements, representing another considerable long-term investment of resources. West Sussex SSD is contractually responsible for providing all placements and has consistently organized these to begin on time – possibly a nationally unique achievement. Placements are made available through the partnership but are the domain of the agency. Thus, the partnership has not been undermined by becoming the battleground for control over placement resources.

Jordan (1988) sees partnership as based on trust with some pooling of resources and integration of roles. Partners must also be able to mobilize the resources required to meet sufficient of their common goals for each to be satisfied. Jack (1995) suggests that it is often hoped that the act of collaboration might improve the resources made available to a project. In the West Sussex partnership, all these threads are brought together within the remit of practice learning co-ordinators.

West Sussex SSD has a long-term strategic commitment to training and developing staff, despite financial constraints. This was demonstrated by their investment in full-time study supervisors for CSS and has continued with the provision of four full-time equivalent practice learning co-ordinators (PLCs) for the DipSW.

A PLC is an experienced and qualified social worker and practice teacher who maintains an overview of the practice of a group of students, called a PLC group, throughout the programme. The general pattern has been that a student's PLC acts as their practice teacher in the first year. In the second year PLCs act as a link between the DipSW, the student's practice teacher and the placement. Each annual student intake is divided into four PLC groups. In the first year, one college tutor is paired with each PLC, enabling effective working relationships to develop. In the second year, students are allocated different tutors, depending on their chosen practice pathway. Every term each student, their respective PLC and tutor are among the personnel who attend that student's progress meeting. Among PLCs many tasks, it is pertinent to mention the following:

1. The former study supervisors for CSS were key members of the team that drew up the DipSW's first validated document. PLCs continue to share responsibility for programme reviews and revalidation with Institute lecturers.

2. At the selection stage, each student is jointly interviewed by a PLC and an Institute lecturer, both having an equal say in the process and outcome.

3. PLCs and Institute lecturers are represented on the Programme Management Group and the Programme Board and all PLCs attend the DipSW Examination Board.

These details illustrate how the PLCs provide the students' key integrative experience and how the college and the agency are jointly involved in all the key processes in the programme. Reactions from other programmes to the size and significance of the contribution made by these agency staff suggest that this may be unusual; in our experience it is crucial to the reality of joint working.

Teaching and Assessment

The West Sussex DipSW has been strengthened by achieving clarity about the respective contributions of agency and academy in teaching and assessment. The core principles are that:

- one assesses what one teaches, so agency teaches and assesses practice and academy teaches and assesses theory.

- practice and theory are not separate entities so every assessed piece of work must include both theory and practice or experience, albeit in differing proportions, and must demonstrate the ability to make links between theory and practice.

These principles are epitomized by the most substantial elements in the programme:

- the Professional Practice modules which run across both years, with 20 credits in year one and 30 credits in year two, and which must be passed

- the Assessment and Planning in Practice module, 20 credits in year one, and the Independent Practice Study, with 30 credits in year two

towards a total of 120 credits per annum.

The Professional Practice module occupies a central role in any professional programme. There are many elements that contribute towards this module, such as:

- placement or supervised employment
- supervision with a PLC, a practice teacher, a tutor or an on-site supervisor
- college sessions with formal taught input, discussion and reflection
- individual and group supervision
- visits of observation
- written practice records and practice diaries
- progress meetings.

The taught college sessions are jointly planned, delivered and evaluated by a team of two PLCs and two tutors. Thus supervision and the college input on professional practice may come from a tutor and/or a PLC, from academy and/or agency. However, as befits a Professional Practice module, the assessment of the student's practice is the responsibility of their practice teacher. Such a report draws on many forms of evidence, including reports on visit/s of observation from tutors. After moderation by a group of practice teachers, they select a sample of reports for consideration by a CCETSW approved external assessor who is also an Institute external examiner.

The other substantial elements are also underpinned by practice. Assessment and Planning in Practice and the Independent Practice Study are the most significant written assignments in their respective years. Both integrate theory and practice through the analysis of a student's intervention in a verified practice situation. Because of their pivotal and integrative role, these assignments are marked independently and then moderated by each student's PLC and tutor. In this context, moderation means that academy and agency separately assess the assignment against the objectives and jointly agree a grade for the piece of work as a whole.

The terms of reference that the programme has developed for its Practice Assessment Panel also reflect the core principles on the teaching and assessment of theory and practice. While the academy attends the Panel, which is chaired by a PLC, it is clearly in a minority. Robust quality assurance procedures have been developed which ensure the Panel's right to make direct recommendations on the assessment of practice to the Examination Board. This Board operates within the domain of the academy, yet the authority of two external examiners who are also CCETSW approved external assessors enables the dual award to be approved simultaneously. Thus the programme has clearly acknowledged that the assessment of practice is the prerogative of the agency and this is endorsed by the highest authority of the academy.

Looking to the Future

Power in partnerships

When looking to the future of the West Sussex DipSW, rather than examine power relationships between agency and academy, it is more stimulating to consider who, in the broadest sense, the programme's partners should be. Earlier reference was made to employers as prospective purchasers of the eventual product of education and training and thus, it is implied, entitled to influence the educational and training process. This approach to partnership 'derives from an underlying ideology of consumerism' that is concerned with 'the power to purchase in a welfare economy regulated by market forces' (Braye and Preston-Shoot 1993, p.41). I anticipate that students will increasingly experience themselves as purchasers and consumers of their chosen educational programme, as they combine study and paid work to gain and pay for their qualification.

The West Sussex DipSW is also increasingly interested in developing the role of service users and carers as consumers and providers of the programme. As Hastings points out in Chapter 6, no group can have a greater investment in the production of effective social workers than those who will experience their practice. Service users already contribute to the provision of DipSW programmes in the following ways:

1. CCETSW requires that student social workers are observed interacting with service users to provide evidence of competence.

2. Evaluative feedback from service users contributes to practice teachers' reports.

3. The experiences of service users and carers has always been an essential element in students' assignments.

4. Increasingly the teaching material that draws on these experiences is taking the form of autobiographical and other forms of service user controlled material.

5. Service users and carers are always positively evaluated by students when they contribute as visiting lecturers.

Nevertheless, however service users and carers contribute to this process, power remains almost exclusively in the hands of the professional educators. The West Sussex DipSW has therefore earmarked funding to employ a project worker to involve service users more fully in the delivery of training to the programme's students. It is anticipated that this will include enabling service users to participate in setting the agenda for their contribution and introducing the service user perspective in aspects of the programme other than direct training. I hope this collaborative development will eventually contribute towards the development of structures that recognize service users and carers as genuine partners in social work training and education. This will only happen if they are allowed to move beyond tokenistic involvement. In turn this will require some sharing of power and cultural shifts, both within the programme's educational and training culture and within the host organizations.

The 'concept of partnership in work with service users and carers' is listed by CCETSW (1996, p.20) as an element of the knowledge base for the core competence of promote and enable, which qualifying social workers must demonstrate. Partnership between participants with unequal power is a current issue in anti-oppressive social work practice (Aymer, Chapter 8). Braye and Preston-Shoot (1993) do not view equal power between participants as a condition of partnership. However, '[partnership] does imply recognition and open discussion of how power is distributed and used' (p.46). Taylor makes a similar point in relation to the position of the student: 'the educator in professional education must hold power as the gatekeeper to the profession, but if such power is openly identified and managed this enables acknowledgement of the power of the student as consumer and encourages a real dialogue to take place' (1996, p.155).

In educational partnerships between agency and academy, both parties have substantial independence and power. Such partnerships can only reasonably expect students to work in partnerships with unequal power if agency and academy can manage this task themselves. Programmes which work towards involving service users, carers and students as true partners in social work training and education offer staff an opportunity to model good practice and generate material to explore with students (Braye and Preston-Shoot 1993).

Expanding the consortium

I anticipate that other agencies will wish to train some of their staff through the West Sussex DipSW. One of the key strengths of the West Sussex partnership has clearly been the effective communication between the individuals involved. Extending the partnership network too far could undermine this cornerstone. Not only would the number of personal relationships probably become untenable, but organizational relationships would be fundamentally altered.

Trevillion and Beresford recognize 'that in some form markets are the context in which social work must operate, and that social workers should understand market mechanisms, even as they try to assert the value of things which cannot be bought or sold' (1996, p.28). This can equally well be applied to social work education. The West Sussex DipSW might decide to protect its small partnership by acting as service providers for others without involving them in the structure. Stagnation could be avoided by responding to other agencies' interests as spot purchasers and by developing the influence and involvement of the ultimate consumers – service users – as outlined above.

However, one danger with such small partnerships is that a lack of diversity might produce a parochial approach. There are no black staff in the core group that teaches the West Sussex DipSW, making it more likely that racism will pass unrecognized, despite good intentions and specific strategies on staff development and mentorship for black students. Another consequence of protecting a small partnership is that this could undermine the aim of involving service users, carers and students as true partners. It will be important to explore what sort of relationships and structures should support this development rather than assume that all parties will wish to make identical contributions.

Conclusions

Key characteristics

Throughout this chapter, certain themes have emerged as underpinning the fruitfulness of the West Sussex partnership between agency and academy. Previous positive collaborative ventures were consciously used as the organizational and personal foundation for this new enterprise. The partnership has remained small, enabling trusting personal relationships to develop in depth and avoiding the need for 'time-consuming and largely pointless formal structures' (Jackson and Preston-Shoot 1996, p.5). Funding from CCETSW has been used to develop the staff team. The common educational and professional goals of the individuals and their organizations have provided a unifying focus at all times. The programme has received sufficient resources, with an outstanding level of input from West Sussex SSD. It has been acknowledged that all staff have transferable skills in development, planning, supervision, teaching and assessment. It is therefore sometimes appropriate that staff operate in each other's arenas. All strategic decisions and key operational matters involve some level of joint endorsement. Equally it has been recognized that it is appropriate for agency and academy respectively to retain exclusive control over certain resources and processes, under the umbrella of the programme.

Working within these parameters has enabled the programme to avoid some potential conflicts. Where conflicts have arisen, revisiting the programme's key principles has generated mechanisms or guidelines for progress. It is hoped that this experience will enable the programme to anticipate the consequences of inequalities of power as efforts are made to extend the concept of partnership to include students and service users. For example, I imagine that students and service users might identify some similarities in their experiences as recipients of the educational and social services systems respectively. As service users begin to play a more prominent role in the teaching and assessment of students within the agency and academy, likely tension points will have to be anticipated and addressed if destructive conflict is to be avoided.

Is partnership essential?

The experience of the West Sussex DipSW demonstrates that partnership in social work education is essential for as long as social work is seen as a profession whose qualification requires:

- substantial practical skills and an in-depth knowledge base
- integration through reflection and underpinning values
- validation by professional and academic authorities.

Theoretically, either partner could purchase the contribution made by the other side, but producing contracts and promoting quality assurance could easily generate the 'time-consuming and largely pointless formal structures' which Jackson and Preston-Shoot (1996, p.5) so abhor (see Wilkes, Chapter 7). The impression I have gained at national conferences is that such structures are associated with large consortia, involving several agencies and academic institutions operating in different towns. In such circumstances organizational relationships become complex, frequently undermining the possibility of personal relationships.

The DipSW review (Department of Health in progress) is examining the number of DipSW programmes, especially those consortia that overlap geographically. Hopefully this review will take account of the number of newly qualified social workers required to maintain the profession. Should it eventually be decided to reduce the number of DipSW programmes, I would urge that this is not achieved by amalgamating existing programmes. Small partnerships are likely to have access to fewer placements and would be well advised to accept this as the limit to their student intake. Not only are small partnerships more likely to develop fruitful organizational and personal relationships, but students will have a greater choice between programmes.

Closing Thoughts

On reflection, the West Sussex DipSW has, in Payne's (1994) terminology, focused on personal relationships within an education and training culture. The West Sussex experience suggests that no linear process can generate the ecosystem required for the growth of a healthy partnership. The shared vision of the competent and reflective practitioner that unites academy and agency is one aspect of the education and training culture within which this DipSW has grown. In turn, this culture is the safe inter-organizational space within which staff are able to work together to develop the networks that enable the partnership to flourish. This is reminiscent of the imponderable chicken and egg question.

However, I suggest that if host organizations are not overtly hostile, then committed individuals can often make a space for change, or even make a space for deviancy. Within this space, relationships can be developed, networks established and eventually new structures may be formalized. By the time the host organizations are aware of this activity, whatever has grown to occupy this space will need to be sufficiently robust to withstand inspection, perhaps by presenting itself as culturally acceptable to the host organizations.

The experiences of the West Sussex partnership highlight many parallels between education and social work. Both require an appreciation of social, organizational and personal relationships and of power and both require partnership if they are to succeed. Equally, neither will truly flourish in a climate of oppression or mistrust. Partnership is a process and an outcome; it cannot be imposed. Finding ways to model and expand working in partnership provides social work education and training with excellent opportunities to enhance this process in students' practice.

Acknowledgements

No chapter on partnership worth its salt can be the work of one person! This chapter draws on ideas shared and explored by colleagues from both sides of the West Sussex Diploma in Social Work (DipSW) team – the West Sussex Social Services Department (SSD) and the Chichester Institute of Higher Education – over many years. Particular thanks are due to colleagues from West Sussex Social Services who have offered supportive feedback on successive drafts of this chapter.

References

Beresford, P. and Trevillion, S. (1995) *Developing Skills for Community Care: A Collaborative Approach.* Aldershot: Arena.

Bogo, M. and Vayda, E. (1987) *The Practice of Field Instruction in Social Work: Theory and Process.* Toronto: University of Toronto.

Braye, S. and Preston-Shoot, M. (1993) 'Partnership practice: responding to the challenge, realising the potential'. *Social Work Education 12,* 2, 35–53.

Brown, A. (1992) *Groupwork,* 3rd edn. Aldershot: Ashgate.

Cannan, C. (1994) 'Enterprise culture, professional socialisation and social work education in Britain'. *Critical Social Policy 2,* 5–18.

CCETSW (1989) *Rules and Requirements for the Diploma in Social Work: DipSW,* Paper 30. London: CCETSW.

CCETSW (1995) *Assuring Quality in the Diploma in Social Work – 2; Approval, Review and Inspection of DipSW Programmes.* London: CCETSW.

CCETSW (1996) *Assuring Quality in the Diploma in Social Work – 1 Rules and Requirements for the DipSW.* London: CCETSW.

Department of Health (work in progress) Review of the Diploma in Social Work.

Handy, C. (1993) *Understanding Organisations.* Harmondsworth: Penguin.

Jack, R. (1995) 'Post-qualifying consortia: an expensive waste of diminishing resources'. *Issues in Social Work Education 15,* 1, 78–87.

Jackson, S. and Preston-Shoot, M. (1996) 'Social work education: a changing policy context'. In S. Jackson and M. Preston-Shoot (eds) *Educating Social Workers in a Changing Policy Context.* London: Whiting & Birch.

Jones, C. (1996) 'Anti-intellectualism and the peculiarities of British social work education'. In N. Parton (ed) *Social Theory, Social Change and Social Work.* London: Routledge.

Jordan, B. (1988) 'What price partnership? – costs and benefits'. In A. James and D. Scott (eds) *Partnership in Probation Education and Training.* London: CCETSW.

Morris, J. (1993) *Independent Lives: Community Care and Disabled People.* London: Macmillan.

Payne, M. (1994) 'Partnership between organisations in social work education'. *Issues in Social Work Education 14,* 1, 53–70.

Preston-Shoot, M. (1993) *Effective Groupwork.* Basingstoke: Macmillan.

Pugh, G. and De'Ath, E. (1989) *Working Towards Partnership in the Early Years.* London: National Children's Bureau.

Rumgay, J. (1988) 'Teaching social work practice: a partnership between college and field'. *Practice 2,* 4, 334–345.

Taylor, I. (1996) 'Reflective learning, social work education and practice in the 21st century'. In N. Gould and I. Taylor (eds) *Reflective Learning for Social Work: Theory and Practice.* Aldershot: Arena.

Thompson, N. (1995) *Theory and Practice in Health and Social Welfare.* Buckingham: Open University Press.

Trevillion, S. and Beresford, P. (1996) 'The shape of things to come'. *Community Care,* 14 March, 28–30.

Webb, D. (1996) 'Regulation for radicals: the state, CCETSW and the academy'. In N. Parton (ed) *Social Theory, Social Change and Social Work*. London: Routledge.

West Sussex Diploma in Social Work (1990) *Definitive Document for the Diploma of Higher Education / Diploma in Social Work*. Chichester: Chichester Institute of Higher Education.

West Sussex Diploma in Social Work (1996) *Definitive Document for the Diploma of Higher Education / Diploma in Social Work*. Chichester: Chichester Institute of Higher Education.

CHAPTER 6

User Involvement in Education and Training

Miriam Hastings

Introduction

Good work practice in any profession that provides care services needs to be founded on a firm basis of working in close and equal partnership with people using those services. 'User involvement' has been a popular and fashionable phrase during the last two decades. It is often applied without necessarily carrying much real meaning or having any effect on actual work practice or service provision.

In this chapter I shall deal with various issues about user involvement in services and the participation of clients in their own care programmes: how care practitioners might work in partnership; sharing power with clients; empowering clients to express their feelings; and enabling them to make their own choices wherever possible. I want to take a fairly deep and complex look at these questions and the problems they raise, while making my contribution as practical as possible.

Major changes have occurred during the last decade in the provision and organization of care services: the division of roles and responsibilities between purchasers and providers; a growing emphasis on economic efficiency and financial business acumen; and an increasing emphasis on professionalization, particularly within the context of education and training of care workers. During this period of major change a commitment to consumer choice and the involvement of users in the services they receive have become fundamental government principles underlying the development and provision of community care services.

A direct causal connection exists between user involvement in care services and user involvement in care professional education – the two should operate simultaneously. Before a successful policy of user involvement can be developed in care professional training, there needs to be a clearer understanding of what user involvement should really mean in work practice. Until this is understood, user involvement cannot be effectively implemented as a fundamental, structuring principle in care professional education.

I have run many training courses for care professionals in user involvement and empowerment. The most common justification offered by participants for their failure to implement these approaches successfully in their work practice rests on lack of resources. It is important to remember that respect, honesty and the free sharing of information do not cost money, and do more to promote empowerment and self-advocacy for service users than any number of elaborate and ambitious projects. The vital elements necessary for user involvement are the attitudes of the individual care professionals and their manner of relating to their clients.

In this chapter I will begin by considering the problems of involvement for different groups of clients, focusing, because of the limitations of space, on three specific groups of service users who are all particularly vulnerable to having their views ignored: children in care, the confused elderly and people receiving psychiatric treatment for acute mental distress. Rather than becoming too enmeshed in the theoretical concepts of care practice, I will endeavour to offer some exciting and innovative ways forward.

Choice for Children?

It is a hard unpalatable reality that children who come into contact with care services frequently grow up to experience such services again as adults – whether mental health services, social services, or penal and probation services. If we can find more effective ways of addressing the needs of children, they may be able to experience a less damaged adult life.

Under the Children Act of 1989, care practitioners are required to listen to children and accept the child's version of his or her life experience. They are required at least to act as if they believe any account the child gives of abuse or exploitation, even if they may actually have some doubts. They are also required to explain to the child the care options available, and to endeavour to find out the child's choices and wishes concerning the care they might receive.

While in principle this is clearly a desirable policy, there are enormous obstacles that prevent children from expressing their real feelings and wishes. It is true of all children, but most particularly of children in difficult life situations, that they react to the adults around them. Whether a child feels very anxious to please and therefore says what they think the adult wants to hear, or whether the child is full of rage and driven by an impulse to punish and so says what they think the adult does not want to hear, they will usually respond to the power of the adult rather than being able to focus on themselves and their real feelings.

A guardian ad litem commented to me that the principle of user involvement was well understood, but there was little or no understanding of exactly how to put this principle into practice. He cited his experience of chairing statutory review meetings. He said that a child's social worker would usually appreciate the need for the child to be present at the review and would lead the child into the room to join the team of professionals. It frequently became evident that the children had no idea why they were present, what the review meeting was for, what decisions were being made or how those decisions would affect their lives. The children were often scared and frequently bored, and after they had fidgeted restlessly for several minutes, their social worker would ask them if they had had enough. Given a response in the affirmative, the worker would lead the child out again with little or nothing achieved.

The guardian was concerned at the lack of advance planning and preparation this demonstrated. He pointed out that children need to be given time and attention by their care workers to enable them to participate in their own care review meetings. The format and function of the statutory review should be explained fully beforehand, and children need to be helped and encouraged to formulate and express their wishes. He admitted that it was often extremely difficult to win children's confidence and to enable them to express their feelings honestly and openly.

Guardians ad litem are now required to obtain feedback from children once they have finished working with them. An assessment form is provided by the courts for this purpose. Again, this is an example of the principle of involvement being recognized but the practice being inappropriate. Most children find the assessment form intimidating, boring and inaccessible. The practitioner cannot help them fill in a form designed to assess their own work practice. One of the most successful ways to overcome this problem has been to provide the child with a walkman-style dictaphone to use while alone in an empty room. Many children found this an empowering and enjoyable way of expressing themselves, and have not only given useful feedback, but also valuable new insights into their feelings and life experiences. Care practitioners might equally try offering children, especially teenagers, the chance to make 'video diaries' as a popular and useful means of expression and communication.

These methods are not so practical with very young children, but creative forms of self-expression could still be adopted. Most small children love painting and drawing. The care professional could ask them to paint a picture of the practitioner and of the care service (or other aspects of their life) and then get the child to talk about the paintings, recording the conversation on a cassette tape.

It would also be much easier for children using care services to give feedback and assessment of those services if they were brought together to share their experiences and to talk about them in a group. If they could make complaints and offer ideas and suggestions for improvement of services as a team they would feel more confident and less intimidated or vulnerable.

We live with a legacy from the past when children were regarded as the property of adults. While most people would agree this is an undesirable and damaging attitude to hold towards children, our culture still functions along those lines – and this applies also to care services. In fostering and adoption, for example, confusion exists about whom the service is really for – in whose interests and for whose benefit. Realistically, the child can be allowed little choice because options are so limited.

There is no care service where this is more evident than in mental health, whether we consider mental health services for children or adults. In relation to children and mental health, one major problem lies in the invisibilization of children's mental distress. We live in a culture that seems unable to accept acute mental distress as being a reality for young children. The hard truth is that user involvement for any client group will not be able to exist in a real way until the whole culture of care services has changed – and, indeed, the wider culture of our society.

Working with Older People who are Confused

As with children, it is extremely alarming how the mental distress of elderly people is invisibilized and neglected. As Hancock (1998, p.10) puts it, 'Our society is ageist; mental health services also discriminate by age.' Distressed and confused elderly service users are often viewed as being incapable of making any decisions at all and consequently totally denied a voice of their own.

While the ageist attitudes prevalent in our society detrimentally affect all older service users, the more vulnerable the mental and emotional state of the elderly person, the more silenced and invisibilized are their needs and rights to compassionate and respectful treatment. For example, the elderly mental health service user is more likely to be given invasive forms of treatment such as electro-convulsive therapy (ECT). One of the damaging effects of assumptions that confused older people are incapable of expressing their views is that the care professional fails to make any real effort to communicate with the client.

The term 'confused elderly' can be applied to a wide range of people who experience very different problems. These might include acute mental distress, progressive conditions such as Alzheimer's disease and dementia, or confusion and lapses of memory. In all these situations there is evidence to show that individual attention and intellectual stimulation have a positive and beneficial effect on both the mental state and the emotional health of the client.

John Killick's work using creative writing with elderly people with dementia, is a perfect example of the kind of ideas I want to explore and discuss to show how care professionals can find innovative ways to hear and communicate with their clients.

Since 1993 John Killick has been working as a writer with people with dementia in residential nursing homes. In his collection (1997a) of very strong and beautiful poems, 'You Are Words: Dementia Poems', he has drawn directly from conversations shared with people with dementia. His approach relies on active and respectful communication, encouraging clients to talk about themselves and their lives, listening to them carefully and attentively, however mentally confused they appear to be. With the permission of the clients, he records his conversations with them and later pares away all superfluous and repetitive words, so that he is often left with very powerful and moving statements that frequently become a form of poetry.

He is anxious to stress that he never adds anything to the clients' words – they are all their own. In his extremely interesting introduction to the poetry collection, John Killick explains that the poetic quality of the language used by the clients directly results from their dementia and its effect on their mental processes:

> A significant characteristic of the speech of many people with dementia is the direct expression of emotion. The disease has a dis-inhibiting effect ... At the same time intellectual capacities are diminished, and rational language proves elusive. Suddenly talk blooms with metaphor, allusion, the currents of feeling are reflected in rhythm and cadence. (Killick 1997a, p.7)

His response of listening to and valuing the client's words, rather than dismissing them as meaningless and incoherent, has a profoundly positive and beneficial effect on the client's mental state: 'Without consulting them, without listening very hard to what they are trying to tell us, we can't have any notion of what their needs may be' (Killick 1997b, p.14).

To work with service users, rather than working on them or for them, requires a practitioner to experience and inhabit the client's reality. Most care professionals interpret and explain their clients' words and actions according to their own experience and understanding of the world. Until they stop imposing their perception and version of reality upon their clients, real communication – and therefore real partnership – will remain impossible.

These principles for good work practice are equally as important in work with clients experiencing acute mental distress, and I shall now move on to discuss issues around user involvement in mental health services. Once again, communication and respect are vital elements.

I have been running therapeutic creative writing workshops for women survivors of mental distress and child abuse for seven years and I have found that acknowledging and valuing their experience, listening to and respecting their words, are an essential part of the healing process.

Working with Mental Health Service Users

Who writes the script?

The key to a successful working partnership between a mental health service practitioner and client lies in an insightful understanding of the nature of a 'professional relationship', and how that might affect the roles and the interaction between the two people concerned.

It might well be argued that the whole notion of a care professional essentially renders an equal working partnership between practitioner and client impossible. I would question whether user involvement can ever be a real possibility while practitioners cling to a concept of professionalism which prevents an equal and honest relationship existing between practitioner and client. The sad reality remains that the majority of care practitioners do not relate to their clients as themselves. Their family and friends would have difficulty recognizing the persona they adopt when at work.

A psychiatric social worker told me that she was very conscious of always wearing a 'metaphorical white coat' in her work practice. This was becoming so entrenched that she had begun to notice it was increasingly difficult to take off this mental uniform in other areas of her life. Her mother, for example, was elderly and needing more support and she found herself automatically relating to her mother as if she was a client. Feeling uneasy about this, the social worker asked me what I thought about her finding it so hard to 'be herself' with her mother. I asked her whether she had considered trying to relate to her clients at work *as herself*, in the way she was relating to me, rather than as a different 'professional' person. Interestingly, she was adamant that it would be neither possible nor desirable to practise as a social worker without this clear sense of role playing.

The argument usually raised in favour of adopting a professional persona relies on the need for boundaries between worker and client. Clearly, boundaries are necessary to protect clients from exploitation and abuse of any kind. But while adopting a role as someone with no weaknesses, needs or problems, who knows what is best for their client and has all the answers, may serve to make the practitioner feel more confident, in control and better equipped to deal with the demands of work, this may be at the cost of undermining the confidence of the user and rendering them powerless, inadequate and unable to cope.

Obviously, when working with clients who are in acutely distressed and disturbed states, it is not appropriate to tell them of personal problems or to disclose our own distress – at least while clients are in a state of crisis – but it is important to be honest with ourselves and not to hide behind a protective barrier of professional inviolability and power. All care service clients (and I think this particularly applies to children as well as adults using mental health services) will be aware when a care professional is not being genuine. Their ability to trust and communicate with the professional will be seriously undermined and damaged.

Another major problem created by care practitioners adopting a separate professional mask or persona in their work practice is the response it tends to elicit in their clients. It sets up a dynamic where the user is under pressure to adopt a corresponding role to the one presented by the practitioner. This means the user will respond to the professional as 'a user', not as themselves, and the practitioner will only be presented with the aspects of the client's personality and character that fit the stereotype of a mental health service user. Since service users are as varied, complex, and profound as most human beings, this means the professional does not get to know more than a fraction of the client's identity.

I have seen this process happen on many occasions with some amusement and much dismay. As a survivor of the mental health system who now runs workshops and teaches courses for users of mental health services, I have the privilege of meeting many users on a basis of equality and friendship. I get to know their many strengths and abilities as well as their difficulties and vulnerabilities. Frequently I have seen a user I know well having to interact with a care professional. They take on a persona I do not recognize, presenting themselves as inadequate, pathetic or in need of guidance, in response to the 'caring' approach of the practitioner. Not only is adopting such a role damaging to the self-image and identity of the user, but there is the additional danger that they may be offered inappropriate services. Care practitioners cannot expect to provide suitable services if they do not fully understand their clients as rounded and complex individuals.

It is important to realize how much a practitioner needs to listen to people in acute distress and crisis – even when the client does not appear able to talk rationally and coherently. Constant communication can only be maintained if the practitioner is prepared to spend time listening attentively, trying to empathize with the client and enter into their experience. The user's account of what is happening to them should be respected and taken seriously. If the practitioner knows what is going on for the client, usually their most bizarre behaviour or incoherent statements begin to make some sense and become easier to understand.

It is also important to realize that experiences not recognized as 'normal' by the majority of society, such as hearing voices or seeing visions, are not necessarily a serious problem or a sign of disturbance or 'illness'. If the client is bothered by hearing voices, spend time talking about the voices and try to understand what the voices mean. Do not immediately assume that the client needs medicating or admitting to hospital. Sometimes, both client and practitioner can learn a lot about what is going on in the user's life and about what is really causing their distress from listening to their voices. Therefore the voices should be treated with respect. Being afraid of acute mental states in clients will damage the practitioner's ability to communicate and the client's ability to trust that practitioner.

If care professional students are educated by user trainers who have experienced acute mental crises, the students will be able to learn that mental health service users in crisis are ordinary people, the same as themselves, and as a result will treat clients going through an acute crisis with more respect, insight and sensitivity.

Mental Health Service Users and Care Professional Education

To make partnership an essential element in good practice, we need to place the concept of partnership as the fundamental basis of care professional education. Use of language, for example, is an essential part of meaningful communication. Educators of care professionals must stop relying on, or teaching students, inaccessible, incomprehensible, specialist language in a misguided attempt to emphasize the professionalism of the discipline. The true care professional is one who freely shares information, resources and power with their clients.

Training and education of care practitioners must teach students an understanding of the need for a working partnership with clients, based on respect and equality. It should facilitate the development of an ability to communicate honestly and openly with clients. These abilities and skills can be taught successfully by those who have themselves experienced acute distress and have used mental health services. There are a great many local mental health service user and survivor groups, as well as national networks such as MINDLink and Survivors Speak Out, who have members willing and able to take an active part in training care practitioners.

The need for active user involvement in care professional education and training applies not only to users of mental health services, but to all care service clients. So let us now consider some of the implications and issues concerning such involvement.

User Involvement in Care Professional Education

In spite of the stated government policy of a commitment to consumer choice and involvement in services, there is no care professional training which incorporates user involvement as a fundamental structuring principle, informing all aspects of care practice. At best, user involvement is an 'add-on,' an extra or an afterthought. At worst, it is altogether absent from care professional training.

To implement the government policy of user involvement in a manner that will be effective and successful, service users need to be actively involved in the training and education of care professionals, and this involvement needs to work on several levels. Inviting individual users as 'guest speakers' on professional training courses, to give isolated talks, has been happening already for some time, although not on the majority of courses. Significantly, some courses that used to invite such speakers have now dropped the practice. While this approach may be helpful, it is not adequate on its own. Service users need to be involved at all stages of planning and running professional care education, including the examination and assessment of students.

Overcoming the Obstacles to User Involvement

Professional care educators have expressed anxieties about the involvement of service users on training courses and some seem threatened by such involvement. The most common reasons offered for not involving users include: the question of representation and who is a representative user; how user trainers can be incorporated into professional training courses; how users could qualify to work in an equal partnership with other educators; and finally, how educators would pay users for their involvement. Although these obstacles should not actually apply to user trainers more than to any other lecturers, let us consider them carefully.

The question of representation is the most frequently voiced, not just by educators but also by care professional students. It is of course a complete red herring, since there are no representative service users any more than there is one stereotypical care practitioner or care professional educator. There are only individual users who are able to offer their expertise and particular valuable insights.

This criticism is as erroneous as claiming that any other course lecturer is unrepresentative. I think it reasonable to expect care practitioners and care professional students to be able to apply information from the particular to the general, especially since this is a form of intellectual functioning necessary for good work practice. It also raises the point that user trainers are not just users of care services, they have many other skills, experiences and abilities which they can usefully bring to care professional training when they are not limited to a 'user trainer' pigeon-hole.

The second common objection to employing user trainers lies in the question of how educators might work with service users on courses that are becoming increasingly based on academic and theoretical teaching. The fear is sometimes expressed that user trainers would be too practical and subjective, and their involvement would lead to a lack of professionalism in care practice training. This fear stems from a misunderstanding of the nature of professional expertise and from a lack of confidence in the position which the care professions occupy among other scientific disciplines in the higher education academy.

The debate about whether social work training should be more theoretical and research based or more practical and competence based is considered elsewhere in this book (Chapters 1, 3 and 4). I believe a less academic, more practice-based approach is of greater value, particularly when the user perspective is fully considered and recognized. With the dissolution in the next few years of the Central Council for Education and Training in Social Work (CCETSW) and the establishment of National Training Organizations and a General Social Care Council (GSCC), the debate is likely to be resolved one way or the other. While it might be anticipated that service users will have a voice on the GSCC, unless they are given a leading role in the training and education of care professionals – including a significant part to play in the assessment of students – this will have little real effect on daily practice.

Service users are the experts on their own needs and experiences and on the care services that are required. User trainers can bring many urgently needed new skills and concepts of good work practice to the educating of practitioners. Once professionals have recognized that learning from service users does not undermine or jeopardize their professionalism, we should begin to see an improvement in care professional education.

In relation to the building up of a useful body of knowledge that can provide a theoretical basis for education, many service users, and groups representing users, have done and are doing their own research which can begin to offer a body of theory that is user centred and user led. As Cheetham says in Chapter 4, there are a number of users and survivors of psychiatric services who have progressed through the higher education system. Some are now doing their own research into understandings of and treatments for mental distress (Faulkner *et al.* 1998). More funding is urgently needed for such user-led research, which might usefully provide a body of meaningful theory and knowledge for future care professional education.

The final question of payment for user trainers will only be raised by care professional educators who have personal difficulties sharing power with service users. Even to consider paying a user trainer differently to any other trainer is clearly both insulting and disrespectful. The point generally made is that the user trainer may be receiving benefit and not entitled to reasonable remuneration. Obviously, this is not the business of the employing educator – it is up to the user trainer to resolve. Many users and ex-users who work as trainers are actually self-employed and working to earn their living, or else they are involved in self-advocacy groups who can receive the money on their behalf. If educators really believe in equality and user involvement, the issue will not even be raised.

This leads us on to the wider question of sharing financial resources. It is remarkable how many care agencies and service providers will talk at great length about user consultation and involvement and about the importance of encouraging responsibility and decision making on the part of service users. But at the suggestion of actually handing over money to users they panic and cannot cope with the idea at all. The funding and promoting of user-led services has been sadly neglected by care service providers, yet there are examples worldwide of such services offering excellent alternatives to those controlled and run by professionals. O'Hagan (1993) gives a valuable survey and analysis of such user-led services in Europe and the USA.

Another concern raised by care professional educators centres on specific issues concerning particular groups of service users. While some groups have made great efforts – and not without a certain success – to be involved on training courses, others, who need more advocacy for promoting their interests have so far been neglected. Representatives of people with physical disabilities, people with learning difficulties, notably the group called 'People First' and some survivors of mental distress and psychiatric treatment have been involved in care professional training in limited ways – usually by providing guest lecturers for one-off sessions and workshops. The problem is that, inevitably, the people who offer this kind of involvement tend to be the more self-confident and articulate. This certainly does not invalidate the usefulness of their contributions, but it does raise the question of how less confident and more disabled service users might be empowered and involved in care professional training. It also becomes easier for care professional educators and students to dismiss the contribution of users on training courses as 'unrepresentative'.

It is here that the involvement of service users in the design of training courses, and in the supervision and assessment of students can provide a way forward. Users who feel unable to give a lecture or run a workshop for a large group of care professional students may feel confident about sitting on a consultation panel to help design and plan a training course syllabus. They are also more likely to feel able to work with an individual student, supervising practical work, discussing their studies with them and advising them. I suggest that every care professional student should be allocated two user supervisors, drawn from two separate client groups, who would work closely with the student throughout the course. These supervisors should be paid at a realistic rate for their time and expertise and the report they give of the student should count for at least 25 per cent of the student's final assessment. Even in care work with children, or with users who have literacy problems, this system of supervision can work if the ideas I suggested earlier of using cassette recorders, video diaries, etc. are adopted to enable the supervisors to make their reports.

The participation of service users in the final assessment of care professional students is essential and invaluable, since they can offer unique insights into the work practice of the student not available to anyone without direct experience of using services.

Development and Support of User Trainers

It should be recognized, however, that there are serious implications for any level of user involvement and for the way it might be successfully introduced. The most important of these is the need for adequate, supportive training for the service users and how to provide this most effectively. Service users inevitably come from an experience of being powerless in the face of authoritarian and frequently insensitive service provision. Before user involvement can become a reality, professionals must acknowledge the power imbalance that exists between service users and service providers. Real involvement will mean that users need supportive training in a range of areas: personal development of self-confidence; assertiveness and communication; training in practical skills, such as how to design and facilitate training workshops; learning how to participate on committees; learning how to plan and deliver lectures; and how to draw upon subjective experience and apply it in more generally useful forms. This training will ideally be delivered to service users by their peers, since this will in itself prove empowering and encouraging and will challenge the unequal user-professional power dynamic. There are many service users and ex-users now successfully offering training to other service clients and care professional educators. I have been involved in running three such training courses for service users in two separate London boroughs (Tissier 1993). User participants, following and completing training of this kind, will soon form a group of local service users who are both willing and able to contribute to care professional education in a major way.

Once service users have been offered and have followed this kind of training and are actively contributing to care professional education, they need ongoing support and encouragement – both from professional educators and from each other. They also need to see that their contributions are given real recognition and validity. It would be a constructive step for care professional educators to establish advocacy groups that would work closely with the professional training courses, where user trainers and consultants could raise any difficulties they encountered and where they could offer ideas and suggestions for improvements to the course.

Conclusions

For user involvement to become a reality in service provision, we need to teach care professional students the essential qualities of respect for their clients, the necessity of developing partnership with their clients based on equality and the ability to communicate with their clients openly, sensitively and honestly. We also need to enable care service users to develop self-respect, assertiveness and the ability to express themselves confidently and constructively.

With all care service client groups, we need to find ways to break the silence – imaginative ways that will enable service users to express their individual needs and wishes. This will necessarily involve using initiative and creativity and will require an ability on the professional's part to understand the world from their client's perspective, so that they can use the most accessible and attractive means of self-expression to communicate with their particular client group. Every service user, however alien and confusing the practitioner might find their means of expression at first contact, can be empowered and enabled to express their perceptions and emotions in constructive, meaningful and creative ways.

The most important point I want to emphasize is that all service users, whatever their difficulties and disabilities, can communicate meaningfully and with insight if care professionals are willing to hear them. This communication includes the client's experience of and feelings about the work practice of the professional. If practitioners genuinely want to improve their services and to involve their users, they will make every effort to discover their clients' opinions of their work practice and will take serious note of the judgements their clients pass on to them as practitioners. We all find criticism painful to hear, especially when we feel we have invested a great deal of time and genuine effort into our work. But for care professionals it is vital that we listen to and accept criticism, both in order to improve our work practice and, since care services are inevitably based on power relationships, so that we can give power back to our clients.

Until service users are enabled to play a major role in the education and training of professionals, user involvement will remain a notional idea in care work practice. We need service users to participate fully in designing, managing, teaching and assessing on care professional training courses.

Acknowledgements

I would like to thank all the care practitioners who agreed to discuss their work with me during the writing of this chapter. I greatly appreciated their openness, honesty and the valuable insights they shared with me concerning their work experience.

References

Faulkner, A., Wallcroft, J., Nicholls, V., Blazdell and Treitel, R. (1998) 'The right to ask questions'. *Open Mind 91,* 14.

Hancock, M. (1998) 'Nobody's priority'. *Open Mind 90,* 10.

Killick, J. (1997a) 'You are words: dementia poems'. *Journal of Dementia Care.*

Killick, J. (1997b) 'Communication: a matter of life and death of the mind'. *Journal of Dementia Care, 90,* 14–15.

O'Hagan, M. (1993) *Stopovers On My Way Home from Mars.* London: Survivors Speak Out.

Tissier, G. (1993) 'Turning the tables'. *Community Care,* 24 June.

Suggested Reading

Crepaz-Keay, D., Binns, C. and Wilson, E. (1998) *Dancing with Angels: Involving Survivors in Mental Health Training.* London: CCETSW.

Trevillion, S. and Beresford, P. (eds) (1996) *Meeting the Challenge: Social Work Education and the Community Care Revolution.* London: National Institute for Social Work.

CHAPTER 7

Quality Assurance

Julie Wilkes

Emergence of Quality Assurance (QA) Discourse

Why did quality discourse from 1980s business consulting get co-opted into the world of social work education in the UK? How have education professionals responded to this process? What now remains for social work education to achieve in quality assurance (QA)?

Quality discourse in western management science was promoted during the late 1970s by consultants and applied researchers writing primarily for people in the organizational development and consultancy field (Baker 1980; O'Toole 1979; Peters 1978; Ouchi 1981; Ouchi and Price 1978). Their theme was the enhancement of competitiveness by emulating 'Japanese' cultural style in business organization, placing an emphasis on cultural values, flexibility and service outcomes. Hand-in-hand with these theories, new forms of financial accounting and audit were being introduced in the USA and Europe, creating mini-markets within and between firms, to sharpen the profitability of the production process. These markets were regulated via the use of quality indicators, to explain why and to whom contracts were awarded. Long-standing contractual relationships between suppliers and manufacturers were reviewed to ensure that each component was supplied as cheaply as possible, working to minimum standards. To help them compete in this environment, quality management theory was promoted to senior managers as the next step forward from the tired old ideologies of scientific management, human relations and rational systems theory. The 'excellence' school argued that neither chains of command nor bureaucratic rulemaking would attain the kind of flexible and inventive practices that could be achieved by working to quality norms. For whole industries, the language of quality provided a participative ethos of continuous improvement to ward off the dangers of alienation that might otherwise arise from splitting off and outsourcing parts of the manufacturing process, and the scramble for contracts.

The quality movement was born out of the contradictions facing US profitability and the desire to maintain competitiveness for western manufacturing (principally of cars) in an international market. Yet over the past 20 years it has found its way into areas of work far from manufacturing and which at one time would have been hard to imagine as markets, including the world of social work education. The reception of this idea has nevertheless grown and now all areas of government in the UK are subject to quality systems. However, the education literature shows considerable mistrust of 'quality speak', which may go some way towards explaining many social work education professionals' compliant but relatively minimalist and sometimes rather grudging involvement in QA processes. A serious obstacle to their engagement, I will argue, is an unhelpful set of commonplace theories in everyday use about how political discourse works. Although to be a professional is to declare a concern for standards in the profession in which you practise, social work professionals have tended to dismiss QA either as fashionable buzzwords or as a non-negotiable bureaucratic 'regime of truth'. They have therefore missed certain opportunities to shape their own worlds and those of service users and students. In addition to these obstacles, perhaps customer views are not always seen by professionals as straightforwardly synonymous with their own interests. Finally, from my own observations I have noted how QA systems can at times be used by social work educators to defend positions that are not compatible with a quality service to students.

Reception of QA Ideas in Education

A review of the QA literature in health and social work reveals that, in the UK, public sector professionals have tended to view sceptically the prospect of quality assurance – as a fad, an American import and an encroachment of business practices and ethics derived from the Thatcher/Reagan years on very different kinds of service in a very different context (Hart 1997). Suspicion focuses on the language of quality assurance and some clearly regard the new buzzwords as things of the surface and therefore transitory and relatively meaningless. Others treat the new terms as if they carried inherently political agendas, rather as a virus carries disease, which should be handled carefully, but at a distance, and preferably by specialists. When the specialists visit to carry out their testing, they are then vehemently resented for their intrusion. UK academics identified the discourse of quality control as another form of scientific management, designed to facilitate the insertion of employers' instrumental agendas into academic curricula (Hartley 1995).

The developments were seen as systems of surveillance designed to make education more instrumental and less free to define its own purposes (Parker and Jarry 1995).

Even among those who seize upon and promote quality initiatives, there is a perceived 'dissonance ... between what professionals, managers and elected representatives say they do and how organisations behave' (James 1994, p.200), resulting in confusion, anger and disappointment. James regrets that quality assurance has been viewed as part of a right-wing managerial programme and believes that this factor has impeded radical improvements in services. Having spent several years approving and reviewing quality assurance arrangements for social work training, and investigating complaints into social work programmes for CCETSW, I would share some of James's disappointment. While complying with top-down QA demands, social work educators have rarely taken opportunities to assert professional goals from the bottom-up via quality assurance systems, or to make professional issues a legitimate part of the new accounting systems.

This managerial slant is also clear from the implementation of quality initiatives in UK local authority social services departments (SSDs). James notes that the Social Services Inspectorate found, via an inspection, that SSDs were using quality initiatives primarily as a means of financial restraint; secondly as a demonstration of policy achievement; and only thirdly as a mechanism to enhance services to users (James 1992). In observing what differences QA implementation makes, it can appear as if the agenda is de facto managerial. It remains to be seen whether the *Quality Protects* initiative (Department of Health 1998) will have a more radical effect in practice.

Need for an Action Theory of Discourse

Everyday common-sense notions of the way in which political language works can deter the involvement of service users and professionals. Both advocates and detractors of quality systems point to the social and political effects of words and deeds, the operations of discourse and its relationship to the social world. Whether you sign up to quality rhetoric or see it as window dressing, you are looking at the relationship between language and action. Nevertheless this relationship is often alluded to rather than explained; both sides lack an adequate explanation of the relation between talk and action. Just as it is not safe for professionals to dismiss quality assurance as a new fad, neither is it possible to ascertain the political direction of discourse from its semantic components alone. Because of the stress on language use in the critiques of quality assurance, these matters are significant to our involvement with quality initiatives and warrant closer examination.

Discourses are often viewed as structures of thought, with political biases, and it is common for people to attribute particular powers to them. They are often described as if they are set up to work in the interests of a section of society, which is just what happens in the descriptions in the academic critique of quality assurance already cited. These claims derive, however, from a theory of discourse that minimizes the role of people as creative interpreters of their social worlds. In critiques that focus on the importance of language, there is a tendency to rely heavily on post-structuralist or Foucauldian ideas about discourses as 'regimes of truth' promoted by particular interest groups, as if stored in some collective socio-psychological reservoir, to be drawn on to promote sectional interests. However, people are not dupes of their own language. They recognize and take account of particular ways of talking and can discern such things as self-interest, hard sell and irony in interpreting what they are told. They also transform language as they use it; it does not pass through them unscathed. Who participates in this transformation is key to the work of quality systems.

The infinitely flexible discursive facility of language makes ample provision for language users to remodel a concept in order to take particular positions, to insulate themselves against possible accusations, to render their accounts plausible, according to their creative deployment of terms. This is not only the prerogative of the right wing. This process is continuous through the minutiae of everyday conversations in organizations. Once an idea enters the world of language, it can always be subverted, in the sense that subversion is an everyday interpretative feature of human exchanges. 'People can perform actions, and say things, for the kinds of actions they will be taken to be' (Edwards 1997, p.99). Though this 'taking as' quality of interpretation provides the mechanism by which certain kinds of political talk are recognizable, by the same token people can and do construct an argument pursuing the opposite goal by borrowing moral positions, terminology or criteria from its rival position. Quality assurance provides exactly the same argumentative resources for social work education professionals, students and service users as it does for auditors and senior managers.

Studies of implementing quality systems have shown how quality initiatives, far from working unidirectionally on the side of management control, cost cutting, or instrumentalism, have opened up new possibilities for equality initiatives and professional creativity. They have enabled professional staff to gain ground in improving services and in pursuing valid grievances of their own, particularly where management practices had failed to live up to their own quality rhetoric, using the customer voice as a persuasive resource (Rosenthal, Hill and Peccei 1997; Webley and Cartwright 1996). Before returning to the opportunities provided by a quality system in education, it is worth examining how quality assurance discourse is being used to manage the key post-war dilemma about the provision of health, social services and education in the UK public sector.

The Wider Quality Agenda

The circumstance and timing of the adoption of the new quality systems in health, social services and education give an indication of their practical function. Behind the incontrovertible goal of better services and the obvious populism of increased customer involvement, quality rhetoric provides argumentative resources to help reconcile a seemingly antithetical agenda: that of reducing central public spending, supplementing or eventually replacing it with local private or charitable sources of finance, while maintaining centralized government control over the sensitive nature of this transfer process and of the services provided. Responsibility for provision is being devolved to the lowest possible level, while accountability is retained at the highest. The way many quality systems are set up provides exactly the type of discursive resources suited to this kind of political task. Quality discourse lends itself to the provision of a public account for difficult decisions about scarce resources, that is, whether particular organizations sink or swim. This type of account reduces personal risk for the decision-makers, as it presents as a science and can be taken therefore to be independent of personal interest or bias. Quality assurance is being drafted in to manage the public face of the rationalization process, by providing a system of accountability wherein one's fate ultimately lies in one's own actions. This is not an inevitable feature of QA, but a discernible trend in the way it is used since its inception in the 1970s.

Increasingly sophisticated quality systems have been playing a key role in managing the transitions of spending in higher education (HE) and in the personal social services across the UK. In HE the crisis of confidence in education, publicized by the training agency and employers' organizations in the 1980s, helped to account for the deregulation of universities. This propelled the established higher education system into competing alongside newcomers whose products were cheaper, shinier and available in many more places. As James says, 'quality can be a substitute for core values when core values are being challenged' (1994, p.211). A similar process is occurring in the delivery of personal social services. For example the *Quality Protects* initiative announced by government in late 1998 promised to reward quality performance and to punish authorities that fall short of government targets. The impact of this system of accounting on professionals is important; it is significantly shaping their environment and behaviour. I have argued that there has been a tendency among professionals to avoid involvement in the setting of quality goals and targets. This has compounded the problem of distance, as the goal setting has largely been left to bureaucrats (government organizations and quality specialists) and the divide from local interests is reinforced.

The Alternative: Professional Quality QA

The key to achieving a desirable outcome in quality assurance activity is the professional facilitation of user voices in the establishment of baseline standards, so that standards are clearly derived from a bottom-up view about the kinds of services that are wanted (see Hastings, Chapter 6). There also needs to be more flexibility and innovation in the methods for gathering data, taking into account the circumstances of the stakeholders in whose interests the process claims to operate. Another aspect requiring scrutiny is that of analysis, of turning data into information. I will discuss some examples of problems arising in the design of QA systems in social work programmes to illustrate how quality systems could be improved.

Three Stages of Professional QA: Standard setting, analysis and action
GENERATING BASELINE STANDARDS

Standards need to be set for the most basic aspects of provision. Sometimes fundamental areas are most easily overlooked. In many cases, data are routinely gathered but standards for interpreting these data are never set. For example, universities require particular forms of subject monitoring, as does the statutory regulator in the case of a professional social work award, and the Quality Assurance Agency is set to continue in this vein with the regulatory assistance of the General Social Care Councils. A universal feature of baseline data for monitoring purposes is wastage and attrition rates. CCETSW currently publishes an annual stewardship report in which national average attrition rates for qualifying training are summarized. Despite this, many social work qualifying programmes set no quality standards for attrition. In the process of five yearly reviews by CCETSW where students are interviewed, in those programmes where attrition is high this is one of the causes of greatest concern to DipSW students.

The most damaging effect of a high attrition rate on a learning programme is the impact on the learning culture both for the victims and, in some ways more importantly, the survivors of the process (see Weinstein, Chapter 9). The experience of sitting alongside fellow learners and watching large numbers of them disappear creates the antithesis of an empowering culture. Students report becoming fearful, compliant, focused on concealing learning needs rather than drawing attention to them. Quite apart from the effect on the learners, agency partners regularly report that for them, professional social work training is an extremely resource intensive activity. It requires a high resource commitment from pressured employers to collaborative arrangements and placement provision. They do not wish to see large numbers of first-year placements used for students who will not qualify. Yet when asked to account for the high numbers of candidates who fail or withdraw, programme staff often explain their losses as a feature of their high standards and of their positive commitment to equal opportunities. They are prepared to run a high level of risk in their decisions about intake, in the hope that the positive qualities embodied in some less able students may not be excluded from the profession. This is a complex argument; it could be taken to be an expression of principled concern for disadvantaged groups. It could also be taken as an unscrupulous bid to maintain cloaked as an equalities issue. Whichever argument rings more true, in the absence of any openly agreed quality standards for attrition, programmes are in a position either simply not to report on this aspect or to produce any retrospective analyses of their results. The quality system allows this gap to remain open and its value contested. The group that consistently does not contest the desirability of this situation is the students. This example shows that even the most basic measurements for QA of standards need to be developed at the outset, in consultation with all stakeholders, and the purpose behind them agreed prior to data gathering and analysis.

DATA GATHERING

Categories generated by bureaucrats are not likely to reflect the common-sense version of quality as understood by people using education provision. Systems all too often take the form of paperwork and reporting arrangements, which may not be immediately recognizable to the people they claim to represent. Quality systems will tend to reduce variation in order to generate countable instances and it can appear as if the generation of quality education is to do with eliminating variation. What is essentially a function of reporting can be confused with a desirable goal. In a typical quality system an authorized person will use a finite number of classifications to generate data by interpreting the fit between available categories and material gathered. This is an important gatekeeping role, as only the person authorized to do so can generate valid data. Thus, what people say and do is turned into something measurable. In this process, variation will be eliminated except that generated by the categories of the system, which becomes the only variation of significance. The outcome of the audit system might look as if it supports the purposes of its designer, but in practice it is a product of interpretation at several levels: the groups that count as relevant to respond; response rates among those groups; how responses are elicited; who is authorized to complete the return; and how data are turned into information at various levels of the system. These should all be matters of tremendous significance to professionals.

What counts as data is a key issue for reporting. In quite serious cases of concern to CCETSW, it is not uncommon for complaints about the same issues over long periods of time to have escaped attention in formal quality reporting. On closer inspection, the quite sincere rationale offered is that each problem raised is unique, contingent, different in some way from its predecessors. Although there is truth in the assertion, by viewing each complaint singly their cumulative impact as part of a pattern is missed. There are easy parallels to draw between this style of problem solving and child protection enquiries. Data only become meaningful when set in a history of other relevant instances.

Although all interests are, in theory, represented in a quality system, in practice much depends on the way it is organized. Too often in quality returns the only voice heard is the voice of the authorized respondent. While this person may indeed occupy an advantageous position in relation to the many interests represented, the reality of their position is that while there will be things that only they can see, there will also be things that only they cannot see. To address the problem of (hidden) perspective, it is important to devote programme time to gathering data for quality analysis. This might include more imaginative methods, such as group and pairs discussions, in order to address the way the dynamics of the respondent body or individual fears of retribution may inhibit or distort responses. Reporting too could take a more direct or collective form. Somehow the demands of the bureaucratic system have to be temporarily set aside, in order for quality agendas to represent actual experience.

ANALYSIS AND ACTION

It is evident, from five years of quality monitoring by CCETSW of social work consortia, that immediate operational issues tend to prevail, at the expense of longer term planning and analysis. The predominant picture is one where thinking at consortium level is lost in the minutiae of everyday operations. The problem with this level of response is that it is likely to treat events as one-off contingencies and to pre-empt reflection on them with the urge to find solutions. It is well known from social work practice that these kinds of responses tend to curtail the assessment of need in favour of the imposition of a particular kind of service. So it happens with complaints from students that their settlement, often framed in a procedural way, takes priority over accurate listening. A number of key points emerge from several years of dealing with students' complaints:

1. Students wish to be heard and have their concerns taken seriously. Many feel that this does not always happen because the person who should be listening cannot risk hearing what they say because of the consequences for their own position. Staff are sometimes perceived as unwilling to acknowledge how a student feels in case they may have to act on it. This alone can at times create an avoidable escalation of a process.

2. Students learn a great deal from witnessing what happens to others. Episodes of staff–student conduct are sometimes mistakenly regarded by staff as private business, when they are in principle the legitimate concern of the learning group. Everything that happens on a programme of learning, particularly the micro-level interchange such as the way a message is delivered, plays a part in setting the power culture of the programme. Poor or missing communication can become a habit, so that it is no longer recognized as such.

3. Recourse to formal procedure is almost always a measure of despair. It signals a breakdown of trust and confidence in the provision's ability to deal fairly and responsively. A small proportion of such cases do unfortunately arise as part of a mental health crisis for the student, but in the majority of cases, irrespective of the validity of the substance of the complaint, there is something important to be learned about the environment in which it arose.

4. Measures that empower students are, paradoxically, the key to the resolution of complaints. In the main, where programme staff induct properly and develop and take time to explain complaints procedures, the generation of serious complaints is prevented.

With these points in mind, in the context of operational pressures acknowledged earlier, it is easy to see that the kind of measured and reflective analysis needed of quality issues is sometimes hard to find.

Conclusion

Quality systems are here. Rather than being subject to them, professionals have a responsibility both for their own closer involvement and for the representation of the users of their services. To see a system as unidirectional is part of the process that makes it so. The question of what counts as data is fundamental to a professional approach to quality. Our knowledge base from other contexts can help us to create innovative methods of enabling user voices to be heard, both in generating information and in making it mean something. Much information is collected, but in the absence of standards it remains unanalysed and of little use to the people supplying it. If standards remain in the hands of QA specialists they remain arbitrary. This does not have to be so; quality systems could provide a vehicle for the promotion of interests closer to the heart of social work.

References

Baker, E.L. (1980) 'Managing organisational culture'. *Management Review 69*, 8–13.

Department of Health (1998) *'Quality Protects' Initiative.*

Edwards, D. (1997) *Discourse and Cognition.* London: Sage.

Hart, W.A. (1997) 'The qualitymongers'. *Journal of Philosophy of Education 31*, 2, 295–308.

Hartley, D. (1995) 'Teaching and learning in an expanding higher education system (The MacFarlane Report) – a technical fix'. *Studies in Higher Education 20*, 2, 147–158.

James, A. (1992) *Committed to Quality: Quality Assurance in Social Services Departments.* London: HMSO.

James, A. (1994) 'Reflections on the politics of quality'. In A. Connor and S. Black (eds) *Performance Review and Quality in Social Care (Research Highlights in Social Work No 20).* London: Jessica Kingsley Publishers.

O'Toole, J. (1979) 'Corporate and managerial cultures'. In C.L. Cooper (ed) *Behavioural Problems in Organisations.* Englewood Cliffs, NJ: Prentice Hall.

Ouchi, W.G. (1981) *Theory Z: How American Business can Meet the Japanese Challenge.* Reading, MA: Addison-Wesley.

Ouchi, W.G. and Price, R.C. (1978) 'Hierarchies, clans and theory Z: a new perspective on OD'. *Organisational Dynamics 7*, 24–44.

Parker, M. and Jarry, D. (1995) 'The McUniversity: organisation, management and academic subjectivity'. *Organisation 2*, 2, 319–338.

Peters, T.J. (1978) 'Symbols, patterns and settings: an optimistic case for getting things done'. *Organisational Dynamics 7*, 3–22.

Rosenthal, P., Hill, S. and Peccei, R. (1997) 'Checking out service: HRM and TQM in retailing'. *Work Employment and Society 11*, 3, 481–503.

Webley, P. and Cartwright, J. (1996) 'The implicit psychology of total quality management'. *Total Quality Management 7*, 5, 483–492.

CHAPTER 8

Teaching and Learning Anti-racist and Anti-discriminatory Practice

Cathy Aymer

This chapter aims to provide health and care professional educators with ideas and questions that can be converted into practical strategies to improve the quality of services to users. This teaching and learning can occur in the university or the practice setting. Both anti-racist practice and anti-discriminatory practice have an important historical context within social work and this context will be examined briefly. The emphasis, however, will be on the future where I will attempt to bring together best practice to reflect on how we can develop ideas for moving into the new millennium. I will be drawing on my experiences of working with diverse groups of social work students since the mid-1980s.

There are some key questions that need to be asked in order to define the terrain I intend to traverse:

1. How have we dealt with issues of racism, discrimination and inequality in the past?

2. Which ideas and methods have worked successfully and which have not?

3. What is the impetus for change that causes us to seek alternative ways of approaching these issues in a more productive manner?

4. How can we devise a model for the future that can relate theory to practice and be applied in our work with students, service users, managers and practitioners?

5. How can we continue to recognize the diversity of the profession and of the student body and devise ways of thinking that liberate them and us from the conflict and 'stuckness' that has typified relationships in recent years?

6. It is easy to identify the hindrances to progress such as anger, guilt, accusation and recrimination. Nevertheless, how can we, in the process of learning, understand the similarities and differences of a complex series of inequalities but strive to avoid a 'hierarchy of oppressions'?

This is an opportune moment to be asking these questions, for although social work may feel that it has long dealt with them, the whole country has been made aware of their importance in very forceful ways. The McPherson Report (1999) into the murder of Stephen Lawrence, a young black man, concluded that, among other things, there was institutional racism throughout the police force. In March 1999, a report into the deaths of prisoners at Belmarsh prison concluded similarly that institutional racism was endemic in the prison service. At the same time an Ofsted Report (1999) suggested that racism in schools led to differential performance of pupils. Following the backlash against feminism (Faludi 1992), Germaine Greer (1999) thought it timely to suggest that a new women's liberation movement is needed. The turn of the century has seen a growth of fundamentalist religions, with certain outspoken views about sexuality and lifestyles, causing gay and lesbian people to feel unsafe. In April 1999 Londoners experienced three bomb attacks targeting predominantly black, Asian and gay communities.

These are important reminders to the social work profession that racism and oppression have not disappeared. Complex issues of anti-racism and anti-discriminatory practice clearly have to be rethought and renegotiated for the new century. In the 1980s, social work education was admonished for its insistence that racism is endemic in British society (CCETSW 1991, Annex 5), and the government insisted that references of this kind had to be removed from the documentation of the social work regulatory body (see Pierce and Weinstein, Chapter 1). Social work thus became rather nervous about 'stating its case.' The lessons to be learned from the McPherson and other reports are that the social work profession should be mature enough to put forward professional arguments about oppression and the nature of society that can withstand the criticisms and machinations of politically more powerful others. In some ways we may have been rather complacent about our advances in these areas and it is necessary to 'rediscover' inequality and oppression. The scope of this chapter is broad. It is my intention that students, trainers and educators will find it a resource for practice in a variety of organizations and communities, health, social work agencies, schools and other care settings. Other professions have much to learn from the sometimes rocky paths that social work has already trodden.

Countering the Political Correctness Lobby?

Despite the fact that the profession has, in principle, endorsed anti-racist practice and anti-discriminatory practice as part of its value base and integrated it into the social work curriculum (CCETSW 1995), there is a residual concern regarding 'political correctness'. At the heart of the criticisms about anti-discriminatory practice is the belief that it idealizes the history and experiences of black people and other minorities, enabling them to feel good about themselves while everyone else feels guilty. In effect, their argument is that 'political correctness' is a standpoint that unconditionally values descriptions of blackness over whiteness; female over male, etc. It was envisioned that the 'thought police' would prevent you from using perfectly ordinary words or from making ordinary jokes in the mistaken belief that someone will be offended. So what if 'they' are offended? 'They' should not be so sensitive. Of course some of the more ludicrous and laughable excesses of the 1980s were bound to produce such a reaction. It is of little consequence now whether anybody ever banned children from singing the nursery rhyme 'Baa Baa Black Sheep'. This is now part of the folklore of political correctness. The political correctness backlash has not, however, restored balance to social workers' perspectives on anti-discriminatory practice. While this backlash is understandable and fairly inevitable, it has served to hinder the development of more sophisticated strategies and interventions that could encompass all the complex realities, rather than the simplified and mythological views of 'other' social groups.

This chapter will argue that we need to find a perspective to heal the rifts in our thinking about 'otherness' and about how we construct relationships between black–white; men–women; gay–straight; religious–secular, etc. The social work profession has to ask questions about how we can create equivalent rather than dominant voices in our endeavour to settle societal differences in a socially complex and multi-layered environment.

This understanding of the differences and similarities that exist between people from various racial, ethnic, cultural, social and religious groups is crucial to achieving a fully functional, diverse professional workforce, or student body which is free from 'internecine warfare'. Weinstein, in Chapter 9, found that black students on social work courses are more likely than their white counterparts to drop out or to fail. When recruiting to programmes or staffing care agencies, organizations need to think beyond just recruiting a diverse group and must focus on retention and team functioning. They need to find ways to maintain a diverse student or staff group by identifying their unique contributions to the profession and incorporating that uniqueness in all aspects of their services, not least their ability to work together and to develop productive methods of communication. To achieve this, the university or agency must take account of the cumulative effect of the poorer life chances that many black people will have experienced.

In Aymer and Bryan (1996) we outlined some of the difficulties that black students face in their interactions with each other and how different groups of black students use different strategies for making sense of their private and public worlds. We examined the role of black lecturers and discussed their potential contribution and effect. We concluded that having a proportion of black lecturers on and around the programme creates a psychological context in which black students can feel a sense of belonging. The presence of black managers in professional contexts will have the same impact.

Learning from History

When discussion began about race and racism in social work in the 1980s, the typical social worker or social work student was white; so too were the lecturers, practice teachers and managers. When a small number of black workers or students were admitted to the profession, the thinking was directed towards the idea of race and the place of black workers within the profession. Drawing on the US experience, black social workers began to question the view that the black family is pathological and to seek explanations for the high proportion of black children in care (Dominelli 1988; Maximé, 1993; Small 1986).

All the welfare services had traditionally been staffed by women, but the development of large social work departments with multi-million pound budgets resulted in men occupying positions of power (Grimwood and Popplestone 1993). This led to important questions being asked about women and the enterprise of social work (Hanmer and Statham 1989). The women's movement left its imprint on the profession.

As the variety of peoples within British society continue to expand, and as an increasing number of people maintain multiple racial, social and cultural identities, and as ideas about race change rapidly, understanding the nature of race and of racism is bound to become more complex. So too must our thinking change about all other social groups. More and more members of minority groups have moved into all positions in the care professions and there are different ways in which they belong or do not belong to an oppressed group.

Over the years social work students, both black and white, male and female have come to view anti-racist practice and anti-discriminatory practice in purely objective terms – as information about other cultures, knowledge about other groups – that have to be mastered in order to work effectively with clients from 'other' groups. This is a distancing activity, a type of cultural tourism. The question is whether social work's long-term experience has left the profession with any better grasp of the complex concepts of anti-racist practice and anti-discriminatory practice. Are communications between different groups any more productive or has the profession decided to rest on its laurels and no longer discuss race, gender, sexuality or other inequalities because of potential conflict and anguish that is caused within groups?

After all, social work, as the first profession to recognize the need for anti-racism and anti-discriminatory practice, has been a leader in providing insight and innovative means of working with poor and disadvantaged populations. Social work agencies have been through many phases of training strategies in order to raise awareness and equip staff with knowledge and skills to counter oppression. Many commentators have pointed to different ways of achieving this (Cheetham 1986; Dominelli 1988; Langan and Day 1992; Thompson 1993)

The literature on race, gender, sexuality, religion and oppression is vast and there is a variety of approaches to studying these very complex subjects, many of which are relevant to care professional training. In this short chapter I am going to concentrate on the theme of identity because I have found it an effective concept to help students understand some of the conflicts, misunderstandings and differences between and within groups.

What is this Thing Called Identity?

I will start with a simple premise that we experience life through association and our identities are shaped by the dynamic interactions between the people we encounter. When difference is perceived between people, their lives are shaped by stories we tell about that difference and the stories we are told about difference. These stories are not just invented, they are negotiated through culture. White and Epston (1990) describe a story as a sequence of events that unfolds over time with a theme or plot that helps to define who we are. They go on to explain that we are multi-storied, but that the dominant story develops over time and attempts to make us single-storied.

The history of black people's lives, for example, has been the history of how our lives have been shaped by the ability of powerful others to construct our reality. In western culture the construction of identities is thoroughly permeated with the erection of binary oppositions such as white–black, man–woman, good–evil, where the first term is regarded as superior and where the second term contains within it features that pose a threat to the first.

Hall (1996) highlights the distinction and the struggle between two models of the production of identities. He articulates the complexity of this debate between modernists and post-modernists by showing that the first model assumes that there is some intrinsic and essential content to any identity which is defined by either a common origin or a common structure of experience or both. Struggling against existing constructions of a particular identity takes the form of a contest between negative images and positive ones, and of trying to discover the 'authentic' and 'original' content of the identity.

The second model emphasizes the impossibility of such fully constituted separate and distinct identities. It denies the existence of authentic and original identities based in a universally shared origin or experience. Identities are always relational and incomplete; they are in process. Any identity depends upon its difference from, or its negation of, the other. As Hall (1991, p.21) puts it, 'Identity is a structured representation which only achieves its positive through the narrow eye of the negative. It has to go through the eye of the needle of the other before it can construct itself.'

Thus the emphasis is on the multiplicity of identities and differences rather than on a singular identity and on the connections or articulations between the fragments or differences. The fact of multiple identities gives rise to what Mercer has called 'the mantra of race, class and gender' (1992, p.34). The challenge is to be able to theorize more than one difference at a time.

Hall (1996) has spoken of 'race as a floating signifier'. Others have spoken of race as an 'empty signifier'. Obviously influenced by Derrida (1978), such a position sees identity as an entirely cultural, even linguistic construction. When I use the term black it is with the tacit knowledge that I am more than just the text, that I have an existence that is rooted in reality and I have a connectedness with other people like myself. This leads me to agree that race is relational, that identities are changing, complex and contingent.

In the 1980s, discussions about race created the representation of a black person as a unitary subject, a single generalized and stereotypical entity. It was evident that something which we call the black experience existed, that it was complex and varied, and that it had many nuances and textures as people lived their lives in situations of oppression and disadvantage within contemporary society. Bourdieu's notion of cultural capital (1977) is important here. He argues that different social groups possess different sorts of knowledge and skill. They share different cultural histories in which they invest, to varying degrees.

The work of White and Epston (1990) highlights how the story that is told about you, in western culture, and the stories you hear about yourself initiate you into memberships of particular clubs. Some memberships are privileged and elevated while certain memberships are rendered invalid and cast down. For black people the 'authorship' of the story belongs with the powerful white group. Re-authoring is a term that I will borrow from these two writers. The notion that it is possible to rewrite our story in our own words and thus become the 'primary author' is an aim of this chapter. Individual identities are shaped and framed by a broader context and, in order to reclaim the authorship of our stories, it is necessary to deconstruct the stories that are told about black people, about women, about minorities, and to understand the nature of the context. But as hooks (1995) points out, we are not speaking of replacing one set of absolutes by another, but it is the experience of learning when one's experience is recognized as central and significant, when one is regarded as a subject not an object. The ways in which we come to know these stories about self and other will be discussed later.

Communication across Differences

Difficulty in communication between any two groups comes about because the emotions and the sense of self are closely connected, but this connection is often to a 'single-storied' sense of self. One of the difficulties has been in the acceptance of multiple identities, no one aspect taking precedence over the other. Furthermore, it means acknowledging that one can belong to an oppressed group and an oppressor group simultaneously. For example, I have often heard black students say, 'I am black first and a woman second'. It would seem to me that it must be possible to be black and a woman simultaneously, plus any other aspects of identity that one chooses, including middle class. Rather than a sequential building up of identity along hierarchical lines, the idea must be to achieve a holistic sense of self where each aspect is important and integral. It should be possible to have a bicultural identity, for example, if you are of mixed parentage (Katz 1996; Tizard and Phoenix 1993).

Whenever people of different races, genders and ethnicity come together, educators and managers can assume that race is an important issue but not necessarily a problem. The very high apparent difference between group members is laden with highly sensitive social meaning. The racism and institutional discrimination found in society at large become a salient part of a group's social reality whenever more than one is present. The ways in which the group develops will depend critically on the group leader's ability to control the situation, which in turn depends on them having:

- a realistic sense of their own ability to cope with concerns and fears regarding race and other social divisions
- the ability to use knowledge and the skills to cope with racially charged situations in a sensitive and non-defensive manner

- an understanding of the sources of racial tension in groups such that, as leader, they can:
  - have a critical awareness of the racial dynamics in the group
  - anticipate sources of group conflict based on all types of social divisions
  - seek innovative and creative solutions to problems.

A Personal Case Study: The Meeting of Religion, Race and Sexuality

My observation of some of the changes within social work student groups between the 1980s through to the turn of the century has helped me to develop effective strategies for teaching about issues of race, sexuality, gender and other inequalities. These changes have to be understood in the context of developments in the wider society, including representations in the media.

What seemed to be in evidence in the late 1980s was that some social work students were expressing strongly held political views. There was a political discourse about issues of race, gender and class, and in a sense some of the struggles that students had with each other were about the different levels of political awareness that they brought to the ideas under discussion. People were trying to understand the nature of society, of social justice and of oppression at a time before Marxism had been discredited.

During the 1990s I noticed an increase in students with very definite religious views, in some cases, very outspoken religious views. I am not suggesting that there were no students with religious views before, but they were not as vocal in the mid-1980s. This may be true for this social work programme only, but I suspect not. Our programme has a large number of black students of different cultural backgrounds and many, but by no means all, are people with religious views.

A second strand to my thinking is the ways in which black people are represented in the media. There are many different representations but I perceive an increase in representation as sexual stereotypes. This means that there is, generally speaking, both a sexualization of race and a racialization of sexuality. Some of these factors have come together in the dynamics of the interactions between students. In this context, any discussion of anti-discriminatory practice that leads to discussions about sexuality becomes very heated and very charged with accusation and counter-accusation of homophobia on the one hand and religious intolerance or racism on the other. The readiness with which religious students have made negative statements about sexual lifestyles and, in particular, sexual orientation has surprised me. There is a feeling of legitimacy about making these statements because they are sanctioned by religious belief. I recall reading some years ago in Berger's *Ways of Seeing* (1972) that the person with the biggest stick has the best chance of defining normality. Religion has, throughout history, been one of the biggest sticks with which to define normality.

Another aspect is the way that some white students of good will have been upset by the angry reactions of their black colleagues or the hurt that black gay students feel about homophobia from other black students. When white students think that they are doing everything to understand the history of black people and to empathize with their experiences, they may feel angry with the black students for not immediately accepting their understanding and empathy. They do, however, need to recognize the depth of the damage that has been done by racism and colonialism and find a way to acknowledge their own history. Some white students would prefer that we all adopted a form of historical amnesia, and some black students and practitioners would prefer that we did nothing else but remember. The project for social work (and for society at large) is to seek both ways to remember and ways to move forward, to move away from the 'ain't it awful' culture (Aymer and Bryan 1996).

Are There Acceptable and Non-acceptable Views for Professionals?

Anti-discriminatory practice is sometimes described simplistically as 'valuing diversity'. However, it is more complex than that. If people say, 'my religion allows me to say that', to make statements that are considered to be discriminatory by other people, is this acceptable? On the one hand, social work values have a religious strand as well as a strong humanistic tradition, not just the Judaeo-Christian tradition but other religious traditions as well. These define our world view. When these debates come about, I believe that people are asking a number of questions:

- What systems of beliefs are allowable for the care professions in terms of what people can or cannot adopt as their world view?
- Are all belief systems and world views acceptable in care practice?
- What is the role of the educator (in university or practice) in changing people's views? How do we make sense of the different positions that they hold?
- Are different sets of beliefs allowed to rub along together, side by side?

- How do world views get discussed in relation to anti-discriminatory practice?
- How should we look at and try to understand these different belief systems and the positions that people can take?

As discussed earlier, the abilities of the group leader are brought into focus in these discussions. One of the reasons that I am particularly interested in this is that I started off my earlier life in a very religious way, but I left this behind a long time ago. I have to ask myself whether we really leave things like our religious upbringing behind or do I have a tendency to be antagonistic towards some religious views precisely because I have left them behind.

These personal questions are necessary to enable me to look at and make sense of my own reactions. I do believe that all religions are, by their very nature and definition, organized systems of controlling and monitoring people's thoughts and actions. As I try to think through my own beliefs I must, at the same time, try to help students to think about what it means for them to hold certain beliefs. The vital question to ask students to explore is: How did you come to know what you know about the world, about yourself and about other people and what do you believe about them? In this way students are asked to think at a deep level about their taken for granted notions of 'truth' and 'normality' and, hopefully, to see their narrow and deeply problematic nature within our society.

Teaching Strategies: Ways of Knowing and Experiencing Self and 'Otherness'

I shall set out to offer a paradigm that informs thinking at a trans-cultural level and not just a model that provides specific strategies for ant-racist and anti-discriminatory practice. Such a model might serve to replace rather than preserve the difficulties which have divided social work students from each other and, later, from the clients and communities with which they work. I shall introduce three different types of exercises that assist students to consider their views about the 'other' social group. These are tried and trusted exercises used over many years with different generations of students and practitioners. People have always engaged with them and learnt many lessons about themselves and others.

Exercise one: Ways of knowing positions

The conflicts described above between social work students, whether they derive from political, religious, feminist or other viewpoints, occur when people believe that there is one authority, a truth, and that it is single, it is absolute and it is concrete. Instead of continually confronting the strongly held beliefs, it is useful to help students understand how they came to the position they have reached. Belenkey *et al.* (1986) undertook extensive research, speaking with women about a wide range of subjects, to determine what they described as different 'ways of knowing'. These are summarized below because I have found them so useful as a means of deepening students' understanding of thought processes and belief systems.

Ways of knowing positions (adapted from Belenkey *et al.* 1986)

SILENCE

Experiences the self as both deaf and 'dumb', without any capacity for receiving knowledge from others. Words are seen as weapons, rather than as a means for sharing meaning

RECEIVED KNOWING

The source of knowledge is external, residing especially in authorities who know the truth. Truth can be embodied in words. Truth is single absolute, concrete, and factual, so it is either right or wrong, true or false, good or bad.

SUBJECTIVE KNOWING

The source of knowledge is located in the self. Listening to one's own inner voice becomes primary as knowledge is now seen as based on one's own personal experiences and intuition. There are multiple truths and multiple realities and all are equally valid, but mine is absolutely right for me. Truth is personal and private and probably incommunicable.

PROCEDURAL KNOWING

Knowledge is acquired, developed and communicated through the deliberate and systematic use of procedures. There are two forms: separated mode and connected mode.

Separated mode

Focuses on analysing and evaluating different points of view or arguments. It is abstract and analytic. Objectivity is achieved through detachment, by adhering to impersonal standards and 'weeding out the self'. Feelings are seen as clouding thoughts. The goal is to construct truth – to test, prove, disprove, convince and be convinced.

Connected mode

Focuses on trying to understand and experience another's perspective, another's reality, and to be understood. This is narrative and holistic rather than argumentative and analytic. Objectivity is achieved through attachment, adopting the other's perspectives. Feelings are seen as illuminating thought. The goal is to construct meaning, to understand and be understood.

CONSTRUCTED KNOWING

Knowledge is understood to be constructed, and the knower is assumed to play a role in shaping the known. Both separate and connected modes of discourse are used, possibly integrated into a single approach. The goal is to understand the contexts out of which ideas arise and to take responsibility for examining, evaluating and developing systems of thought, and to attend to their implications for action. The goal is to care about thinking and to think about caring. (Adapted from Belenky, M.F *et al.* 1986.)

Within any group involved in discussing anti-discriminatory practice issues, all these positions emerge in some way or other. The exercise asks students to consider all these 'ways of knowing' and to explore their own positions with respect to knowledge about the self and the other. The notion of '*silence*' is particularly significant as a means whereby people can be silenced or can silence themselves. Some students will readily understand how they have been placed in this position by their experience of oppression.

The most interesting position in terms of the intersection between religion, race and sexuality is '*received knowing*'. It is inevitable that religious positions put people into this way of knowing position. If we go on to look at the other positions, '*subjective knowing*' states, 'This is my belief, this is my personal standpoint and it is unquestionable!' '*In my experience*' gives a statement validity but it is also a two-edged sword because that validity takes on the status of truth. But, ultimately, it is paradoxical. To talk of 'my experience' in that way is a rhetorical form that is irreducibly social. After all, communication is never an individual phenomenon, its origins are social and its goals are social.

The aim of the exercise is to ask students to look at knowledge in a particular way and to step back and ask themselves the questions:

- How do I come to hold this belief and to know what I know?
- How do I come to have beliefs in certain directions and not others?

What we try to do in this exploration is to separate belief from knowledge. Belief is a simple story that explains why the world is the way it is. Simple stories are very useful because they reduce our anxiety and are very calming. Knowledge is about complexity. One has to be quite flexible to take into account the many complex theories and explanations about why the world is the way it is. As professional educators, we are not laying down 'right' or 'wrong' beliefs. We maintain the rights of everyone to hold their own personal beliefs. Nevertheless, we are saying that care professionals who have to deal with complex problems in a diverse community must be sophisticated enough to cope with complex knowledge. It is not possible to undertake the role with a single story or a narrow view of the world.

Exercise two: Case study

One tried and trusted way of getting people to think about what they do is to ask them to analyse a case study. Case studies should provide situations with different levels of ambiguity about individual or structural causes of the problems presented. Case studies with low ambiguity suggest just one aspect of the protagonist's identity at any one time. For example, a person is black and nothing else. In contrast a high ambiguity situation contains a complex combination of the protagonist's identity, personality and/or behaviour towards other actors, the organization or society, with different levels of ambiguity about individual or structural causes of the problems presented. An example of a high ambiguity case study might be:

> *I am a black, female lecturer of Caribbean descent who meets with a male Asian student in his practice placement agency. His practice teacher is a white Jewish woman. The main user group is white, female and elderly. The student is having difficulty in his placement in the area of professional competence. What assumptions are being made and what types of discussions should this grouping have about anti-discriminatory practice?*

This approach helps to bring the discourse of power back into the client–worker relationship, into the student–practice teacher relationship and into the practitioner–manager relationship. This is an issue of politics. There is an imperative in social work to be more 'scientific' and 'rational' (Macdonald 1997) which implies knowing something that is 'permanent', 'true', 'universal' and 'essential' about the 'other'. This is simply not possible. We cannot totally transform political questions into technical ones. The client and the social worker, the student and practice teacher, the lecturer, the student and the practice teacher have each other's perceptions and resources to work with and, I would argue, not much more. Thus the nature of these multiple identity relationships takes on paramount importance. We have to maintain the need to be able to combine an experiential and affective component with the cognitive content as a positive way of developing a successful curriculum about inequality and oppression.

Exercise three: Trading places (week 1)

This exercise encourages students to imagine what it is like to be a member of a different group. These groups are women, black and minority ethnic peoples, lesbians and gay men, and disabled people. Students are divided into groups but we make no assumptions other than the most obvious, i.e. the group of women will consist of men, and the group of black and minority ethnic people will consist of white people. The other groups will be distributed randomly. Each group considers the following questions and writes down answers on a flipchart:

- What do you generally hear about your group, both positive and negative?
- How does this make you feel?
- What does your group experience (both positive and negative) when you come to a social work agency to ask for help or for a service?
- What indicators does your group look for to give you some confidence that this is an agency that is aware of, or relevant, to your needs?

Students then give feedback from all the groups on their discussions. Throughout this exercise it is stressed that participants *must* speak in terms of we, i.e. we would feel, we would hear rather than 'they' would feel. (Time for this exercise is 45 minutes.)

The aim of this exercise is to get the students to think about and experience what it feels like to be someone else, to put themselves in someone else's place, to think about how other people are treated on an institutional and personal level. Students are asked to think about how they relate to 'others' and how the stories that are told about others affect their views of and interactions with them.

Trading places (week 2)

- In groups of four discuss the links between your individual experiences of oppression and others' experiences of oppression. What links can be made from the trading places experiences of your group and the experiences of the other groups? (20 minutes)
- In the whole group give feedback on the discussions in the small groups and consider what this means for your work with clients. (20 minutes)

The aim of this exercise is to enable students to make the links and connections between their own positions and those of others, to move beyond their personal experiences. They are then able to look at similarities and differences in terms of the impact on the individual, to move away from a hierarchy of oppressions and to consider their own positions with those of their clients.

Conclusion

The problems of racism and discrimination may have changed over the years, but they are far from resolved. At the turn of the century genocide and ethnic cleansing are still international phenomena; sectarian murders have not yet ceased in Northern Ireland; racial and homophobic murders, harassment and discrimination are rife throughout Britain; and there has been a backlash against feminism, especially in the form of moral attacks on single parents. Black service users continue to receive sub-standard services from health and social care agencies and black people in the care professions often face discrimination on their education programmes and in their agencies.

Anti racist and anti discriminatory strategies must be multi-dimensional – political, economic, social and educational – if they are to achieve significant change in life chances for many oppressed groups. The educational strategies outlined in this chapter are designed to promote better communication and understanding between the diverse groups involved in providing and receiving services. Care professional educators who have thoroughly explored their own belief systems and have developed a sophisticated understanding of others' will be more likely to provide the support needed to enable students from oppressed groups to fulfil their potential. Qualifying professionals who gain this understanding will be more able to engage in meaningful partnerships with the full range of service users and thus improve the appropriateness and responsiveness of the services offered.

References

Aymer, C. and Bryan, A. (1996) 'The experiences of black students in higher education: accentuating the positives'. *British Journal of Social Work 26*, 1–16.

Belenky, M.F. Clinchy, B., Goldberger, N. and Tarrule, J. (1986) *Women's Ways of Knowing: The Development of Self, Voice and Mind*. New York: Basic Books.

Berger, J. (1972) *Ways of Seeing*. London: Penguin.

Bourdieu, P. (1977) *Reproduction in Education, Society and Culture*. London: Sage.

CCETSW (1991) *Rules and Requirements for the Diploma in Social Work*, Paper 30. London: CCETSW.

CCETSW (1995) *Assuring Quality in the Diploma in Social Work 1 – Rules and Requirements for the DipSW*. London: CCETSW.

Cheetham, J. (1986) 'Reviewing black children in care: introductory note'. In S. Ahmed, J. Cheetham and J. Small (eds) *Social Work with Black Children and their Families*. London: Bartsford.

Derrida, J. (1978) *Writing and Difference*. Chicago: University of Chicago Press.

Dominelli, L. (1988) *Antiracist Social Work*. London: Macmillan.

Faludi, S. (1992) *Backlash: The Undeclared War Against Women*. London: Chatto and Windus.

Greer, G. (1999) *The Whole Woman*. New York: Doubleday.

Grimwood, C. and Popplestone, R. (1993) *Women, Management and Care*. London: Macmillan.

Hall, S. (1991) 'The local and the global: globalization and ethnicity'. In A. King (ed) *Culture Globalization and the World System*. London: Macmillan.

Hall, S. (1996) *Representation: Cultural Representations and Signifying Practices*. London: Sage.

Hanmer, J. and Statham, D. (1989) *Women and Social Work: Towards a Woman-Centred Practice*. London: Routledge.

hooks, b. (1995) *Yearning: Race, Gender and Cultural Politics*. Boston: South End Press.

Katz, I. (1996) *Social Construction of a Mixed Race Identity: Mixed Metaphor*. London: Jessica Kingsley Publishers.

Langan, M. and Day, L. (1992) *Women, Oppression and Social Work*. London: Routledge.

Macdonald, G. (1997) 'Social work research: the state we're in'. *Journal of Interprofessional Care 11*, 1, 57–65.

McPherson, W. (1999) *The Stephen Lawrence Inquiry*. London: HMSO.

Maximé, J.M. (1993) 'The importance of racial identity for the psychological well-being of black children'. *ACPP Review and Newsletter 15*, 4, 173–179.

Mercer, K. (1992) *Welcome to the Jungle: New Positions in Black Cultural Studies*. London: Routledge.

Ofsted Report (1999) *Raising Achievement in Ethnic Minority Children*. London: HMSO.

Small, J. (1986) 'Transracial placements: conflicts and contradictions'. In S. Ahmed, J. Cheetham and J. Small (eds) *Social Work with Black Children and their Families*. London: Bartsford.

Thompson, N. (1993) *Anti-discriminatory Practice*. London: Macmillan.

Tizard, B. and Phoenix, A. (1993) *Black, White or Mixed Race*. London: Routledge.

White, M. and Epston, D. (1990) *Narrative Means to Therapeutic Ends*. New York: Norton.

CHAPTER 9

Selection and Retention of Social Work Students

'The Best Workers and the Best Human Beings'

Jeremy Weinstein

Setting the Scene

At the beginning of the century, social workers recruiting students were told 'The best workers must be the best human beings, those whose conduct of their own lives is most nearly what we wish the conduct of all lives to be' (Gow 1900, p.110, cited in Jones 1983, pp.87–88). Fifty years on, it was argued that a student selected to train should have the strongest 'identification with the ideals and objectives of his profession as well as with the group he serves. He must have an unwavering conviction as to the worth of the ends of his work' (Towle 1954, p.vi, cited in Jones 1983, p.87).

More recent authors (Lousada 1993; Parton 1996), whose texts critique contemporary social work, remind us of just how lacking we now are in this sense of professional self-confidence. We retain few concepts of what the 'best human being' might look like, or the 'worth of social work', let alone how one might dovetail into the other. Nonetheless the questions remain relevant for social work programmes which hold a crucial gatekeeping role in selecting future social workers. Chapters 1 and 3 trace the history and debates about the nature and purpose of social work education. Different views about the purpose of social work and the purpose of training inevitably influence opinions about the kind of student programmes should recruit.

A strong lobby during the 1970s urged the recruitment of students whose backgrounds would better reflect the communities they serve. The mainly white, middle-class recruits of the 1960s, although they rarely failed their social work courses, were accused of failing their clients, especially ethnic minority groups, because of their lack of understanding or relevant life experience. CCETSW and social work programmes responded to this by introducing equal opportunities into recruitment procedures and promoting social work as a career for mature students.

Following this development, concern began to be expressed in professional circles that access may have been made too easy and that once students were on a course their success seemed guaranteed. Indeed the simultaneous initiatives of the Diploma in Social Work (DipSW) and the accreditation of practice teachers, established in 1989, were intended precisely to introduce more rigour into the assessment process of both academic work and professional practice. These initiatives clearly had an impact in that it began to be more common for students to fail a social work programme.

How well students do is, of course, related to the quality of the students selected and, if the process is not managed well, the price is high (Wilkes, Chapter 7). As one tutor comments, failure is 'not just a private grief. Its consequences reverberate round the student and staff groups and the placement agencies' (Munro 1995, p.23). The debate among academics therefore returned to the selection process: had it become too lax? Had the reduction in the competition for places, combined with an over-eagerness not to discriminate, led the admissions tutor to take on anyone who applied?

Less account seemed to be taken of the issues that arise once students are on the programme. The rapid expansion of higher education during the 1980s, the abandonment of the individual tutorial on social work programmes and the large lectures replacing small seminars significantly reduced the individual support received by social work students. The institutional racism faced by black students, once they had gained entry to programmes, also received insufficient attention.

Issues of recruitment and retention are explored in this chapter through the experiences of one inner-city, postgraduate social work programme based in a new university. The selection process and its intended outcomes are described and compared with other care professional programmes within the same university whose tutors are struggling with similar dilemmas. Previous research about selection procedures on social work courses is examined, together with research undertaken with respect to professions and mature students in further and higher education.

The results of four cohorts of social work students are examined to see whether or not success on the programme and rates of retention and attrition can be related back to factors identifiable at the point of selection. It also considers the relative chances of black and white students to succeed on the programme. While the research is limited, because time available for the project did not allow for providing adequate controls for all the variables, important questions are raised and proposals made about how the selection and retention processes might be strengthened.

Problems of Attracting and Retaining Social Work Students

The crisis in social work education, with all its ramifications, is debated elsewhere in this volume. What is important to note here is the continuing uncertainty about the role of social work in the mixed economy of welfare. Postgraduate programmes (such as the one researched in this chapter) are currently challenged both philosophically, with NISW (1998) questioning the benefits of training at this level, and practically, since the number of bursaries for postgraduate students is decreasing (THES 6.6.97); and their long-term future is in some doubt.

What is known is that fewer people want to train as social workers: in 1998, 6220 applied for 4900 places, a decrease of 35 per cent compared to 1995.

The figures for applicants on the DipSW programme researched here provide a clear indication of this over a four-year period (see Table 9.1.)

Table 9.1 Applicants to DipSW programme 1995–98

Year	Applicants	Interviewed	Offered	Accepted	Enrolled
1995	355	100	40	38	23
1996	378	209	40	32	28
1997	270	73	30	28	24
1998	248	131	26	25	25

These tensions are not unique to social work. A *Guardian* report (12.6.98) on admissions to universities is headlined 'Students turn away from 'caring' degree courses: Rush for subjects with prospects of more lucrative employment'. The article details the significant drop in applicants for such subjects as primary education, environmental science and sociology.

Figures from CCETSW also suggest that once on a programme progress can be difficult. In 1996–7, out of a total number of 4446 students, 120 failed (2.7 per cent), 52 withdrew (1.7 per cent), 921 were referred or deferred (20.7 per cent). On the postgraduate programmes the figures were: 1157 students, of whom 24 failed (2.1 per cent), 14 withdrew (1.2 per cent), 171 were referred or deferred (14.8 per cent) (CCETSW 1998).

Again this is not a problem just for social work programmes. The struggle of 'non-traditional' students, seeking to survive within the education system, has been well researched. The conclusions are that mature students bring 'a much larger and more complex baggage of commitments ... when these are combined with the psychological demands of academic study they produce, for some, intolerable stress' (McGivney 1996, p.110). The debate about how tutors respond to this level of need is outlined below and returned to in the conclusion of this chapter. Another key factor that has contributed to the drop-out rate for all students in higher education has been the phasing out of student grants and their replacement by loans.

Debate about Selection Methods

These concerns serve to emphasize the importance of selecting students who are sufficiently robust, personally, professionally and academically, to progress through a professional training. Within social work it has been argued that tutors are managing selection systems that are both uneconomic and inefficient out of 'nostalgia and fears for the consequences of change' (Bridge 1996, p.13). They are uneconomic in that interviews are expensive to set up, in addition to the cost in terms of time that has to be spent on reading application forms, responding to letters from disappointed candidates, and organizing panels with representatives of programme providers.

Selection processes are inefficient even with the changes that have been introduced. Thus Bridge critiques the traditional psychodynamic model that was dominant for so long when interviews were unstructured explorations of personal and professional themes. The discussion might be graded on a numerical scale, but with little standardization within interviews, or across interviewees, and no training offered in their use. The point is made that the therapeutic approach, which carries with it a willingness to take calculated risks with vulnerable individuals, militates against the assessment role with its demands for clear and consistent criteria. Bridge remains equally concerned with the subsequent introduction of equal opportunities, with an emphasis on preprepared questions, linked specifically to professional and academic requirements and intended to signal a shift 'from subjective to objective, public criteria and ... reduce the risk of personal prejudices influencing judgements' (1996, p.9). Bridge argues, however, that because these are actually based on 'implicit rules ... related to gender, class and ethnic backgrounds' (1996, p.10) they remain subjective and discriminatory. Munro (1995) also concludes that interviews are a poor indicator of success on social work programmes; that subsequent performance on the programme correlated with previous academic performance and the ratings of the personal statement, whereas 'interview ratings did not correlate' (1995, p.21).

Munro and Bridge argue, therefore, that research provides clear indicators at the point of entry of probable success on a social work programme. This gives overriding significance to the quality of the previous academic experience over prior professional experience. They found that the more successful students had degrees from old universities rather than the new universities and polytechnics and within the old universities group, students with higher classified degrees did better. Those without a social science degree appeared to do slightly better.

These findings allow Bridge to argue for an alternative to the individual interview for all applicants. Instead she suggests a process consisting of a combination of paper exercises, taking into account the screening of application forms, references and personal statements, and open days to help applicants make informed choices. If there are any queries about an applicant, paper selectors can correspond with candidates, but this is an exception rather than a rule.

The London School of Economics programme, where Bridge was based, subsequently closed down with only one intake selected by paper alone. Nonetheless Bridge (personal communication) remains very positive about the experience, arguing that there was no significant decrease in student standards as compared to previous cohorts.

The case for paper selection is clearly an attractive one. In 1998 a significant minority of DipSW programme providers did not routinely offer candidates individual interviews. Some relied entirely on paper exercises, either the application form alone, or further written material provided by candidates. Elsewhere, paper selection was the prime option, but candidates could be interviewed individually to clarify concerns. Other programmes offered a mix of written exercises and group discussion and interviews where service users were involved (Social Work Advisory Service 1997).

Debate about Retention

While the issue of selection is being debated within social work there is less attention paid to the problems of supporting students through the programmes once they have been chosen. For this, one needs to turn to related fields. In nurse education changes in training and recruitment of large cohorts of students have led to tutors feeling less intimate, less able to identify with student groups (Reid 1998), confused as to whether they are primarily educationalists or whether they also carry a pastoral and counselling role. The subsequent confusion can lead to a system which meets no one's needs (Wilson 1996).

Turning to a different group, McGivney (1996) has usefully researched the experience of students in further and higher education who are nontraditional entrants. These are often older black women returning to study, who may have some similarities with a significant proportion of social work students who share some of the same 'intolerable stress' (p.110). This research shows that withdrawal rates tend to be higher in the first year of a course. McGivney suggests that if these students are simply acknowledging that they have embarked on the wrong course at the wrong time, then the act of leaving is a positive move. Nonetheless most of her work is focused on supporting students successfully through their studies and she emphasises three key phases: pre-course preparation; immediate transition period; on-course support.

PRE-COURSE PREPARATION

The college must provide clear information about:

- the workload (nature and timing of assessments, dates of semesters, etc.)
- pre-reading
- opportunities to talk with past or current students
- student-centred pressures that might impede an individual's progress
- how the programme is relevant to previous experience and will build appropriately on earlier educational attainments.

IMMEDIATE TRANSITION PERIOD

This demands good inter-student and staff-student interactions, with the former possibly facilitated by peer support and self-study groups. A clear period of induction is also needed, reiterating the importance of pre-course material setting out the nature and demands of the work.

ON COURSE SUPPORT

The continuing well being and progress of mature students depends to a significant extent on good staff–student relations and the provision of practical and personal support. Their experience has to be recognized and incorporated into curricula and course work.

The lessons of the research are that institutions need to take into account the realities of the outside commitments of mature students, especially women's continuing family responsibilities. Central to this are the tutors who offer students encouragement to continue their learning, 'the key attributes of such a person are friendliness, availability and interest in the student' (McGivney 1996, p.133). It is also suggested that staff, tutors and administrative staff alike might need to be 'prepared to go beyond a narrow interpretation of their role' (McGivney 1996, p.134).

Experience of one progamme: the DipSW selection process

The selection process on the postgraduate programme researched here has remained essentially the same within the 'living memory' of tutors. It seemed a 'good enough' process, if an exhausting one, until in one cohort a number of students failed or left the programme, occasionally with accompanying disruptive behaviour at the university and the initiation of a series of complaints and threats of legal action. There were further concerns about the number of referrals and deferrals in academic work and that black and ethnic minority students seemed to be affected disproportionately.

The process has three components: the initial application form, the interview day (consisting of a timed essay and a group interview) and the individual interview. Throughout, in order to meet the requirements of the regulatory body (CCETSW 1995), it is the knowledge, skills and values that applicants already have that are being assessed. Those offered places have to undergo a police check.

APPLICATION FORM

The application form is the first stage, with details checked against the basic criteria in the CCETSW handbook: a minimum age of 24, a first degree (or an equivalent professional qualification in, for example, nursing or teaching) and at least two years' experience in some aspect of social work. Since most applicants normally gain their experience in settings which carry little statutory power, the admissions tutor is looking for indications that a candidate is working to a high professional level. Unfortunately, work references are generally bland or evasive and so it is the candidate's personal statement that needs to provide the main evidence. This is generally too brief to develop a detailed picture, with anti-racist and anti-discriminatory issues often omitted or dealt with in quite a cursory manner. The application form, therefore, is viewed as offering only the barest information, useful only for the initial sifting and decisions about who to invite to the next stage.

TIMED ESSAY

The interview day starts with a timed essay, a case study drawn from the candidate's own work, which is then marked for fluency, an ability to analyse and to relate theory to practice within anti-racist and anti-discriminatory social work values. This is seen as a test of a candidate's ability to write lucidly and under pressure.

GROUP DISCUSSION

A group discussion follows, led by a tutor and an agency representative, based on a short article on some aspect of social work. The discussion is included because of the importance of being able to operate in groups, both in social work practice and in the college-based programme. Candidates are marked on their ability to contribute without dominating, their understanding of wider issues in social work and their anti-racist, anti-discriminatory practice.

INDIVIDUAL INTERVIEW

Finally, there is an individual interview conducted by a tutor and an agency representative who, ideally, represent a mix of race and gender. The interview includes set questions and supplementaries that may arise from the personal statement and/or the reference. Candidates are asked:

- to describe a good piece of work and one that has gone less well
- what led them to a career in social work
- what they are bringing from their previous studies
- what recent reading had most helped their thinking about social work
- how they are preparing for returning to study on a social work programme
- whether they have a criminal record.

All the pairs of interviewers meet to make their decisions, with the discussions strengthened by the various perspectives on offer: tutors anticipating what it might be like to teach the individual; agency representatives reflecting what it might it be like to have them on placement. The essay and feedback from the group interview are drawn upon and a decision is made to reject, accept or place the candidate on the waiting list.

POLICE CHECK

For successful candidates, the final stage is the police check which the university, not being an employer, contracts out to a local authority. A candidate who has a record is then invited in for a further interview with the local authority representative and the course director. Together they make a decision based on the nature of the offence, how recently it had occurred, how the candidate explains the circumstances surrounding it and what s/he has learnt from the experience. For example, one candidate had committed a number of thefts over a very short period of time arising, as he explained it, from excess drinking at a time of personal crisis. He had subsequently received treatment for his alcoholism and his work manager confirmed that the candidate was a good employee and had been strengthened by the experience. He was offered a place. One candidate, relatively recently convicted of shoplifting, had her place deferred until she could evidence how she had distanced herself from the life style that had led to the offence. As a final example another candidate admitted three convictions for violence and the police check revealed further, more recent undeclared offences. This, plus the fact that two of the attacks had been on his partner, meant that he was refused a place.

Those involved in the admissions process are being asked to make difficult value judgements and, on this programme, discussions with employers have revealed very real differences in what are seen as acceptable or unacceptable offences. CCETSW has no authority to set rules to aid these discussions but does advise programmes to warn students with a criminal record that a place on a programme does not guarantee acceptance on placements or future employment.

Comparison with other Professional Programmes in the University

Comparisons with other programmes within the university, incorporating the vocational and the academic and operating at both graduate and postgraduate levels, show interesting similarities and differences. The programmes are health promotion (HP), occupational therapy (OT), nursing studies (NS), radiography (R) and community health care (CHC). These courses share with social work the concern to assess fully the knowledge and skills of potential students. The values element is not always as readily acknowledged but is often implicit.

Pre-interview

All the courses require evidence of a candidate already having achieved appropriate educational levels, although most have mechanisms for considering nontraditional students, either through a portfolio (OT) or a pre-course essay (HP). Many tutors are caught up with offering a good deal of support and general career guidance at this stage, whether via telephone contact and/or tutorials and workshops to help with portfolio preparation.

Prior experience is paramount. Thus a candidate for the HP programme must be already working in some area of health promotion or have experience in a related area such as teaching, nursing or social work. OTs also have to be already working in the field, as an OT assistant or technical instructor, under the direction of a qualified OT. The NS candidates need experience in a caring role, whether in a paid capacity or as a main carer within the family. In CHC, candidates would need at least two years experience in professional practice 'sufficient to have consolidated pre-registration experience'.

The collaborative aspect is played out differently in that representatives from the agencies may not be present in the actual interview, as in social work, but candidates on the OT programme can only be offered a place if they have won secondment in a separate interviewing process. The radiographers have clinical staff involved in the interview.

The interview

Many candidates have to complete an essay on the interview day. The group component is important in many programmes. The radiographers only conduct group discussions, but for the others the group is intended to complement rather than replace the individual interview. In OT the individual interview is seen as a test of competency in English and 'maturity of ideas, communication and interpersonal skills'. To this list is added, for NS students: 'awareness and interest in exploring equal opportunity issues', further, evidence of an ability to 'contribute to the group learning process' and 'demonstration of their interest in valuing people's individual experience and at the same time grasping the contextual nature of that experience'.

The interview is often cited as a two-way process with opportunities for candidates to meet staff, ask questions and see the environment and resources. Certainly no tutor can envisage not interviewing. One tutor argues strongly that application forms say how much experience candidates have but not the impact, nor how candidates reflect and make sense of what they have seen. In his view, the course begins at the interview. One tutor comments on the improved retention rates on her programme, which she puts down to tutors being clearer about their rationale for selection. However, she adds that 'it still feels like we're operating from our guts'.

Analysis of the Data Relating to the DipSW Programme: A Comparison of the Progression Rates of Four Cohorts of Students

This research was undertaken to explore the possibility of improving and rationalizing the selection process on the DipSW programme. Four cohorts of students were compared to see if factors identified at the point of selection indicate subsequent success or difficulties on the programme. These factors were:

1. The entry requirements of this programme: (a) a minimum age of 24 by the time the student starts on the programme; (b) a degree or equivalent qualification; (c) at least two years' experience in some aspect of social work by the time the student starts on the programme

2. Factors identified by the research of Bridge (1996) and Munro (1995) as indicators of subsequent success: (a) the class of degree; (b) whether gained at a new university/polytechnic or an old university; (c) whether the degree was in a relevant (social sciences) or non relevant subject. (It is important to acknowledge here that the programme researched by Bridge was an academic Masters programme that used traditional examinations, while the programme in our study was a postgraduate diploma with continuous assessment. It is these kinds of variations between DipSW programmes (see Rowlings, Chapter 3) that make systematic research on this issue difficult.)

3. Additional factors relating to (a) racial origins and (b) gender of students: this arose from the tutors' impression that social factors, especially in terms of race, were having an undue impact on students' progression through the programme.

The first two cohorts were subjected to a more detailed study in which all the above data were examined to see how far they could relate to grades given to assignments, whereas the study of the latter two cohorts was an additional piece of research and only pass/fail/deferral rates were considered.

Rates of withdrawal, failure and deferral taken cohort by cohort
FIRST COHORT

The first cohort consisted of 28 students, 14 black students and 14 white students of whom 4 black students and 3 white students, a total of 7, failed to complete. Two withdrew, one black male left early in the programme giving no reasons, one white woman withdrew early in the placement, disillusioned with social work. Two deferred, both were white women, one became pregnant, the other left because of stress and neither returned to the programme. Three, all black women, failed, two not submitting work and leaving acrimoniously.

SECOND COHORT

The second cohort consisted of 22 students of whom 4, 2 white and 2 black, failed to complete. One, a black woman deferred but subsequently returned and completed the programme. All four withdrew in the course of the first year. One black student cited personal reasons, and another three (two white and one Asian) expressed concerns about the nature of social work and or the programme/university. All fulfilled the entry requirements, were mature (over 30) and had good previous experience. According to the information recorded at the point of selection they had impressed the interviewers.

THIRD COHORT

The third cohort consisted of 31 students of whom 17 were white and 14 black. Five failed to complete, two black and three white. No one withdrew. A white woman who became ill on the final placement deferred and subsequently rejoined the programme but still failed to complete. One white woman failed at the end of the second year, three failed at the end of the first year, two black students and one white.

FOURTH COHORT

The fourth cohort consisted of 24 students of whom 15 were white students and 9 were black students. Seven failed to complete of whom three were white and four black. Two withdrew, one black man and one black woman, both offering personal reasons. Five failed. All of these were at the end of the first year and consisted of two black women and three white students, one female and two males.

TOTAL

The total number of students in the study was 105 of whom 60 were white and 45 were black. Table 9.2 shows a summary of the non completion rate overall, and for white students and black students.

Table 9.2 Non completion rates				
	No. of students	Withdrawals	Deferrals	Fail	Non-completion total
Total no. in study	105	8 (8%)	4 (4%)	12 (11%)	24 (23%)
White students	60	3 (5%)	3 (5%)	5 (8%)	*10 (16%)
Black students	45	4 (9%)	1	7 (15%)	*11 (24%)

*1 deferred student completed on recovery from illness.

Results related to qualifications, gender, race, age and previous experience

Qualifications

In the first and second cohorts there were no significant differences in terms of class of degree. However, nobody with an upper second failed, although two withdrew. Most students had lower seconds but two students with thirds did well. In the third and fourth cohorts there was a wider spread of class of degrees and results indicated a stronger relationship between the class of first degree and subsequent success on the programme. No student with an upper second failed, while, of the eight students in these two cohorts with third class degrees, five failed. The factors of old or new university or nature of first degree appeared irrelevant.

Gender

There were no significant differences in terms of gender in any of the cohorts.

Race

In both the first and second cohorts, a more detailed study of referral and deferral rates and grades attained was undertaken. Black students were less likely to be referred but their scores were lower. This amounted to an average 57.7% (a C grade) as compared to 60.4% (a B grade) for white students. In the third cohort there was no racial imbalance in pass, fail or deferral rates. However, in the fourth cohort black students were more vulnerable. Four of the nine students failed to complete whereas the comparative figure for white students was three out of fifteen. Table 9.2., which considers the total number of students in the study, shows a worryingly higher risk of black students not completing the programme and that black students overall are almost twice as likely as white students to fail. However, as this was not a consistent picture in each cohort, other variables may have played a part.

Age

In the first three cohorts there were no discernible differences in age of students who passed and students who failed. The average age for both groups was 33. However, in the fourth cohort the older students seemed to do better. The average age of students who passed was 35 (ranging from 24 to 53) and those who failed was 28 (ranging from 27 to 31).

Previous experience

In the first and second cohorts, the research found that the longer in practice, the higher the grades. In the third cohort, the normal prerequisite of two years' previous experience was relaxed; some 40% had a year or less experience. While some went on to do well on the programme, as a group they were more vulnerable; three of the four failing students fell into this category. In the fourth cohort there was no discernible difference with passing students averaging 4.5 years experience and students who failed averaging five years.

Students who join the programme in the second year from other courses

A group of students, six in total, joined the second year from other programmes (having failed the course or the other programme having closed down). This group has not been included in the above data but is worthy of comment because of their likely problems both in terms of their previous disrupted training experience and integrating into an already existing cohort. Yet the experience of the programme is positive. All six students, recruited over the four cohorts, completed the programme successfully.

Using the outcomes of the study to plan for the future

It is difficult to draw hard and fast conclusions from this research because there was insufficient control of all the potential variables. However, some tentative indications arise from the data. Students with a third-class degree or below appear to be more vulnerable to outright failure and, conversely, students with upper seconds or above can be expected to do well. However, the previous university and the subject of the degree made no apparent difference.

Unless the programme reserved places for students with upper seconds in their first degree, this research has not highlighted specific factors that could be used to indicate success or failure from an application form. Those programmes that do insist on an upper second are less likely to attract as many non-traditional students as this programme which has maintained a steady 40% black intake since 1989. The ethos of both the host university and the programme is to recruit from a wide range of backgrounds. Demanding an upper second has been ruled out because it would discriminate against potential students who can and do make excellent social workers.

With very few exceptions, students who successfully complete the first year go on to complete the programme, thus reinforcing McGivney's finding, cited earlier, that the first year is when students are most likely to drop out.

With respect to her conclusions about the care needed by mature students, some social work tutors are cautious about the level of support that is appropriate to offer weaker students. Not only are they more educationalists than counsellors (to echo the debate in nursing education, Reid 1998) but too much cushioning may only serve to raise false expectations of what might be available in the increasingly tough world of social services once they qualify.

With the withdrawals, a worrying eight in total, a minority express concerns about the nature of social work or disagreements with the programme, although, more generally, students seem simply to have been overtaken by life's events: breakdowns in relationships, stress, or financial burdens. Reviewing the files there seem to be no indications of these potential difficulties in the application forms or at the point of interview.

While the gender of students appears to make no difference at all to their chances, black students appear to be almost twice as likely not to complete. There are 50% black tutors on this programme and a very high investment in anti racist and anti-discriminatory practice. Nevertheless, more attention is clearly needed to address these issues. Although age does not appear to be a significant factor, the lack of sufficient previous experience may make students more vulnerable.

Staff involved in selection on the social work programme and on a range of related health and care programmes in the university support the existing interview procedures as helpful; they value having sight of potential students and assessing how they operate on both an individual and group basis.

Having considered the outcomes of the study, the programme remains wary of paper selection only since the current application form provides too slim a body of information for such important decision making. This is even if an application form is a scrupulously honest record of employment and experience and the references are genuine. This is not always a safe assumption as illustrated by CCETSW's involvement in warning of the need to guard against fraudulent admissions (UCAS 1997).

However, this attention to the detail of the selection process may become less relevant if applications continue to fall, leaving tutors with fewer candidates to choose from. The emphasis needs to shift to the mechanisms in place throughout the programme to support students at a time of challenge, personal, professional and practical. Certainly, this research highlights the struggle that large numbers of students, especially black students, have in staying the course. Over the four cohorts, 8 per cent of all students withdrew (compared to a national figure of 1.2 per cent for postgraduate programmes) and 11 per cent failed (compared to 2.1 per cent nationally) (CCETSW 1998).

The tutors on this programme remain somewhat sceptical of these national figures and wonder if like is being compared with like. Based on their informal knowledge, they suspect that their student intake is more weighted with mature students, with their 'complex baggage of commitments' (McGivney 1996, p.110), than other programmes which are not based in the inner city and/or are part of old universities with more generous student–staff ratios.

Having said this, however, there is an urgent need to understand the dynamics of success and failure as they are played out on this programme; to continue monitoring current and future student cohorts in the way that has been initiated in this research, and refining it further. A methodology for this is provided by Cheetham (Chapter 4) whose 'single case design' approach could be applied to evaluating individual student outcomes. Certainly, in terms of individual students, each may have a personal point of crisis, and tutors are now considering means by which each student can be more carefully tracked through the programme. This means taking note of, and being more proactive around, patterns of marks for assignments, attendance in class and tutorials, etc. The information that was seen as important in helping select the student for the programme needs to be retained on file and actively drawn upon to aid the assessment process and develop the student's strengths.

Social work tutors might usefully draw on Wilson's model (1996), from nurse education, which suggests five levels of helping: first, practical help (e.g. setting realistic work plans for assignments); second, giving information (teaching, informing, referring on, etc.); third, listening (allowing a student to ventilate her/his feelings); fourth, challenging (enabling a student to identify her/his problems); fifth, counselling (helping a student to manage her/his problem).

What must also be addressed is the wider culture of the programme, which transcends the experience of an individual. Tutors, as a group, need to become more skilled in recognizing the key and consistent danger points in the life of the programme. There are strong indications that this fits with what McGivney has identified as the pre-course period and the immediate transition period, but discussions with students may help identify other, less predictable, trigger points. Above all, there is the need to improve the academic work, because it is here that students fail, not on their placements. The tutor group is now building the following into the programme: writing workshops, sustained and consistent support in tutorials, a more imaginative range of assessment methods, such as report writing and seminar presentations, thus shifting from an undue reliance on the traditional essay format.

None of this guarantees, in itself, miraculous improvements in students' progression. It does, however, offer a strategy to help students realize their potential while on the programme and find ways to be both self-reliant and to be able to ask for appropriate support. Such skills should stand them in good stead in the world of work once they have gained their diploma.

References

Bridge, G. (1996) 'Minimising discrimination: a case for excluding interviews from selection for social work courses'. *Social Work Education 15*, 4, 5–15.

CCETSW (1995) *Assuring Quality in the Diploma in Social Work 1. Rules and Requirements for the DipSW*. London: CCETSW.

CCETSW (1998) *5th Report on Applications via the Social Work Admissions System, 1997 Entry*. London: CCETSW.

Gow, H.J. (1900) 'Methods of Training 11'. *Charity Organisation Review 8*.

Jones, C. (1983) *State Social Work and the Working Class*. London: Macmillan.

Lousada, J. (1993) 'Self-defence is no offence'. *Journal of Social Work Practice 7*, 2, 103–113.

McGivney, V. (1996) *Staying or Leaving the Course, Non-Completion and Retention of Mature Students in Further and Higher Education*. Leicester: NIACE.

Munro, E. (1995) 'Selecting students for a social work master's degree course'. *Issues in Social Work Education 15*, 1, 21–32.

NISW (1998) *The Careers of Post Graduate Entrants to Social Work*. London: Department of Health.

Parton, N. (ed) (1996) *Social Theory, Social Change and Social Work*. London: Routledge.

Reid, J. (1998) 'I only ever wanted to be a nurse…' Unpublished assignment for Masters in Nursing Studies, South Bank University.

Social Work Advisory Service (1997) *Applicants' Handbook*. Gloucestershire: SWAS.

Towle, C. (1954) *Learner in Education for the Professions*. Chicago: University of Chicago Press.

UCAS (1997) *A Guide for the Prevention of Fraudulent Admissions*. Gloucestershire: Universities and Colleges Admissions Service.

Wilson, T. (1996) 'Levels of helping: a framework to assist tutors in providing tutorial support at the level students want and need'. *Nurse Education Today 16*, 270–273.

CHAPTER 10

Practice Teaching and Learning

Mark Doel

Introduction: From Tugboat to Flagship

It is 1975 and a student, Dawn, is about to start a placement in a social work agency. Accompanied by her tutor, she has been to visit the social worker who will be supervising her, in order to discuss the kind of work she will be doing with the clients. John, the student supervisor, has never supervised before, but it is his turn in the team and he thinks it will be a useful experience if he wants to supervise staff as a team leader in the future. He has been to two half days at Dawn's university to find out more about what is involved. John knows he will have to write a student assessment report on Dawn at the end of the placement and recommend a pass or a fail.

It is 2000 and a student, Ashok, is about to start stage one of his practice learning in the purchasing/assessment unit of an agency which has been approved by CCETSW for practice learning. With his tutor, he has been to visit Hope, the practice teacher who will be co-ordinating his learning opportunities. They will negotiate the details of the placement and the kind of contact Ashok will have with service users. These include how Ashok will demonstrate six core competencies, underpinned by specified values in order to qualify for the Diploma in Social Work (CCETSW 1995), and the kinds of teaching methods Hope will use. She has a post-qualifying Award in Practice Teaching, having submitted a portfolio to an assessment panel, following 150 hours of study. Ashok will gather evidence of his learning and practice and present this in a portfolio, too. It will include evidence gathered directly from service users. His portfolio will be presented to a Practice Assessment panel for a recommendation of 'pass' or 'not yet competent to practise'.

It is clear from these past and present vignettes that there have been considerable changes in the way students learn about professional practice in a work setting, and also in the manner in which their ability is assessed. In this chapter I will explore the details of these changes and attempt to separate rhetoric from reality in a process I will describe as 'practice teaching' from the teacher's point of view and as 'practice learning' from the student's. I will take social work as the home base, but recognize that the influences at play in this discipline are experienced widely in the care professions.

There is no doubt that there has been a concerted effort to make changes in the quality of the experience of teaching and learning professional practice. A number of forces pulling and pushing in similar directions in the UK in recent times have led to an extraordinary change in perspective. At a political level, a succession of high profile scandals in social services departments added fuel to a wider political view that there was something wrong with the welfare state in general and social work in particular, and that the training which social workers received was part of the problem. This 'you're part of the problem' view extends to other professional groups, especially in teaching and health.

In Chapter 6 Hastings describes the growing dissatisfaction of users with services that are not sufficiently responsive to their needs. Increasingly sophisticated consumers have put pressure on professionals to demystify their roles and tasks; users expect to participate as active partners, not as passive recipients, of services. In particular, ethnic minority groups protested about being dealt with on social work courses as one of a number of 'social problems'. The need to combat 'institutional racism', especially as it operates to disadvantage social work service users from black and ethnic minority communities became an urgent priority.

Practices have also faced challenges from managers in health and social work agencies. There has and continues to be a current of hostility towards the academic base of professional practice, especially in social work and nursing, and criticism that new recruits are 'not fit for the job'. In these circumstances, many managers of professionals welcomed changes that placed more emphasis on the practical component and shifted power over the content of the curriculum towards agencies.

Finally, there was dissatisfaction at the professional level. The direction of professional practice in social work was shifting away from psychodynamic explanations (e.g. the psycho-social model) to educational ones (e.g. the task-centred model) and this slowly began to have an impact on the way in which social work practice learning was conceptualized. All of these different tendencies – political, managerial, user focused, anti-discriminatory and professional – signalled dissatisfaction with current practices. This dissatisfaction has had a crucial influence on the way professionals learned their trade.

Resources were diverted to practice teaching and learning. This aimed to improve the training which practitioners could expect to receive before they supervised a student (CCETSW 1996a), the auditing of agencies to ensure that they could provide a suitable environment (CCETSW, 1996b), and structures to encourage post-qualifying training. Although those on board the flagship had different motives for upgrading, the upgrade was very real.

Models of Practice Teaching and Learning

Between 1975 and 2000 education and training providers have significantly improved their approaches to the ways in which students are taught and assessed in practice. Key developments include the following.

Introduction of an explicit curriculum

There is now a greater understanding of what the curriculum for social work practice is, with the content of learning made explicit and shared across settings (CCETSW 1995).

Underpinning of learning and assessment with a clear statement of values

Learners are now expected to be aware of their own prejudices and to understand how these might influence the way they work with different service user groups. Furthermore, they must learn to counter racism and discrimination within the context of their work role. Their ability to integrate anti-racist and anti-discriminatory practice is a core aspect of their self-assessment and the assessment by the practice teacher.

Introduction of explicit methods of assessment

There is now more direct access to the learner's practice because it must be observed systematically by experienced practitioners.

Involvement of users in the teaching and assessment of students

Learners no longer simply practice on service users during their placements but are encouraged to seek feedback from service users and to learn from what they say. In the future we are likely to see the growing involvement of users in the assessment of students (see Hastings, Chapter 6).

Formation of the teaching team

The notion of 'placement packages' has been introduced, with a person who co-ordinates learning opportunities rather than an individual who 'takes' a student. This means that a number of people have access to the learner's practice.

Development of a common language

Practice teachers experience common training programmes that give them a common language to describe and evaluate their teaching, with the potential to learn from each other and to disseminate innovative practice.

Evolution of common structures

The growth of organizations such as the National Organization for Practice Teaching (NOPT) and journals such as the *Journal of Practice Teaching, Social Work Education* and *Issues in Social Work Education* encourage contributions from practice teachers and provide opportunities to disseminate ideas and innovations.

Establishment of interprofessional training programmes

Joint training programmes for practice teachers in health and social work settings have facilitated cross-fertilization of ideas and approaches (Bartholomew, Davis and Weinstein 1996; see also Lowe and Weinstein, Chapter 13).

Approaches to practice teaching and supervising students vary considerably from placement to placement and time to time. These have been characterized in a variety of ways in the student supervision literature. Doel *et al.* (1996, p.4) consolidated them into four basic types: personal growth; apprenticeship; managerial; and structured learning. Although the four models are not locked into a particular era, the apprenticeship and personal growth models are more characteristic of 1975 and the managerial and educational more prevalent in 2000.

Assessment dilemma: Ascendancy of the competency-based approach

The movement to more explicit approaches is also evident in professional practice, where what was once 'mystique' has become more 'technique'. There is an increasing expectation that all professionals will be open about their methods and work with people rather than on them. Although some people interpret this as a lack of trust and a loss of expertise, most would see it as a positive development, respecting individuals as fellow citizens.

In addition to changes in the social climate in which professionals operate, there are two other developments which have a significant impact on the role of professionals. First, there are different expectations in relation to the accountability of professional workers. All agencies are expected to have accessible complaints procedures that must be made available to all service users. Where, previously, conflict was not faced squarely or was handled informally, it is now more likely to be dealt with using formal systems. The increasingly open, individualized and litigious climate means that professional staff cannot hide behind their profession, nor can they expect the same degree of protection as was once possible.

The second change in expectations concerns the profession's own views about what constitutes good practice and how this is assessed. In line with the moves towards greater explicitness, the last decade has seen the ascendancy of the notion of competence, so that good practice has become virtually synonymous with competent practice. Attempts have been made to define 'competence' as specifically as possible, in terms of behaviour or accomplished activities and tasks, so that a profession can have what it considers an objective measure of competent practice. Similarly, novice professionals are assessed against these criteria and must successfully demonstrate their achievements before they are admitted to the profession. This process has been made increasingly explicit, with responsibility for gathering evidence falling on the individual learner, and a growth in structures and systems to formalize the process. Perhaps the differences between current and past practices can best be summarized as shown in Table 10.1.

Table 10.1 Differences between past and current practice

	Past	Current
Process of assessment:	Implicit	Explicit
System of assessment:	Informal	Formal
Emphasis on:	Process	Outcome
Relationships are:	Personal	Contractual
Good practice seen as:	Practice wisdom	Agreed competencies
Evidence primarily by:	Learner's self-report	Observed practice
Assessment consists of:	Written report in general terms from experienced professional (only)	Specific evidence of competence and values gathered by learner and verified by practice teacher (possibly including the views of users)

The explicit system has undoubted benefits. It is less arbitrary because it defines the goalposts and this means there is less scope for oppressive behaviour. Perhaps most significant in the long term is the shared knowledge which is possible when the many transactions between novice and experienced professionals are transparent and available to others, rather than shrouded in what is often mistaken for confidentiality. A profession has the opportunity to learn from itself and to develop better practices.

However, there are costs, too. With the change in the power balance, learners hold a greater degree of responsibility for gathering their own evidence and making their case. The focus on assessing competence can consume much of the teaching and learning time, so that the assessment tail is in danger of wagging the learning dog. The search for increasingly detailed elements of competence could lead to a massive failure to see the larger picture.

Is it possible to hold on to the best of the explicit model while avoiding the costs? In particular, how might we develop methods of assessing practice learning which are detailed and specific, yet holistic and integrated? One of the difficulties with what has become known as the competency approach is that it measures the parts (or attempts to) but not necessarily the relationship between them. Their inter-relationship must be considered when evaluating the impact of a skilled intervention. Professional practice is an ability to operate at a 'meta-level', to make connections that are creative and go beyond the sum of their parts.

With an understanding of the relationships between the parts comes an awareness of the meaning behind them. Skilled, competent behaviour is not context free; it is laden with cultural and situational meaning and can be used to good or ill intent. Professional practice, especially in social work, is essentially self-aware and situation aware. Whereas technicians must keep their eye on the ball, professionals must also keep the players, the playing field and the spectators in sight.

A Department of Health funded project undertaken by Parsloe and Swift for the University of Bristol (CCETSW 1998) devised a schedule for service users to assess the practice of social work students. The criteria, which were developed in consultation with users themselves, returned to fundamentals like warmth and friendliness, reliability, understanding, patience and the ability to give information clearly.

We posed the dilemma as to whether it is possible to be specific and concrete, yet rounded and integrated; in other words to achieve a synthesis of the past and present. There are no simple answers to the dilemma, but we do have some indicators for guidance, described below.

Sampling

Long lists of competences can be dry and dispiriting. Although it might be possible to make a good case that each one is essential, it does not follow that each one needs testing. In the trade-off between time spent learning and time spent assessing that learning, we might be able to make reasonable inferences that competence in this area means competence in that area. It might be more effective to focus on deepening skill in x at the expense of developing the same level of skill in y, because the experience of learning x to a more complex level can be transferred to y. Professional education needs to consider how it samples. Sampling is not a new or radical solution – in effect, we sample all the time, since it is impossible to assess everything. What is needed is a more systematic approach to sampling, backed by research, so that we can do it with more confidence and an understanding of what truly is core and transferable.

Transfer of learning

Related to the notion of sampling is that of transfer. It is important to develop methods of teaching and assessment that encourage the transfer of learning. Also, because learners learn in different ways and at a different pace, it is equally important to vary these methods accordingly (Cree, Macaulay and Loney 1998). The learning experience needs to be integrated with the learner's previous knowledge, encouraging the learner to make connections and providing opportunities to put the learning into practice. When these opportunities for direct practice are not available, practice teachers need to find innovative ways to simulate these experiences as I will explain below.

'Signposted portfolio' approach

An example of an innovative attempt to square the circle of detailed elements of competence on the one hand and a broadbrush, integrated whole picture on the other is provided by the 'signposted portfolio' project (Doel and Sawdon 1995, 1999). Learners are asked very specific questions about discrete areas of their learning and professional practice. The project has discovered that the precise wording of these 'signpost' questions guides the way learners present their work. The advantage of this approach is that it keeps the assessment tightly focused, while allowing the learner the creativity which is lost in the 'tick-box' approach. The signpost questions are separated into descriptive and evaluative ones, which mirror notions of reflective practice and the learning process so that the assessment itself becomes part of the student's learning task (Schön 1987; Yelloly 1995, p.61). The signposted portfolio approach requires the learner to think how best to sample their own practice.

LINKING THEORY AND PRACTICE

There is no doubt that the partnerships which were forged between agencies and colleges to provide the DipSW have done much to alter the perceptions that the course is shorthand only for what goes on in the educational establishment. After all, half of a social work programme takes place in social work agencies. However, the gap will only be fully bridged when the conceptual gulf between theory and practice is likewise filled. There are many ways to bring the two closer, such as the involvement of agency personnel in teaching at the college, but the breach is essentially perceptual, frequently characterized by identifying theory with college-based learning and practice with agency-based learning. This is a false dichotomy.

Theory-free professional practice is no more possible than value-free professional practice. The distinction lies between theory which is explicit (and therefore presents itself to challenge or confirmation and builds as the professional community listens to itself), and theory which is implicit (and therefore is not perceived as theory, but becomes encoded as practice wisdom and fails to put itself to the test). This is not to suggest that practice wisdom is necessarily wrong or inferior, just that we have no way of knowing. Initiatives have been established to change this by introducing the notion of 'evidence-based practice' and by encouraging more systematic monitoring of outcomes as described by Cheetham in Chapter 4.

The development of the 'researcher-practitioner' is a significant breakthrough, both in perceptions and in practices (Fuller and Petch 1995; Hart and Bond 1995; Powell 1996). A slowly developing tradition of finding out what works, or what works better, rooted in everyday practice, is likely to benefit both the quality of theorizing and the quality of practice. Asking the question 'what works?' and attendant contextual questions such as 'how do we define what works?' and 'who defines it?' is essential. In terms of innovative education and training, we can only recognize what is innovative when we know what is commonplace. Innovation is only of value if it works and if there is robust research evidence that it will continue to work in a variety of settings.

Methods of practice learning: potential for innovative practice learning opportunities

We began this chapter by reviewing how practice teaching and learning have progressed from 'tugboat' to 'flagship'. The increased self-confidence implied by this metaphor is amply demonstrated by the expansion of methods of practice teaching and learning; the development of pro-active teaching rather than simply 'supervising' is perhaps the most dramatic of the changes I have been documenting. Moreover, these changes appear to be widespread and not confined to a few pioneer practitioners. A survey of teaching methods used by practice teachers in the West Midlands revealed an enormous variety and breadth which would have surprised John, our student supervisor of 1975 (Birmingham 1998).

The questionnaire used in the Birmingham survey clustered 54 different 'action techniques' into five general categories, borrowed from Doel *et al.* (1996, p.129). These categories were: Hardware (e.g. audio, video); Written (e.g. critical incident analysis); Experiential (e.g. simulations); Graphic (e.g. cartoons); Printed (e.g. articles). In addition to the 54 named techniques, the 81 respondents mentioned a further 26 techniques not specified in the questionnaire. The most heavily used techniques were in the Printed, Written and Experiential categories, and the least used techniques in the Hardware and Graphic categories. However, in addition to the use of conventional techniques such as policy documents (95%), discussions (94%), and case summaries (90%), there was evidence of experimentation with less conventional techniques, such as the use of novels (21%), sculpting (20%) and photographs (11%). The survey was conducted anonymously, so there is no reason to suppose any enticement to over-report.

This rudimentary survey was designed to take a snapshot of the quantity and spread of action techniques used by practice teachers with students, and a picture emerges which would probably be unrecognizable to the student supervisor of yesterday. However, it is more of a sketch than a detailed picture, because it does not reveal how these different techniques are used, in what circumstances or to what effect. More research is needed to study the quality as well as the quantity of action techniques and their effects on the student's learning and professional practice.

One way of illustrating the use of innovative techniques is to explore how a practice teacher might help a student to learn about a particular aspect of practice, using different techniques – one from each of the five general categories mentioned earlier.

Hope, our present-day practice teacher, has been impressed by a study that suggests that learners are strongly influenced by the images they have of their profession. These images are highly influential in shaping what students extract from their pre-service training, how they think about their profession and the kind of professional they think they will become (Gould and Harris 1996, p.226). The study compared student teachers and student social workers and found that the former had much more specific and concrete imagery than the latter, probably because the trainee teachers had all been consumers of teaching in a way that the social work trainees had not. The social work students were more defensive about poor media image, but saw their professional practice in a broader political context than the student teachers. Having read the article, Hope considers it important to help Ashok, a student social worker, understand both the significance of the idea of imagery and develop an awareness of his own imagery. Since this is not a specific competence or requirement, it has been negotiated with Ashok and his tutor as an addition to the placement agreement, because of Hope's belief about the impact it has on the way students frame their knowledge, learning and practice.

The obvious method would be to ask Ashok to read the article [Printed category], ready to discuss with Hope at the next supervision session [Experiential category]. Hope knows that this would appeal to Ashok, who takes a highly intellectual approach to his practice, but she does not feel it would challenge him. For this reason she considers a number of other options:

- She could gather photographs [Graphic] of people cut out from magazines and newspapers [Printed] and ask Ashok to describe what he considers their line of work might be and why.

- In supervision, Ashok could be asked to close his eyes and call forth imagery and metaphor [Experiential] which he associates with the social work profession.

- He could be asked to weave a story [Written] in which he links the experiences in his life so far which he feels are the most relevant to what social work is and what social workers do.

- Ashok could watch video excerpts [Hardware], in which social workers are depicted in popular TV soap operas, and script his own alternative [Written].

- Hope could arrange for the practice nurse and her student at the health centre to join Hope and Ashok in a 'quickthink', using the flip chart [Graphic] to tease out the stereotypes which nursing and social work have of each other.

- The article could be introduced afterwards, to consolidate the learning and to use as a framework to understand the way his professional practice develops during the placement.

None of these potential methods are right or wrong, but some will be more effective with this particular student in this particular context. Some will take minimal time to prepare; others will depend on the practice teacher gathering material along the way, like a magpie. The fact that Hope considers a range of possibilities is evidence that she is a proactive practice teacher.

What happens when opportunities do not arise naturally in the workload? A comparative study of arrangements for clinical placements found that larger intakes of Occupational Therapy students had led to thinking afresh about the required practice learning experiences, instead of being overwhelmed by the problem of finding placements (Alsop and Donald 1996; Health and Care Professions Forum 1997, p.10). The potential for simulated as well as live teaching and learning is already being realized in the training of social work students and was discussed as early as 1972 (Meinert 1972). Social work skills workshops were a common feature in the early 1980s as tutors in academic settings tried to recreate the situations that occur in practice agencies (Hargie, Saunders and Dickson 1981). Since then, the focus has been increasingly on simulation in practice settings, not necessarily trying to recreate practice, but using exercises, activities and video prompts to help learners think about professional practice in creative, 'left-brained' ways. Often, the point of the simulation is not to recreate practice, but to help learner (and teacher) to reconceptualize their practice by throwing it into a different relief. This has the opposite effect of the 'sitting by Nellie' apprenticeship approach, because it encourages critical reflection on existing practices by both learner and teacher.

Well-known examples of simulations are in-tray exercises, in which the learner is presented with a number of 'Monday morning' situations or messages and must make decisions about how to handle them (Doel and Shardlow 1998, p.99). The exercise is used to tease out the criteria which the learner is using to decide priorities. Similarly, 'what if?' exercises are used to introduce a new factor into an existing situation; perhaps the student is working with a white family and is asked how their work might differ if the family was black.

Can simulated learning ease the crisis in the availability of placements, by providing opportunities to learn about professional practice (and to be assessed for this practice) without the resources needed from an agency? The example that is often quoted is the air-flight simulator, in which trainee pilots learn to handle distressed airplanes without the hazard and expense of actual flying time. I have argued elsewhere that simulation has an important place in practice learning, but that there are two critical elements absent from simulated learning – the sense of imminence or immediacy which live learning provides and, perhaps more significant, the sense of responsibility (Doel and Shardlow 1996).

Context of Practice Learning

In addition to the wide range of teaching methods available, there are innumerable settings and arrangements for practice learning for care professionals. The sequencing of practice learning may be in a full-time, intensive block or concurrent with learning in the college (for example, three days in the agency and two in college). Some learners depart for their practice learning towards the beginning of their course, others later on. The pattern for social work students of a 50–day Stage 1 placement and an 80–day Stage 2 placement is mandated centrally by the accrediting body, CCETSW. Clinical practice learning in nursing tends to consist of more and shorter periods in different settings.

There is a difference in philosophy between an approach which sets store by gaining as much experience as possible of different types of the professional practice in question, and an approach which sees the setting as more of a backdrop for learning about core general practice. Social work education has moved increasingly to the latter, although social work practice is witnessing greater divergence and specialism, both in terms of the client groups and between providers and purchasers.

I have used the term 'learner' in this chapter in preference to 'student' or 'trainee' in order to position education and training for professional practice in a broader scheme: not just a training to do certain tasks, but a discipline of intellectual inquiry. This wider framework also helps us to consider teaching and learning as an activity that goes beyond an apprenticeship for a particular set of tasks. However, there is a danger of a rift between the vision of what could be and the reality of what is. Provision of quality placements by practitioners who hold post-qualifying awards has to be set alongside a chronic shortage of available placements. Many students rely on 'on-site' supervisors, who may be inexperienced in teaching practice, backed up by an 'off-site' practice teacher; not all practice teachers in England and Wales are accredited. Enthusiasm for innovative methods of teaching and learning is tempered by knowledge of the crisis conditions in many of the agencies and hospitals offering placements; a learning opportunity is more likely to be lost for lack of a desk than lack of a CD-ROM player. In these circumstances, the mother of invention might indeed be necessity, with creative and innovative practice arising from the gap between what is and what could be.

Conclusion

Reinventing the wheel is a wasteful and dispiriting activity. Now that we have a language by which to describe the experience of practice teaching and learning we have an opportunity to spend our time more creatively: to extend the metaphor, using the wheels to build different kinds of vehicles for the learning.

The recent past has been a difficult time for innovation and creativity. There have been plenty of changes, but change is not synonymous with innovation. Behind the rhetoric of flexible packages of care, user involvement, anti-discriminatory practice and inter-professional working has been the reality of resource shortfalls and increasing insistence on a professional practice straitjacketed by procedures. It is important that the innovations in teaching and learning I have described in this chapter (the movement from apprenticeship to educational models) do not widen the distance between what students experience as learners and what practitioners experience as employees. It is imperative that all health and care professionals are able to exercise their professionalism in creative ways, not just in their experiences as learners but also in their everyday practice as qualified staff. Working more closely in partnership with service users will be a key aspect of this creativity.

'Mind the gap' seems to be an appropriate warning for the distance between expectations and reality. We see the effects of this in the health service, where the original 1940s founders believed that the demands on the service would diminish as health care improved. Quite the reverse has occurred, with people's expectations of what is considered healthy far outstripping the ability of the NHS to satisfy them. We must take similar care that expectations of practice learning are realistic.

I have argued that an approach to teaching and learning which loses sight neither of trees nor wood is essential to produce the rounded professional capable of delivering the proper safeguards for competent practice. The process of teaching and learning should reflect this kind of professional practice; in other words, it should also be experienced as creative. Work is where most of us spend our time; work could be the great revolution of our times, where we experience a sense of quality and creation. As a society we certainly have the technology and the resources to move beyond the routine to the innovative. Do we have the will or the dare?

References

Alsop, A. and Donald, M. (1996) 'Taking stock and taking chances: creating new opportunities for fieldwork education'. *British Journal of Occupational Therapy 59*, 498–502.

Bartholomew, A., Davis, J. and Weinstein, J. (1996) *Inter-Professional Education and Training: Developing New Models.* London: CCETSW.

Birmingham (1998) Creativity in Practice Teaching – Conference organized by West Midlands Regional Forum of DipSW programmes (forthcoming: Doel, M. (ed) *Creativity in Practice Teaching and Learning.* Whiting and Birch).

CCETSW (1995) *Assuring Quality in the Diploma in Social Work.* London: CCETSW.

CCETSW (1996a) *Assuring Quality for Practice Teaching 1.* London: CCETSW.

CCETSW (1996b) *Assuring Quality for the Approval of Agencies for Practice Teaching.* London: CCETSW.

CCETSW (1998) *Report of a Conference on User Involvement in Education and Training.* London: CCETSW.

Cree, V.E., Macaulay, C. and Loney, H. (1998) *Transfer of Learning: A Study, Social Work Research Findings No. 20.* Edinburgh: Scottish Office Central Research Unit.

Doel, M. and Sawdon, C. (1995) 'A strategy for groupwork education and training in a social work agency'. *Groupwork 8*, 2, 189–204.

Doel, M. and Sawdon, C. (1999) *The Essential Groupworker.* London: Jessica Kingsley Publishers.

Doel, M. and Shardlow, S.M. (1996) 'Simulated and live practice teaching: the practice teacher's craft'. *Social Work Education 15*, 4, 16–33.

Doel, M. and Shardlow, S.M. (1998) *The New Social Work Practice.* Aldershot: Arena.

Doel, M., Shardlow, S.M., Sawdon, C. and Sawdon, D. (1996) *Teaching Social Work Practice.* Aldershot: Arena.

Fuller, R. and Petch, A. (1995) *Practitioner Research: The Reflexive Social Worker.* Buckingham: Open University Press.

Gould, N. and Harris, M. (1996) 'Student imagery of practice in social work and teacher education: a comparative research approach'. *British Journal of Social Work 26*, 223–237.

Hargie, O., Saunders, C. and Dickson, D. (1981) *Social Skills in Interpersonal Communication.* London: Croom Helm.

Hart, E. and Bond, M. (1995) *Action Research for Health and Social Care: A Guide to Practice.* Buckingham: Open University Press.

Health and Care Professions Education Forum (1997) *A Comparative Study of the Arrangements for Clinical Placements.* London: H&CPF.

Meinert, R.G. (1972) 'Simulation technology: a potential tool for social work education'. *Journal of Education in Social Work 8*, 3, 50–59.

Powell, J. (1996) 'The social work practitioner as researcher: learning about research'. In P. Ford and S. Hayes (eds) *Educating for Social Work: Arguments for Optimism.* Aldershot: Avebury.

Schön, D.A. (1987) *Educating the Reflective Practitioner.* San Francisco: Jossey-Bass.

Yelloly, M. (1995) 'Professional competence and higher education'. In M. Yelloly and M. Henkel (eds) *Learning and Teaching in Social Work: Towards Reflective Practice.* London: Jessica Kingsley Publishers.

CHAPTER 11

Making Connections in the Curriculum: Law and Professional Practice

Michael Preston-Shoot

Introduction

The prospect of studying law not uncommonly provokes distinct unease among social work students. Qualified practitioners find contacts with the law stressful (Jones, Fletcher and Ibbetson 1991) and believe that they have little credibility in legal circles (Department of Health 1994; Foster and Preston-Shoot 1995; Preston-Shoot, Roberts and Vernon 1998a). Practice teachers experience as daunting their responsibility for teaching and assessing social work law (Preston-Shoot, Roberts and Vernon 1997) and express reservations about their competence. The reasons for this picture are varied but include:

- a fear of ignorance and of being out of date, while conscious too of the breadth of knowledge to be covered

- a recognition of contradictions, including a mandate to practise which is neither clear, consistent or comprehensive

- unfamiliarity with legal settings, procedures, language and methodology, contributing to feelings of vulnerability and of being deskilled

- increasing judicial scrutiny of practice, provoking images of being prosecuted or judged, at a time of growing awareness of the limitations of the work context

- holding responsibility, say for child protection, without sufficient power to prevent abuse or to prevent harm to a vulnerable person

- an ambivalent relationship with authority (Cooper 1992), and scepticism about whether the law is punitive or helpful on welfare questions

- insufficient time devoted to law teaching (Marsh and Triseliotis 1996)
- lack of training and limited resources with which to manage practice complexity.

These feelings, practice experiences and questions of knowledge interact and reinforce each other. While the legal framework might be perceived as providing opportunities to achieve particular goals, this is accompanied by uncertainty, insecurity and a recognition of dilemmas, conflicting imperatives and competing ideologies contained in the mandate to practise. Marsh and Triseliotis (1996) report worryingly high levels of lack of confidence among newly qualified social workers when, coincidentally, their managers prioritize knowledge of law and procedures.

Other health and welfare professionals also encounter the law in practice, or work in a context where the law provides an underpinning mandate. Health visitors and paediatricians, for example, may be required to give evidence in care proceedings. General practitioners and psychiatrists may become involved in the compulsory admission to hospital of a person with a severe or enduring mental illness. Psychologists and occupational therapists may be involved in assessments and the provision of guidance, advice or therapy. Questions of consent and a duty of care underpin their work.

The purpose of this chapter is to provide health and welfare professionals with tools to enable students to engage with the law in their work. The same tools will also be useful for staff development and supervision. These tools, located in a conceptual framework concerned with the interface between law and professional practice, revolve around key questions, exercises, cases and materials. They are designed to assist students, practitioners and managers to make sense of their practice.

Making a Beginning: A Self-audit

Teaching and learning can usefully begin with a self-audit of expertise, gaps in knowledge, and images of law or lawyers derived from feelings, experience and knowledge. This self-audit invites students, practitioners and managers to evaluate:

- their knowledge and understanding of law, including the distinctions between statute, case law, guidance and regulations
- their ability to convey to others their knowledge, understanding and practice of their legal mandate to practise

- the resources needed and available to improve confidence and knowledge, for instance, circulars, journals, law reports and peer support
- the availability of training to update their knowledge of the legal mandate to practise, and to assess the competence of students and staff with this mandate.

The self-audit could then proceed to rank the degree of agreement with statements about the extent to which the law facilitates the achievement of professional goals. Thus, in relation to social work, to what degree:

- does the law endorse social work values?
- can the law be used to achieve social change?
- does the law protect vulnerable people and meet their needs?
- can the law promote equality?
- does the law provide redress and accountability?

The self-audit can also invite perspectives about the relationship between lawyers and other professionals, and about the degree to which their interests, roles and responsibilities converge or diverge. Thus, to what extent has experience suggested that lawyers are concerned with duties, evidence and remedies, while social workers focus on needs, rights and relationships?

Self-audits are a useful beginning, highlighting initial connections between the law and professional practice, derived from experience, knowledge and feelings. They can indicate training needs and, as a regular staff development tool, enable learning to be reviewed and changes in perception mapped.

Locating and Debating the Place of Law in the Curriculum

Social work students, prior to qualification, must demonstrate an understanding of the legislation relating to the country in which they train. One of the practice competences they must achieve is to work in accordance with statutory and legal requirements and to carry out orders of the court (CCETSW 1995a). Law is the only subject discipline where the rules and requirements for qualifying training specify how courses must approach teaching, learning and assessment of students' knowledge base and skills. Students must demonstrate their understanding and application of the law through formal written assessment.

Programmes of qualifying training must provide students with opportunities to apply and deepen their understanding of legislation in practice. This highlights the responsibility of practice teachers for learning and assessment. Accreditation programmes are provided to ensure that practice teachers are able to plan and develop learning opportunities, which will enable students to practise within the legal and procedural framework (CCETSW 1995b).

This centrality of the law within professional practice continues with post-qualifying training (CCETSW 1997). Candidates studying for appointment as Approved Social Workers must be able to apply knowledge of mental health and other relevant legislation, and to locate their practice within the law and associated codes of practice. A core requirement for the Post-Qualifying Award in Social Work is that candidates must 'evaluate the effectiveness of their practice using a relevant knowledge base, including an understanding of legal and policy contexts and appropriate research'. The general requirements include demonstrating competence in exercising the powers and responsibilities of a professional social worker. These include risk management and the use of discretion. One of the general requirements for the Advanced Award in Social Work focuses on candidates demonstrating critical appraisal of relevant theoretical models, policies and law.

Breadth and depth: a conceptual framework

Immediately, questions arise about breadth and depth. What do practitioners and managers need to know? How much do they need to know? The zone of knowledge and of practice can appear indeterminate. Without a conceptual framework, practitioners and trainers may sense the theoretical and practice insecurity of uncertain content and unclear or elastic boundaries. However, a map has been developed with which to frame and understand the relationship between law and practice (Preston-Shoot, Roberts and Vernon 1998b). It has three components:

1. *The relevant legal rules.* These subdivide into social work law (the statutes, guidance, and judicial decisions which provide or clarify a social worker's mandate to practise) and social welfare law (the statutes, guidance and judicial decisions with which social workers must be familiar if they are to respond appropriately to people's needs).

2. *The relationship between the legal rules and professional values.* This involves consideration of where professional values, such as confidentiality, partnership, self-determination, and anti-discriminatory practice are endorsed, required, or challenged by the legal rules.

3. *Administrative law.* The focus here is on the principles for decision-making, and how complaints procedures, judicial review, case law and the Ombudsman have commented on practice and/or interpreted the legal rules.

This conceptual framework provides a recognized body of knowledge. It illustrates how practitioners and managers operate in a defined and legitimized area of activity, and how both social work values and the principles of administrative law create a context for ethical and legal practice.

Exercises

Various exercises may prove useful as learning opportunities for practitioners and students, to contextualize this conceptual framework for themselves. They could take the job description and person specification for the post they hold and consider the following questions. What knowledge of social work law and of social welfare law is necessary? How might administrative law illuminate the decision- making required in this post? What skills are needed to perform the social work law job, and the social welfare law job, well?

A further self audit could be undertaken, this time on the degree and origins of difficulty which students and practitioners experience with various skills for practising social work law and social welfare law. Topics here could include:

- identifying and applying legislation, guidance and regulations
- managing practice dilemmas and the relationship between law and values
- making decisions about when, how and why to act
- risk assessment, and using evidence in advocacy or when taking protective action
- working in partnership
- managing multiple accountability
- working with lawyers
- challenging an agency's practice and policy statements
- practising social work law and social welfare law anti-oppressively.

This self-audit can be used both to define learning requirements and to set an action plan (Braye and Preston-Shoot 1997) for personal development.

These two exercises will enable the completion of a third, namely the articulation of an academic curriculum and a practice curriculum for this setting. Templates for both have been outlined elsewhere (Ball *et al.* 1995). The purpose here is to make the relationship between law and practice accessible in a particular setting, and to encourage reflection and critical analysis. For example, CCETSW (1995a) has identified six core competences for qualifying training. Evidence indicators for these competences can be identified for particular settings that involve knowledge, understanding and application of the law. Table 11.1 gives an example of how these might be mapped.

Table 11.1 Six core competences and evidence indicators

Core competences	Evidence indicators
Communicate and engage	Identify authority, the powers and duties underpinning action
Promote and enable	Assist service users to participate in decision-making. Provide information in accessible formats
Assess and plan	Undertake a needs assessment in the context of relevant legislation and local procedures
Intervene and provide services	Provide or secure services to achieve goals
Work in organizations	Demonstrate an understanding of access to records legislation and policies and forms of redress
Develop professional competence	Demonstrate clarity about reasons for decisions in the context of legislation

Other professional groups will also need to know about the powers and duties which provide their specific mandate to practise, and the laws which impact on the lives of their clients. Doctors must be familiar with the law concerning consent to treatment; nurses with their holding powers under the Mental Health Act 1983; and youth workers with health and safety legislation. Youth workers should be familiar with appropriate adult provisions, education law, and criminal justice legislation; occupational therapists with community care law and guidance; and doctors with child protection procedures. All professional groups should be concerned with administrative law, since this governs the relationship between law and professional practice and sets standards of decision-making that could be relevant if liability for subsequent outcomes is contested. Both health authorities and social services departments have had judicial review against them for failing to follow Department of Health guidance.

The Law and Professional Practice

The conceptual framework and exercises help to locate the law in relation to professional practice and to build new learning from current practice. However, the nature of the relationship between law and professional practice should also be debated. CCETSW's rules and requirements, when locating the law so centrally within academic and practice curricula, appear not to envisage any dilemmas or contradictions, for example, within the law itself, or between legislation, policy guidance and professional values and social work goals. Unease with legalism has been fully discussed elsewhere (Preston-Shoot 1996). Essentially, it centres on several key questions.

First, is the law an adequate or oversimplified response to the complexities and challenges of people's lives, and to the dilemmas and difficulties encountered in practice (King and Trowell 1992; Pietroni 1995)? Second, does the law express commitments, for example, to partnership, which encapsulate rather than solve the dilemmas of practice (Kaganas, King and Piper 1995)? Third, is the law limited in the degree to which it can be used to challenge government policy, and interpretation by agencies of it? How effective is the accountability and redress it offers to service users? Fourth, does reliance on legalism, expressed through procedural guidance and the articulation of standards, replace research-informed practice and hinder professional judgement? To what degree does legalism assume that agency policies accurately reflect statutory powers and duties, and how should practitioners and managers respond when invited to act unlawfully or in ways contrary to sound practice? Finally, to what degree is the law an inconsistent and insufficient mandate, which sits uneasily with some social work values, neglects some disadvantaged or vulnerable people, and ignores or even compounds many of the difficulties experienced by service users?

If professional education and training is to retain its relevance, meeting the needs of employers must not be allowed to extinguish such critical questions. Charges have already been levied that practice is increasingly characterized by poverty of provision and meanness of spirit (Utting, quoted in Ellis 1993), and of losing human contact as its core purpose (Drakeford 1996). Moreover, one lesson from inquiries into intra-agency and multi-disciplinary decision-making is that ethical principles and legal requirements can sometimes be vulnerable to organizational imperatives and agency cultures.

One way to encourage critical reflection is through the use of case studies that encapsulate the dilemmas and demands of practising social work law and social welfare law. Working through a case enables learners to identify the relevant powers and duties that provide an explicit mandate to practise, together with judicial interpretation of them through case law. Other areas of law relevant to the situation, which may help to shape an intervention, can also be explored.

Health and welfare practitioners practise according to ethical and professional values. Confidentiality, partnership, self-determination, and anti-discriminatory practice are examples. Working through cases in training enables key values for practice to be identified, together with the degree to which the law, and associated guidance, specifically endorse and/or require such values-based practice, or appear to undermine established professional values. This approach will clearly illustrate the practice dilemmas which professionals regularly encounter, because neither values nor the law, separately and in their interactions, are necessarily coherent or consistent. It will also demonstrate the complexity of inter-professional co-operation since the relevant legal rules for different professional groups may create duties which do not neatly converge, or where different groups may place greater emphasis on specific values.

The possibility of practice being scrutinized by non-judicial authorities and by the courts should draw attention to principles and standards for decision-making, the knowledge required to understand a situation, and the skills needed to conceptualize, negotiate and implement the options derived from this understanding. From this discussion it will be possible to identify what is being addressed (needs, rights, risks); why (values, legal mandate); how (skills, intervention); and when. The task is explicitly linked to law, values, and knowledge for practice, and requires the thinking through of how to manage or resolve dilemmas, contradictions or tensions in practice.

Making Sense of Practice

Competent practitioners should be confident, credible, critical and creative. They should be confident because authorities do not always interpret relevant legal rules appropriately in operational policies and procedures; and because social work should be concerned with counteracting inequality and social exclusion, with preventing harm, and with securing social justice, equal opportunities, and quality of life.

They should be credible because decision-making authority may be held by others, for example magistrates with sentencing powers or managers with responsibility for resource allocation, to whom convincing arguments must be presented if the language, methodology, values and goals of social work (professional practice) are to prevail.

They should be critical because of the contested relationship between law and practice, and of the need to make professional practice accessible to others. Available guidance and codes of practice are not always clear. Equally, there remain unresolved and challenging questions about the nature, remit and goals of welfare services. There are questions of ethics, justice, rights and needs, and how these are balanced with each other without being compromised. Social work (and other professional groups) have a political role here (Barclay Report 1982). They should not take existing policies as given, but assess their impact on people's lives.

They should be creative because the relevant legal rules represent opportunities and/or threats to the people with whom practitioners work. Creative because of the need to determine the balance to be uniquely struck in each case in the face of practice dilemmas such as needs versus resources, rights versus risks, and autonomy versus protection, a process which requires understanding of social work and legal goals. Creative because the mandate to practise can be characterized by ambiguity and incompatible demands, ideologies, orientations and expectations. One response may be to emphasize a polarity, to adhere to a fixed viewpoint, such as legalism or bureaucracy. Informed and effective practice demands detailed consideration in each case of different possibilities.

When, how, how far, and for what purpose to intervene are central practice questions, involving ethics, justice, needs, rights and the law. The challenge for education and training is to enable practitioners to develop an ethical and active practice, which adopts a sceptical position, weighs up value choices, engages in critical reflection, challenges received ideas, asks awkward questions, and opens up the exploration of possibilities. There has been a marked improvement in teaching law on qualifying social work programmes (Ball *et al.* 1995; Marsh and Triseliotis 1996), but of what might this innovative and effective approach be comprised?

Academic Curriculum

An outline academic curriculum has already been published (Ball *et al.* 1995), although this must be regularly updated as new legislation is passed and implemented. This guidance, and subsequent research into training outcomes (Marsh and Triseliotis 1996), confirm the necessity of a common foundation course on the major statutes and their associated regulations and guidance, with particular pathways providing specialist additional input. That said, legal issues and analysis should also permeate other academic teaching. There are at least three reasons for adopting such a 'law lens'. First, students cannot appreciate working in organizations without evaluating agency definitions and implementation of the mandates for assessment and service provision, or their openness of decision-making and recording, against the relevant legal rules and the judgements of the courts and the Commissioner for Local Administration (Ombudsman). Second, students cannot fully understand the connections between theory and practice, or choose between different methods of intervention, without considering the legal context. Issues of consent, and of the respective rights of parents and children or of users and carers, are examples here. Third, it is impossible to focus on values, such as partnership, confidentiality, or self-determination without exploring the extent to which, and when, the law upholds them. For example, practitioners must understand why and when the law places limits around confidentiality.

Case studies

Case studies are effective tools for learning and assessment (Braye and Preston-Shoot 1991; Eadie and Ward 1995). When accompanied by questions, they enable students to identify relevant legal issues, to clarify their role and task, to frame and understand dilemmas and value issues, and to determine the purposes of intervention and the relationship of the law to these. Carefully chosen, case studies can bring alive moral and ethical dilemmas, can expose hidden value assumptions in the law, and can uncover the deep emotions that practice can generate, thus providing an active illustration for the importance of supervision. They can promote the integration of theory and practice, since students have to draw upon knowledge and skills for effective understanding, assessment, decision-making and intervention.

Source materials

The use of case studies may be developed in two further ways. Students can be asked to read source materials, such as case law, codes of practice or guidance documents, and to give presentations which identify the material's status in law, key themes, definitions of competence, and their implications for practice. Research and presentational skills are developed, in addition to skills linking the law with practice. A further benefit derived from studying source materials is the recognition, particularly when reading majority and minority judgements from the Court of Appeal and House of Lords, or when tracking how one issue has been (re)interpreted over time, that the law (like social work) occupies a contested space. Because of the way it is constructed, it is open to definition. It provides some room for manoeuvre or opportunity for the exercise of professional judgement and argument, as well as a framework to which agencies and practitioners must adhere. Reading judgements, for example, about the rights of young people to consent to treatment, or whether authorities may take resources into account when making decisions about which services to provide, or how abused women who murder their partners are to be treated by the criminal courts, can demystify the law. The process can illustrate how, in relation to social policy, courts wrestle with the relationship between the law and social issues, monitor the (arbitrary) actions of government and authorities, push the boundaries of what is relevant to decision-making, and give legitimacy to social work activity and concerns.

Scenarios

Staged scenarios can also be used. Here, students are given a case outline, perhaps a referral. Their task is to undertake an assessment and to formulate a recommendation on subsequent intervention, with reference to law, knowledge base, and values. For example, they may be given a request for an assessment for residential care for an older person. The first task here is to identify and record the legal mandate that underpins options in such a case, and to research the guidance that might have a bearing on it. Tutors act as supervisors and can provide on request information about the legal mandate, and available guidance, in response to specific questions. They can also provide, again in response to specific questions, information that is held by other parties (relatives, professionals and neighbours) involved in the case. The final task is to make a recommendation for a care package, identifying the values and knowledge used to justify their actions, the dilemmas encountered and how these were resolved.

To summarize, this extended use of case studies can provide opportunities for:

- identifying what the law says about the process and content of decision-making, for instance, about people's involvement in decisions that affect their lives

- using the law to achieve change

- managing discretion and multiple accountability when deciding the relationship between the law and social work activity in any given situation

- compiling a resource bank of cases, references, journal articles, media reports, and summaries of guidance documents

- developing enquiry, assessment, decision-making and intervention skills

- applying social work and legal knowledge to negotiate dilemmas and conflicts that arise in practice, and formulating professional and legal justifications for action taken.

Practice Curriculum for Interim and Final Assessment

Once again, an outline curriculum has been published (Ball *et al.* 1995) but practice teachers often appear to be unaware of a formal practice curriculum and feel that they are operating in a vacuum (Preston-Shoot *et al.* 1997). The practice curriculum should provide guidance on competence in social work law at both interim and final assessment, with practice teachers involved in defining these competences and accompanying evidence indicators. This approach will help practice teachers and students to be clearer about what is required.

The distinction between interim and final competence is one of progression as shown in Table 11.2 overleaf. It moves from identifying prior learning from experience and newly acquired theoretical knowledge, to learning from doing (Braye 1993); from practice to critical analysis of that practice and its context. Students progress from knowing what, to managing roles and purposes; and from gaining information and applying understanding to events, to deciding what needs to happen and why, and managing the practice dilemmas and values dilemmas involved (Braye 1993). They might perceive the law not only as a system of regulation and control, but also as a means of effecting change for, and with, service users and carers.

Learning opportunities can then be identified and described, together with the indicators which might suggest progression towards the achievement of particular competencies. Learning opportunities could include cases, the discussion and working through of scenarios, or critical incidents drawn from practice experience, group work, and the critical analysis of agency procedures and policies. Key questions can then guide the use of these opportunities for teaching and assessment:

1. What areas of social work law might be relevant in this learning opportunity?

2. What areas of social welfare law might also be relevant?

3. What professional values might be relevant, and how might they interface with the legal knowledge required?

4. What skills will this learning opportunity require of the student?

5. What tensions might arise between the law, professional values and agency policy?

6. How will you approach the first and subsequent supervision sessions in relation to this learning opportunity?

7. What would be your expectations of a first/second year student?

Table 11.2. Distinction between interim and final competence

Interim competence	Final competence
Ability to identify legal concepts and to understand the division between legislation, regulations and circulars	Ability to be confident, credible, critical and creative in using the law
Ability to understand the legal framework and the principles underpinning it, in relation to cases	Being conversant with the relevant legal rules and skilled in using them
Ability to use authority in practice	Ability to explain one's authority to service users and professionals
Ability to identify what anti-discriminatory practice requires in a legal context	Ability to integrate anti-discriminatory practice with practising social work law
Ability to identify the roles of different professionals and agencies, and where these are located in legal powers and duties	Ability to manage the inter-professional context of work – networking, teamwork, negotiating roles, establishing value systems and partnerships
Ability to use off-the-peg responses to assessment for services	Ability to plan an intervention on the basis of an assessment; ability to construct individually designed solutions
Ability to identify people's rights	Ability to balance the rights of different individuals involved and the interests of society
Ability to identify the relationship between legal responsibilities and professional values; ability to identify points of multiple accountability	Ability to manage the tensions between welfare and other considerations, such as resources and justice; ability to manage multiple accountability by knowing which values guide practice in what circumstances and making informed decisions
Ability to collect information and analyse it against the legal mandate and social work role	Ability to use evidence in constructing a case; ability to engage in effective advocacy

For instance, practice teachers and students could discuss a critical incident in relation to questions such as confidentiality, an ethical duty of care, or authority and decision-making. A practice dilemma could be analysed with reference to professional values, messages from research or inquiries, and different possible orientations to practice.

Thus, student and practice teacher are in the realm of linking law, values and practice with opportunities to learn and assess the knowledge and skills with which practice dilemmas, multiple accountability (to the practitioner, the law, professional norms, and an employing agency), and discretion are managed in the context of regulation, procedures and standards.

What knowledge would suggest research informed practice? What skills would suggest the application of this knowledge in analysis, assessment and decision-making? It is possible to look at the needs, risks, rights and responsibilities of those involved, and the skills with which competing interests might be balanced.

It is possible to look at social work values and identifying what these might mean to those involved, how conflicts between different values might be resolved, and how the law might assist practitioners and managers to practise according to these values. Students and practice teachers can reflect on how, in the context of a learning opportunity, they would describe value positive practice, management, policy and service. Where relevant, they could consider the effect of the multi-disciplinary context on their values, and how they might manage any tensions that arise.

Supervision can also identify those statutes that permit, require or monitor intervention, and the implications of this for social work tasks and role. Learning opportunities might easily provide experience of seeking change within and between organizations, and of working in partnership with service users, carers and professionals. Supervision thereby locates practice within the legislative framework, and looks for justifications in terms of law, values, knowledge, and definitions of good practice for chosen interventions.

Conclusions

Recent research (Marsh and Triseliotis 1996) found, unsurprisingly, that a good knowledge of the law contributes to confidence and a greater sense of readiness for practice. They also found, more worryingly, that a quarter of respondents were involved in legal proceedings within one month of qualified practice, and experienced a steep decline in knowledge and confidence regarding legislative areas not used regularly because of increasing specialization. This effect of specialization was also reported by practice teachers (Preston-Shoot et al. 1997) as a concern in relation to their competence in meeting CCETSW's requirements on teaching law within qualifying training.

These findings reinforce several key messages. Individual competence, whether of students or practice teachers, depends on organizational competence. Training providers and employing agencies must provide access to information, circulars, guidance documents and case law, and regular updates on the law and its implications for practice and training. Support, supervision and debriefing are crucial in helping practitioners to manage the anxiety, ambiguity, uncertainty and pressure which accompany the legal mandate to practise, and to learn from practice. Increasing specialization must not be allowed to obscure the fact that, when working with children and their families, knowledge of community care or mental health law may be necessary. The converse is also true. Whatever organizational divisions are created, service users and carers do not necessarily conform to such apparently neat agency boxes. A breadth of legal knowledge remains necessary, as well as depth in specialist areas, an observation on which courts have made critical comments when finding agency decision-making inadequate. Finally, it illustrates the importance of a critical perspective on agency practice. While employers have become more central in shaping social work training and practice, their practice itself has been subject to highly critical comment by courts and government inspection teams.

Currently, these messages apply to only a minority of practice teachers (Preston-Shoot *et al.* 1997). Too much is being left to individual initiative. More positively, the tripartite definition of social work law provides a framework for connecting the law and professional practice. The approaches to the academic curriculum and practice curriculum described in this chapter take forward existing good practice. They represent opportunities not just for imparting knowledge but also for assessing how that knowledge is experienced, conceptualized, assimilated and implemented. Most importantly, they begin to demolish some of the intellectual and emotional barriers that have previously characterized the relationship between social workers and the law.

References

Ball, C., Preston-Shoot, M., Roberts, G. and Vernon, S. (1995) *Law for Social Workers in England and Wales. Guidance for Meeting the DipSW Requirements.* London: CCETSW.

Barclay Report (1982) *Social Workers, Their Role and Tasks.* London: Bedford Square Press.

Braye, S. (1993) 'Building competence in social work law for the Diploma in Social Work'. In M. Preston-Shoot (ed) *Assessment of Competence in Social Work Law.* London: Whiting and Birch.

Braye, S. and Preston-Shoot, M. (1991) 'On acquiring law competence for social work: teaching, practice and assessment'. *Social Work Education 10,* 1, 12–29.

Braye, S. and Preston-Shoot, M. (1997) *Practising Social Work Law,* 2nd edn. London: Macmillan.

CCETSW (1995a) *Assuring Quality in the Diploma in Social Work – 1. Rules and Requirements for the DipSW*. London: CCETSW.

CCETSW (1995b) *Assuring Quality in Practice Teaching*. London: CCETSW.

CCETSW (1997) *Assuring Quality for Post Qualifying Education and Training – 1. Requirements for the Post Qualifying and Advanced Awards in Social Work*. London: CCETSW.

Cooper, A. (1992) 'Anxiety and child protection work in two national systems'. *Journal of Social Work Practice 6*, 2, 117–128.

Department of Health (1994) *The Children Act 1989: Contact Orders Study*. London: HMSO.

Drakeford, M. (1996) 'Education for culturally sensitive practice'. In S. Jackson and M. Preston-Shoot (eds) *Educating Social Workers in a Changing Policy Context*. London: Whiting and Birch.

Eadie, T. and Ward, D. (1995) 'Putting a "scenario approach" to teaching social work law into practice: one year's experience on a Probation APP'. *Social Work Education 14*, 2, 64–84.

Ellis, K. (1993) *Squaring the Circle. User and Carer Participation in Needs Assessment*. York: Joseph Rowntree Foundation.

Foster, B. and Preston-Shoot, M. (1995) *Guardians ad Litem and Independent Expert Assessments*. Stockport, Tameside and Trafford GALRO Service and the University of Manchester.

Jones, F., Fletcher, B. and Ibbetson, K. (1991) 'Stressors and strains amongst social workers: demands, supports, constraints and psychological health'. *British Journal of Social Work 21*, 5, 443–469.

Kaganas, F., King, M. and Piper, C. (eds) (1995) *Legislating for Harmony. Partnership under the Children Act 1989*. London: Jessica Kingsley Publishers.

King, M. and Trowell, J. (1992) *Children's Welfare and the Law. The Limits of Legal Intervention*. London: Sage.

Marsh, P. and Triseliotis, J. (1996) *Ready to Practise? Social Workers and Probation Officers: Their Training and First Year in Work*. Aldershot: Avebury.

Pietroni, M. (1995) 'The nature and aims of professional education for social workers: a post modern perspective'. In M. Yelloly and M. Henkel (eds) *Learning and Teaching in Social Work*. London: Jessica Kingsley Publishers.

Preston-Shoot, M. (1996) 'A question of emphasis? On legalism and social work education'. In S. Jackson and M. Preston-Shoot (eds) *Educating Social Workers in a Changing Policy Context*. London: Whiting and Birch.

Preston-Shoot, M., Roberts, G. and Vernon, S. (1997) '"We work in isolation often and in ignorance occasionally." On the experiences of practice teachers teaching and assessing social work law'. *Social Work Education 16*, 4, 4–34.

Preston-Shoot, M., Roberts, G. and Vernon, S. (1998a) '"I am concerned at the possible level of legal input expected from practice teachers." Developing expertise in teaching and assessing social work law'. *Social Work Education 17*, 2, 219–231.

Preston-Shoot, M., Roberts, G. and Vernon, S. (1998b) 'Social work law: from interaction to integration'. *Journal of Social Welfare and Family Law 20*, 1, 65–80.

CHAPTER 12

The Assessment
of Professional Competence

Judith Croton

Introduction

Throughout this book there are examples of significant developments in the
way that care professional education and training is structured and delivered.
In this chapter I hope to contribute to this by considering issues involved in
the assessment of students and candidates. How do we know that students
have learned what we set out to teach them? How can we be sure that
professionals undertaking post qualifying professional development are
increasingly competent? Can we be confident that assessment systems treat
students and candidates fairly and equally? Can we lay claim to national
standards at each level of provision?

Although many of the principles of good assessment practice endure,
regardless of the nature of provision, it cannot be assumed that assessment
systems, usually designed for testing knowledge acquired in the classroom,
will necessarily be relevant when applied to the assessment of work-based
competence. In any system where the main emphasis is on outcomes, that is
the knowledge, skills and attributes of individual workers, rather than on the
inputs of curriculum and expertise of teachers, it is assessment that carries the
main responsibility for quality. No one can be deemed to be professionally
competent unless that competence has been tested. Public, not to say
employer, confidence rests implicitly on effective assessment of that
competence.

I begin by considering the principles of effective assessment practice as
they relate to professional education. I move on to discuss a range of methods
by which candidates can demonstrate evidence of their competence and ways
of ensuring that assessment is fair. The chapter concludes with an
examination of the role of standards, external scrutiny and regulatory bodies
to ensure consistency of assessment systems. I look in some detail at the

assessment of work-based learning at post-qualifying level as well as considering good practice in assessment as it affects qualifying students undertaking practice placements. Although my experience and many of the examples are drawn from social work education, the issues discussed will be relevant for and familiar to all providers of professional education and training.

Assessment of Competence

The concept of competence

Some of the arguments about the concept of competence do not need repeating as they are set out in Chapters 1, 2 and 3 and referred to by authors throughout the book. By now, it should be clear that although competence-based assessment is not exclusively about observed performance, the assessment of professional competence is concerned with work-based assessment, not simply with workplace assessment. All training for care professional awards involves some element of assessment in the workplace but this forms only part of the evidence required for demonstrating competence.

Social work education is not alone in moving away from curriculum-based provision towards education and training expressed in terms of learning outcomes or competences, with the linked requirement to develop assessment methods fit for the purpose (Brown and Knight 1994; Brown, Bull and Pendlebury 1997; Otter 1992). Unfortunately, antipathy towards competence-based education and training has largely obscured the critique of much existing assessment practice in higher education and overshadowed work to develop relevant, manageable and credible assessment systems (Atkins, Beattie and Dockrell 1993; Brown *et al.* 1997). Nevertheless, significant progress has been made in the development of appropriate assessment methods for work-based education (Evans 1990).

The main purpose of assessment leading to professional qualifications is *summative*, to satisfy the requirement that an individual has met an identified, minimum standard. But it can also have a *formative* role, in providing feedback on progress and to guide future learning. This is particularly significant at a time when there is increasing interest and government commitment to continuing professional development and lifelong learning (see Chapter 14). With the introduction of modular and credit-based programmes of learning, candidates may undertake summative assessment at a given point, which becomes formative for the next stage of learning. The recognition of national vocational qualifications (NVQs) in Care at level 3 as an entry qualification to social work or nursing qualification training is an example of this development.

The regulatory bodies for external qualifications define assessment as 'the process through which evidence of candidates' attainment is evaluated against agreed criteria to provide the evidence for an award' (Qualifications and Curriculum Authority 1999). It is the means of making a judgement about an individual based on evidence, either about their competence as a beginning professional, or at a particular stage in their professional development. Brown and Knight (1994) claim that although objectively sound assessment does not exist, in practice, there are a number of conditions which, if present, give a firm base to any system.

Competence and capability

It might, perhaps, be helpful to adopt Eraut's (Eraut 1994; Eraut and Cole 1993) use of the term *capability* to describe the attributes required of a beginning professional and even of one who is undertaking structured professional development. It might get us off the 'hook' of the increasingly sterile debate about competence as a description of 'minimum achievement required', while higher education seeks 'mastery' and excellence. Eraut takes the dictionary definition 'the quality of being capable', uses the term to examine the development of professionals and extends it to suggest that it:

> refers not to the state of already being competent but to the capacity to become competent ... capability has a present orientation and refers to the capacity to perform the work of the profession: capability is both necessary for current performance and enables that performance ... capability can be said to provide a basis for developing future competence including the possession of the knowledge and skills deemed necessary for future professional work. (Eraut 1994, p.208)

This definition, which encompasses knowledge and understanding, personal qualities and cognitive processes, fits very well with the definitions of professional competence set by awarding bodies such as the Central Council for Education and Training in Social Work (CCETSW) or the English National Board for Nursing Midwifery and Health Visiting (ENB). It works equally well at qualifying and post qualifying levels. Both capability and competence are constructs that cannot be directly observed but must be inferred from evidence (Eraut 1994; Wolf 1989). Their assessment or measurement must, therefore, be directly linked to their definition.

Principles of Effective Assessment

Reliable assessment

The first issue to consider when identifying appropriate systems for the assessment of professional competence is *reliability*, that is, to ensure that any assessment outcome describes the phenomenon being assessed and is not an artefact of the measure being used (Brown and Knight 1994). Reliability requires that the judgement made confirms that the candidate's evidence will be of a consistent standard in a range of different contexts. To be reliable, assessment must be consistent between candidates, over time, and between assessors of the same or similar evidence. A repeat test should also produce the same results (Rowntree 1987) and should be readily verifiable by external assessors (Bridges 1994). Equally important is that the work of different candidates will be treated in a similar manner. 'Marker reliability is important because, ultimately, it is about justice' (Wolf 1993, p.18); reliable assessment is central to anti-discriminatory practice.

Maintenance of consistent national standards depends on the reliability of markers over time, between candidates and between markers and assessors. Most candidates will experience more than one episode of assessment and must have confidence that each claim for credit will be dealt with in a consistent fashion. It is suggested that marker reliability is higher when markers are in constant touch and discussion with each other (Wolf 1995b).

Post-qualifying (PQ) awards in social work are gained via registration and assessment by CCETSW approved consortia (CCETSW 1997a). A consortia consists of at least one higher education institution (HEI), working in partnership with one or more service agencies. Candidates must produce a portfolio to demonstrate that they meet the requirements for the PQ award. The portfolio must evidence the candidate's advanced level practice as well as their knowledge against specified criteria.

PQ consortia would normally be expected to have arrangements for close working between markers but this becomes increasingly complex as candidate numbers grow. The minimum requirement for reliability is cross-marking of assessment material and contact between assessors and markers. It is the responsibility of the provider to put such arrangements in place, but consistency can only be assured if the awarding or regulatory body quality assures these processes.

Consideration of a range of evidence can also assist reliability (Brown and Knight 1994). The Qualifications and Curriculum Authority (1999) suggests that the use of a variety of methods helps to ensure that candidates with a preferred learning style are not significantly advantaged or disadvantaged by the assessment process. Care should be taken, however, in the planning of assessment requirements as these have serious workload implications for both candidate and assessor. One example of evidence to meet a competence is unlikely to be enough; three or four examples are likely to be burdensome and counterproductive. Self-reporting by candidates, which is the tool most frequently used on Diploma in Social Work (DipSW) practice placements, can also jeopardize reliability. Shardlow and Doel (1993) offer examples of triangulation that can effectively deal with these dilemmas. They suggest that 'correspondence' between different sources of evidence is the key to reliable judgements of competence.

Valid assessment

The second principle of sound assessment practice is *validity*. This ensures that the system assesses what it set out to assess and relates appropriately to the objective to be measured. Broadfoot (1995) suggests that reliability is more appropriate to 'traditional' forms of higher education while validity is the underpinning feature of competence-based assessment, as exemplified by NVQs. Brown and Knight (1994) point out that valid measures are not necessarily always reliable.

The concept of competence is inextricably linked to *criterion-referenced* assessment – concerned with clearly specified and separately assessed outcomes rather than pass marks or what is called *norm-referenced* assessment. In such a system it is important that a candidate meets all the requirements (criteria), not what grade they achieve or how they do in relation to other candidates (norm referencing). Brown and Knight suggest that the current preference for validity over reliability, as found, for example, in NVQs, is associated with the change to criterion-referenced assessments where it matters that assessment addresses all the criteria, rather than sampling from a range of the candidate's learning.

Jessup (1991) has argued that provided assessments conform to the requirements in the elements of competence and their performance criteria, they will automatically be valid and, being valid, will necessarily be comparable and thus reliable. Wolf maintains that this goal has proved elusive; it is 'a seductive promise of complete clarity' (1993, p.5). Beaumont (1996) also questioned such claims, identifying both valid and reliable assessment as being central to guaranteeing national standards.

Within social work education and training, where both criterion-referenced assessment and programmes based on learning outcomes or competences are now usual, providers need to consider carefully the principles of both reliability and validity when establishing their assessment arrangements. It is particularly vital, where professional competence is inferred from the achievement of a qualification which can lead to 'job reservation' as, for example, in Approved Social Worker/Mental Health Officer (ASW/MHO) training (CCETSW 1993) that assessment does, in practice, measure defined competence (Eraut 1994; Gonczi 1994).

Methods of Collecting Evidence for Assessment

This leads us back to the debate about the nature of professional competence and the kind of evidence that is required to demonstrate it. While it may be relatively straightforward, for example, to assess interviewing skills through direct observation or through the use of video and audio material, this alone would not be a valid method for assessing knowledge and values. Carefully constructed portfolio evidence containing direct observation, source material and critical analysis linked to the piece of direct practice could meet requirements. Similarly, interviewing or counselling skills could not be validly assessed through self-reporting or critical commentary alone (Shardlow and Doel 1993).

Evidence of knowledge

At certain stages in a professional's development it may be necessary to assess knowledge separately from practice. This should, however, be in context (see, for example, Chapter 11 about teaching law). The testing of factual recall is a poor test of knowledge and understanding (Wolf 1989). The capability linked concept of *knowledge in use* is helpful in considering the most appropriate methods of assessing knowledge in professional education (Eraut and Cole 1993). Procedural knowledge, in particular, can be inferred from observation, simulation, case material and so on and there is evidence that expertise and 'mastery' do in fact spring from a wide and detailed knowledge base (Cust 1995).

Simulation exercises can be a particularly useful way of assessing some aspects of knowledge in use, particularly in situations where direct practice is not possible, for example, for child protection on DipSW programmes and with social workers undertaking ASW/MHO training. In such exercises a carefully constructed case history is divided into sections with the total picture emerging over the whole piece. Each section builds upon the information provided in the previous one with candidates working together in small groups (with or without legislation, policy documents, etc. being made available) to respond to questions 'what would you do now?' or 'what further information do you require before making a decision?' Such questions often have no obvious right or wrong answer so they allow candidates to consider the kind of practice dilemmas involving ambiguity and uncertainty that they are likely to experience in the real world of social work. As a result they also allow candidates not only to demonstrate problem-solving skills, knowledge in practice and the exercise of judgement, but also collaborative and presentational skills.

Simulation exercises can also be used as part of formative assessment, returned to at a later date for candidates to reflect upon their learning over a period of time. Assessment takes the form of participant observation and the consideration of written responses. Clear assessment criteria are required, with assessors being carefully prepared to facilitate discussion and to judge all elements.

Evidence of practice competence

Unlike some other professions (Eraut and Cole 1993), social work has quite sophisticated arrangements for workplace assessment at qualifying level (CCETSW 1996a, b). Despite misunderstandings about the nature of competence-based assessment, performance evidence, which can include artefacts produced in the workplace as well as direct observation, remains essential to both formative and summative assessment. The use of trained practice teachers contributes significantly to the reliability of workplace assessment, with material gained through direct observation being used to meet requirements in relation to values, reflection and professional development. The practice teacher has a key role to play in judgements about practice competence and capability (Doel, Chapter 10; Doel and Shardlow 1995). This role, which was originally designed to meet the requirements of the DipSW (CCETSW 1991), has been extended to provide practice assessment arrangements for training practice teachers (CCETSW 1997b) and for other work based elements of the PQ awards.

Skilled practice teachers not only make major contributions to valid and reliable assessment, but can also encourage the critical analysis and reflective practice that are the hallmarks of the competent professional (CCETSW 1998). Within different professions, qualification levels and programme arrangements, practice teachers may have other titles for example: practice supervisors, fieldwork teachers, preceptors or mentors. The recruitment, training and support of people to fulfil these roles is a fundamental element of effective learning and assessment for professionals.

Evidence from service users

Increasing attention is being paid to the involvement of service users in education and training (Crepaz-Keay, Binns and Wilson 1998), but little is yet published about their involvement in assessment (Hastings, Chapter 6; Shennan 1998). Clearly, issues of power and the potential vulnerability of service users must be considered. Nevertheless, with appropriate training and support, users and carers can be in a position to provide feedback on a range of activities that could add to both the reliability and validity of the assessment of practice skills, particularly at the formative stage. This already occurs in some areas of medicine, for example, in the treatment of arthritis where selected patients are specially trained to help doctors develop their diagnostic skills (Patient Partners, personal communication 1998). Notwithstanding the resource and support implications, the existing initiatives involving mental health service users and people with disabilities in training care professionals could be extended to participation in assessment. The practice teacher is likely to play a key role in any such development, as a link between student, service users and assessment requirements (Worsley and Knight 1998).

Evidence presented via portfolio

It has already been stated that work-based assessment is not synonymous with the assessment of performance. Evidence of competence is usually produced in the form of a portfolio which can be described as a collection of material selected by and unique to each candidate/student. Portfolios are usually built up over a period of time and structured to meet the requirements of a particular award (Doel and Shardlow 1995). Although care must be taken to ensure that candidates do not make portfolio production an end in itself, Winter and Maisch (1996) claim that skill in this area does in fact reflect key intellectual and personal competencies.

Written work is an essential component of the portfolio for the assessment of competence and capability. Reports, case histories, assessment plans, etc., as well as more traditional essay assignments, can all explicitly demonstrate the skills of communication, critical analysis and reflection. They can also be used as evidence to infer competence in relation to knowledge, practice skills and values. To be valid, however, there must be clarity as to whether it is content or the ability to write that is being tested. Although written and oral skills are essential elements of professional competence, assessment becomes unreliable when the balance between form and substance is lost.

The assessment of a portfolio, where evidence is unique and where the candidate's practice and academic work are likely to be unfamiliar to the assessor, is a significantly different activity from the assessment of assignments on theory-based programmes where teaching and preparation were undertaken by the assessor. 'Not yet competent' assessment decisions can have serious implications, particularly where candidates are already qualified and in practice.

Where performance is not directly assessed by those responsible for summative assessment, care must be taken to ensure that direct inferences about practice are not made from the construction of a portfolio. In other words, a poorly produced portfolio does not of itself indicate poor practice. The reverse is equally true – that an excellent portfolio does not necessarily mean that practice is excellent.

Evidence assessed by examination

From time to time, when social work training is called into question, the government proposes the introduction of national examinations, for example, in child care. Many professions still retain examinations as a core element of assessment. How useful is this traditional method of assessment in judging professional competence?

The main claim for written examinations is that they can thoroughly test knowledge and understanding of a subject. They have the advantage of being a reliable form of assessment, where all students are given the same range of tasks, with a similar time allocation. Question setters can exercise greater control over the subject to be tested and assessed work will undoubtedly be the authentic evidence of the student.

However, Knight (1995) has described the negative feelings of anxiety and frustration associated with written examinations. There is also evidence that written tests encourage surface learning and question spotting and are unlikely to lead to critical thinking (Atkins *et al.* 1993). Bearing in mind the possibility of superficial 'one-shot' learning and that examinations can only ever sample the student's knowledge, is it acceptable to allow some elements of learning to remain untested?

The key question when considering the use of written examinations, particularly unseen exams, returns to the principles of effective assessment: are they a valid test for the desired learning outcome? Can written examinations fit with a qualification structure requiring professional competence based on the integration of theory and practice, in other words on *knowledge in use*? On a practical level, it would be difficult to introduce written tests into a qualification structure based on learning (and assessment) over time, and possibly in different places, where the collection of portfolio evidence is usually the most valid arrangement.

However, written examinations were originally designed to test the acquisition of knowledge and as such are useful for testing knowledge of legislation where the student/candidate is not yet able to demonstrate understanding and application in practice. Within structured programmes, written examinations may be effective, especially if the subject areas are known in advance and where they precede a period of practice. The outcomes of this assessment can be included in a candidate's portfolio as certificated prior learning.

Methods of Ensuring a Fair Assessment

Sufficiency of assessment evidence

In a system defined by learning outcomes, but where directly assessed performance is not the sole criterion for success, it is particularly important that candidates and assessors understand and recognize the amount of evidence needed to meet each requirement or learning outcome. Portfolio production is still a new assessment tool for many candidates and there is always the temptation to add more and more 'just in case'. Winter and Maisch (1996) introduced a novel method of developing common understanding by requiring tutors in training to gather evidence for an Accreditation of Social Services Experience and Training (ASSET) module. They viewed this as good modelling for candidates which also helped the tutors to clarify a collective view of sufficient evidence.

Sufficiency can also apply to sampling of evidence, as well as to the amount of material required. Educators are conscious of the increasing burden on candidates, but they should not compromise reliability in an attempt to minimize assessment requirements. Most academic programmes will have clear guidelines about the length of essays and assignments. This is not always the case for critical career reviews or reflective practice reports. Reliability and equity can be compromised where candidates in the same consortium are not clear what is required and even more so if practice varies widely between consortia across the UK. Assessment criteria for portfolio production should be designed to reflect appropriate academic requirements in terms of sufficiency.

Currency of assessment evidence

In any system that allows candidates to pursue a qualification over time, currency, defined as the status of evidence in relation to its age or relevance to current practice, must be considered. This is an issue in relation to claims for the accreditation of prior learning or for exemption of elements of taught programmes. In social work, at post-qualifying and advanced levels, claims for credit are normally only allowed for certificated learning less than five years old. In a system where all evidence is accompanied by a reflective and critical commentary, prior experiential learning effectively becomes mediated through current practice, but the origin of the source material has to be identified by the candidate.

Self-reporting

Social work education has traditionally relied on student/candidate reporting, particularly on practice placements. Selective use of self-reporting can make a legitimate contribution to assessment, particularly at a formative stage. Such self-reporting cannot stand alone, but should be supported by other forms of verified evidence (Doel, Chapter 10). A more structured form of self-reporting is oral examination, which if selectively used can also reduce the amount of written material required of a candidate (CCETSW 1998). The two forms can also make a contribution to evidence of appropriate critical analysis and reflective practice. Properly verified witness accounts from service users, colleagues and other professionals can provide additional evidence in areas such as working with groups and of interpersonal and networking skills. Over time assessment criteria will become increasingly sophisticated and the process of self reporting will become a professional skill in itself.

Authenticity and verification of assessment evidence

A major concern for all assessment that relies on portfolio production is *authenticity*. Is the material put forward for assessment genuine and is it the candidate's own work? Is it typical of the candidate's normal work and does it meet the practice standards of the employing agency? At post-qualifying level, where evidence is collected by the candidate over time and possibly in different workplaces, independent verification is required of assessment carried out by workplace assessors and of any secondary material submitted. Self-reporting alone is not adequate to confirm the authenticity of claims for practice competence. Direct observation, reports from colleagues or service users, contribute to verification of evidence.

At post-qualifying level in social work no formal link is required between the assessor and the workplace from where evidence is derived. Good practice therefore demands that practice agencies understand the requirements of work-based assessment so they can support candidates and contribute appropriately to both assessment and verification.

Critical reflection

Brockbank and McGill (1998) assert that critical reflection is a form of self-reporting and as such can be regarded as unreliable. However, the CCETSW takes Schön's view (1983) that reflection and analysis are by definition not simply descriptions of past activity but core skills to be encouraged for all professionals. CCETSW requires candidates to 'demonstrate analysis and critical reflection which informs and influences practice, policy and service provision' (1997a, p.13).

Professional knowledge can never be complete and therefore reflection on experience, in the form of critical commentaries, is not only valid evidence but can also contribute to future practice development (Winter 1993). A well-constructed portfolio will contain a critical commentary that both provides the thread linking the evidence produced by the candidate and reflects the intellectual attributes required at each educational level (CCETSW 1998; Reynolds, McManus and Hilton 1998). Safeguards introduced to ensure reliability in the assessment of other material should also apply here.

Assessment as judgement

Ultimately, assessment is, of course, about judgement. It has even been described as a moral activity, in placing a value on that which is judged (Brown and Knight 1994; Rowntree 1987). We assess in order to make some sort of judgement about people. In vocational or professional education 'fitness to practice' is a crucial element of that judgement. In post-qualifying education and training judgements are also being made about higher order skills such as management, teaching or research. As Eraut and Cole (1993) point out, assessors at this level frequently have to judge responses that quite appropriately begin 'It depends...'. In describing research she has carried out into NVQ assessment, Wolf (1995a) maintains that some assertions made about competence based assessment are simply not true:

> Assessment is believed to require far less in the way of complex judgement than with the opaque criteria employed by traditional school-based or higher education ... nothing could be further from the truth. The inherent variability of the contexts in which competence is tested and displayed means that assessors have to make constant, major decisions. (Wolf 1995a, p.68)

The exercise of judgement can also be described as artistry, in much the same way that Schön (1983) describes artistry in professional practice. Brown and Knight declare that 'there is a science to the art of assessment' (1994, p.27). The scientific element pays attention to theories of reliability, the pre-testing of assessment items, the establishment of schemes for questioning, processing and analysing data. The artistry is apparent in the devising of assessment tasks and the matching of programme design to desired outcomes.

Standards, Standardization and External Scrutiny

Conceptual difficulties in defining knowledge, skills, values and competence lead to difficulties in assessment practice. Differences in interpretation threaten the reliability of assessment, particularly where large numbers of assessors are involved. Standardization is one way of increasing reliability but it can sometimes be at the cost of validity, particularly in relation to portfolio evidence (Atkins *et al.* 1993). To be credible, assessment systems must be designed to reduce variability in assessment outcomes to a minimum. Key elements for achieving this consistency are the assessors, the criteria they work with, national standards and external scrutiny.

Assessors

Wolf and Silver (1986) have described the problem of experienced assessors who ignore detailed assessment criteria when faced with actual practice in the workplace. Winters and Maisch (1996) point out the unfamiliarity both with the candidate's work and with the process of practice assessment that confronts new programme providers. Assessment is most reliable when assessors are given opportunities to work closely together. This is normally attended to at programme and consortium level, but much less so at national or UK level.

Traditional reliance on the 'community of assessors' to be found in higher education (Winters and Maisch 1996) is not sufficient or appropriate in work-based assessment. Here, assessors may be marking a small number of portfolios, all of which are unique, and where they may have little contact with other assessors. Ultimately, it must be the responsibility of the regulatory or awarding body to ensure that assessors are appropriately trained and supported for their task, but all programme providers should regard it as fundamental to assessment activity. This can be expensive and time consuming, particularly in the early stages. Programme providers and PQ consortia who hold regular information sessions for potential candidates, line managers, etc. are not simply carrying out promotional work but are also adding to collective understanding of what is still a new and evolving educational activity. Over time a proportion of today's candidates will themselves become supervisors, tutors and assessors – so developing the expert community which will underpin effective assessment practice.

In the rapidly changing world of social and health care provision, an important issue for the providers of work-based education and training is whether assessors should have the same professional background as the candidate. Wolf (1995a) suggests that same occupational group assessors successfully achieve norm-referenced assessment but are less skilled at assessment against defined criteria. Winter and Maisch (1996) claim this is more a product of unfamiliarity with what is required than inherent inability. The complexity of professional activity demands both understanding and empathy with the values, specific knowledge and skill base of a candidate's work context as well as understanding of the requirements of a particular programme of learning.

Some professional and accrediting bodies may have regulations about this which conflict with increasingly common multi-disciplinary working and training arrangements (see Lowe and Weinstein, Chapter 13). Where it is not felt to be appropriate or necessary to require same occupational group assessment, induction, joint training and support for assessors becomes increasingly important.

Criteria

Valid work-based assessment depends on clear criteria which can be used by candidates as well as assessors. Clarity of assessment criteria, at whatever level they are agreed, contributes to reliable assessment by highlighting areas of disagreement between assessors. The other major advantage is the shift in ownership and responsibility, from 'teacher' to 'learner', for evidence that is provided. Given clear guidance, the candidates choose their own evidence and structure the learning that portfolio production entails. The degree of specificity in criteria is important for both candidate and assessor. With too great specificity the criteria become cumbersome, encouraging the cutting of corners and a 'tick box' mentality. Too little specificity leads to lack of clarity and greater unreliability. While many of the complaints about competence-based education and training centre on the shallow learning that is believed to be encouraged by it (Pell and Scott 1995), other evidence suggests that the self-directed learning involved in gathering and reflecting on evidence is deeper and more relevant to professional roles (Winter and Maisch 1996).

National standards

Reliability and validity in national qualifications require national standards (Eraut and Cole 1993). Occupational standards are one method of providing openness and clarity. Although they are often criticized by the same people who dislike competence approaches (O'Hagan 1996; Pell and Scott 1995), they can provide the basis for higher level professional education and training programmes (Weinstein 1998) and they offer a public statement about professional practice. The introduction of National Training Organizations in 1998–9 led to increasing use of occupational standards across all sectors and a position whereby all occupational qualifications are to be directly based upon, or linked to, occupational or professional standards (Qualifications and Curriculum Authority 1999). By themselves, occupational standards will not improve education and training or improve practice, but they do offer a benchmark and clarity on which to build.

External and independent scrutiny of assessment decisions

Ultimately, it is the interaction between occupational and assessment standards and assessor judgement that is the key to good assessment practice. The former must have clarity and familiarity; the latter must have experience, opportunities for training and networking and be given clear guidelines. The final element is the provision of some form of external assessment or moderation, which has been defined as 'assessment carried out in a manner which is demonstrably independent of any person or persons who might have a vested interest in its outcome' (Qualifications and Curriculum Authority 1999). External scrutiny helps to protect students and candidates by checking the fairness and consistency of assessment decisions. It helps to safeguard standards by checking the design of assessment structures, by monitoring the progress of students and by estimating comparability with standards on similar programmes. The use of external assessors or moderators adds to the rigour of the assessment process and should also contribute to the development of expertise in the assessment of professional competence. Their work may include the external moderation of programme structures and the observation of performance, as well as the more traditional role of independent marker and arbitrator. This should be backed up by appropriate verification procedures.

External assessors and verifiers require guidance and training if they are to contribute effectively to reliable and valid assessment. In social work education and training, external moderation is provided by academic institutions and by CCETSW. There is uncertainty about the future role of externals in higher education and questions asked about their effectiveness in some areas but in the short term at least they are likely to remain essential if assessment systems are to be robust, manageable and credible. External examiners/assessors not only add an important dimension to internal assessment arrangements but they also contribute to consistency across programmes. Most professional bodies are committed to the maintenance of a national or UK standard for their qualifications. This will become increasingly significant at a time of devolution and structural change, but will require both ideological and financial commitment.

Conclusions

Assessment has been described as an art that should contain some of the principles of science (Brown and Knight 1994). With its impact on public credibility, professional status and job reservation, the assessment of professional competence requires clear structures and expertise. Few of today's professionals can expect to undertake one episode of qualifying training to equip them for a lifelong career. Continuing professional development is not simply a fashionable phrase but an absolute requirement on individuals, employers and professional bodies. Many educational and professional bodies are actively developing arrangements for the support and assessment of work-based learning, including the effective involvement of service users and carers. The next challenge will be to develop credible and workable arrangements for inter-professional learning, reflecting new working patterns and the breaking down of both professional and educational barriers.

Today's qualifications in social work are based on definitions of professional competence. If assessment systems are to be fit for purpose they must be based on explicit criteria, valid and reliable. Evidence of achievement must be sufficient, current and authentic. Both structures and processes must be subject to independent and external scrutiny. This should take place within a structure based on rigour, openness and accountability. Programme providers and PQ consortia need clear criteria for all forms of assessment, including portfolios, which can be shared between candidates, assessors, practice teachers and supervisors. Exemplars of 'good enough' assignments and portfolios are a useful resource to enable assessment panels to establish minimum standards. Such measures enhance the credibility of the outcome, assist the maintenance of high standards and are a minimum requirement in terms of fairness to students and candidates.

Safe and accessible assessment arrangements will become increasingly important as continuing professional development becomes a routine expectation. Devolution within the UK makes it increasingly likely that alignment, comparability and compatibility of qualifications will be sought. Only qualifications with robust, clear and accountable assessment structures will be able to meet these challenges.

References

Atkins, M., Beattie, J. and Dockrell, W.B. (1993) *Assessment Issues in Higher Education.* Newcastle: University of Newcastle.

Beaumont, G. (1996) *Review of 100 NVQs/SVQs.* London: NCVQ/SCOTVEC.

Bridges, D. (ed) (1994) *Transferable Skills in Higher Education.* Norwich: University of East Anglia.

Broadfoot, P. (1995) 'Performance assessment in perspective: international trends and current English experience'. In H. Torrance (ed) *Evaluating Authentic Assessment.* Buckingham: Open University Press.

Brockbank, A. and McGill, I. (1998) *Facilitating Reflective Learning in Higher Education.* Buckingham: SRHE/Open University Press.

Brown, G., Bull, J. and Pendlebury, M. (1997) *Assessing Student Learning in Higher Education.* London: Routledge.

Brown, S. and Knight, P. (1994) *Assessing Learners in Higher Education.* London: Kogan Page.

CCETSW (1991) *Improving Standards in Practice Learning. Requirements and Guidance for the Approval of Agencies and the Accreditation and Training of Practice Teachers.* London: CCETSW.

CCETSW (1993) *Requirements and Guidance for the Training of Social Workers to be considered for Approval in England and Wales under the Mental Health Act 1983,* Paper 19.19. London: CCETSW.

CCETSW (1996a) *Assuring Quality in the Diploma in Social Work. Rules and Requirements for the DipSW.* London: CCETSW.

CCETSW (1996b) *Assuring Quality for Practice Teaching.* London: CCETSW.

CCETSW (1997a) *Assuring Quality for Post Qualifying Education and Training – 1.* London: CCETSW.

CCETSW (1997b) *The Practice Teaching Award. Guidance on Practice Assessment for the PTA.* London: CCETSW.

CCETSW (1998) *The Accreditation Handbook.* London: CCETSW.

Crepaz-Keay, D., Binns, C. and Wilson, E. (1998) *Dancing With Angels. Involving Survivors in Mental Health Training.* London: CCETSW.

Cust, J. (1995) 'Recent cognitive perspectives on learning – implications for nurse education'. *Nurse Education Today 15,* 280–289.

Doel, M. and Shardlow, S. (1995) *Preparing Post Qualifying Portfolios: A Practical Guide for Candidates.* London: CCETSW.

Eraut, M. (1994) *Developing Professional Knowledge and Competence.* London: Falmer Press.

Eraut, M. and Cole, G. (1993) *Assessing Competence in the Professions, R and D Series No. 14.* Sheffield: Employment Department.

Evans, D. (1990) *Assessing Students' Competence to Practise.* London: CCETSW.

Gonczi, A. (1994) 'Competency based assessment in the professions in Australia'. *Assessment in Education 1,* 1, 27–44.

Jessup, G. (1991) *Outcomes: NVQs and the Emerging Model of Education and Training.* London: Falmer Press.

Knight, P. (ed) (1995) *Assessment for Learning in Higher Education.* London: Staff and Educational Development Association/Kogan Page.

O'Hagan, K. (ed) (1996) *Competence in Social Work Practice.* London: Jessica Kingsley Publishers.

Otter, S. (1992) *Learning Outcomes in Higher Education.* Sheffield: Employment Department.

Pell, L. and Scott, D. (1995) '"The cloak of competence": assessment dilemmas in social work education'. *Social Work Education 14*, 4, 38–58.

Qualifications and Curriculum Authority, Qualifications, Curriculum and Assessment Authority for Wales and Council for Curriculum, Examinations and Assessment (1999) *Arrangements for the Statutory Regulation of External Qualifications in England, Wales and Northern Ireland.* Pre-endorsement Draft.

Reynolds, S., McManus, M. and Hilton, A. (1998) *A Common Framework for Learning.* Report of the Inter-Consortium Credit Agreement Project. Cardiff: HEDW.

Rowntree, D. (1987) *Assessing Students: How Shall We Know Them?* London: Kogan Page.

Schön, D. (1983) *The Reflective Practitioner: How Professionals Think in Action.* New York: Basic Books.

Shardlow, M. and Doel, M. (1993) 'Examination by triangulation: a model for practice teaching'. *Social Work Education 12*, 3, 67–79.

Shennan, G. (1998) 'Are we asking the experts? Practice teachers' use of client views in assessing student competence'. *Social Work Education 17*, 4, 407–417.

Weinstein, J. (1998) 'The use of National Occupational Standards in professional education'. *Journal of Interprofessional Care 12*, 2, 169–179.

Winter, R. (1993) 'The problem with educational levels (Part 1)'. *Journal of Further and Higher Education 17*, 3, 90–103.

Winter, R. and Maisch, M. (1996) *Professional Competence and Higher Education: The Accreditation of Social Services Experience and Training (ASSET) Programme.* London: Falmer Press.

Wolf, A. (1989) 'Can competence and knowledge mix?' In J. Burke (ed) *Competency Based Education and Training.* London: Falmer Press.

Wolf, A. (1993) *Assessment Issues and Problems in a Criterion-Based System.* London: Further Education Unit, Department of Education and Science.

Wolf, A. (1995a) *Competence Based Assessment.* Buckingham: Open University Press.

Wolf, A. (1995b) 'Authentic assessment in a competitive sector: institutional prerequisites and cautionary tales'. In H. Torrance (ed) *Evaluating Authentic Assessment.* Buckingham: Open University Press.

Wolf, A. and Silver, R. (1986) *Work Based Learning: Trainee Assessment by Supervisors.* Sheffield: Manpower Services Commission.

Worsley, A. and Knight, T. (1998) 'Overcoming the fear: fairness in the joint marking of a case study'. *Social Work Education 17*, 4, 469–476.

Further Reading on Competence

Barnett, R. (1994) *The Limits of Competence.* Buckingham: SRHE/Open University Press.

Burke, J. (ed) (1989) *Competency Based Education and Training.* London: Falmer Press.

Burke, J. and Jessup, G. (1990) 'Assessment in NVQs: disentangling validity from reliability in NVQs'. In T. Horton (ed) *Assessment Debates.* Buckingham: Open University Press.

Clyne, S. (ed) (1995) *Continuing Professional Development.* London: Kogan Page.

Cree, V., Macauley, C. and Loney, H. (1998) *Transfer of Learning: A Study*. Edinburgh: Scottish Office Central Research Unit.

Ford, P. (1996) 'Competencies: their use and misuse'. In P. Ford and P. Hayes (eds) *Educating for Social Work: Arguments for Optimism*. Aldershot: Avebury.

Horder, W. (1998) 'Competence(s) without tears?' *Social Work Education 17*, 1, 117–120.

Issit, M. and Woodward, M. (1992) *Competence and Contradiction in Changing Social Work and Welfare*. Buckingham: Open University Press.

Kemshall, H. (1993) 'Assessing competence: scientific process or subjective inference? Do we really see it?' *Social Work Education 12*, 1, 36–45.

Mansfield, B. and Mitchell, L. (1996) *Towards A Competent Workforce*. London: Gower.

Mitchell, L. and Cuthburt, T. (1989) *Insufficient Evidence? The Final Report of the Competency Testing Project*. Glasgow: SCOTVEC.

Peryer, A. and Peryer, D. (1997) *Human Resources for Personal Social Services*. London: CCETSW.

Phillipson, J. (1998) *Piecing Together the Jigsaws. Making the Most of Mentors and Assessors*. London: CCETSW.

Rogers, C. (1983) *Freedom to Learn for the 1980s*. London: Merrill.

Simoska, S. and Cook, C. (1996) *Applying APL Principles in Flexible Assessment*. London: Kogan Page.

Smith, M. (1996) *Qualified Social Workers and Probation Officers. A Survey carried out by the Social Services Division of ONS*. London: HMSO.

Winter, R. (1994) 'The second dimension of assessment'. In D. Bridges (ed) *Transferable Skills in Higher Education*. Norwich: University of East Anglia.

CHAPTER 13

Interprofessional Education

Helena Low and Jenny Weinstein

Introduction

Successful collaboration between health and social care professionals is increasingly recognized as a necessary part of effective service delivery. The focus of care has moved from institutions to the community and co-ordination of services is essential. To turn this much sought-after ideal into practice, the New Labour government committed itself to establishing the processes and, most significantly, the financial arrangements which would embed integration into the mainstream and 'breakdown the Berlin Wall' between health and social are. The promotion of interprofessional education and training is an important aspect of these developments.

Although interprofessional education has long been advocated as a means to develop collaborative working, single profession courses remain the prevailing model of training. Examples of interprofessional projects reflect an enormous range of approaches depending on their context, the motivation of their leaders and the expectations of their funders. However, the majority rarely survive the departure of their champion or the end of their pump-priming funds. Interprofessional education inevitably remains fragmented and unco-ordinated while it continues to be implemented as pilot projects or short-term specific schemes.

Providing a broad overview of developments, we argue in this chapter that the climate is now right for a more comprehensive and strategic approach to interprofessional education so that it is integrated at qualifying and pre-registration levels and throughout continuing professional education. The barriers to shared learning which faced those who pioneered the work have been well documented and there are now many excellent examples of how they can be overcome. A key strategy has been networking between the many stakeholders who have become supporters of interprofessional education, and understanding the reasons for their interest and the conflicting agendas driving forward the changes. Separate funding systems, cultural divisions and entrenched attitudes of statutory and professional bodies must be tackled if the rhetoric of interprofessional education is to become reality.

It is important that interprofessional education is taken forward on the basis of clear evidence that it is beneficial to service users. Unfortunately there has been only limited research on the outcomes of shared learning. Existing studies tend to evaluate the impact on individual practitioners or professional groups rather than the outcome for service users. While these undoubtedly demonstrate improved mutual understanding and respect, they make assumptions about the likely effect on practice which are not substantiated. The lack of evidence to support interprofessional education is beginning to be addressed. A systematic and rigorous methodology is being developed by the Council for the Advancement of Interprofessional Education (CAIPE) to undertake a review of outcomes from interprofessional education projects and the English National Board for Nursing, Health Visiting and Midwifery (ENB) has also commissioned some relevant research.

Definitions

What do we mean by interprofessional education? A plethora of terms abound in this field (Leathard 1994). The terms are often used inter-changeably but can have quite different meanings for different groups: joint teaching and learning; multidisciplinary teaching and learning; interdisciplinary teaching and learning; integrated learning; shared learning. Gyarmati (1986) argued that a multi-professional approach simply means two or more professions placed side by side accepting joint aims related to a common problem, while interdisciplinary education involves the synthesis and integration of the constituent elements of two or more professions. CAIPE's (1996) definition of multi-professional education is 'when two or more professions learn side by side for a purpose', and interprofessional education is 'when two or more professions learn side by side from and about one another to promote collaboration in practice'. According to Gyarmati, the interdisciplinary approach concentrates on the bases of knowledge, while the multi-disciplinary approach is concerned with the application of that knowledge.

Shared learning is used frequently to describe what happens when one or more disciplines or professions come together in an educational situation. However, to share means 'confidence to give away that which is yours; to possess or use, or endure jointly with others' (*Concise Oxford Dictionary* 1984). It would seem, therefore, that shared learning can only take place when sharing is possible, that is, when individuals or professional groups are willing to 'let go' of their own knowledge and expertise and allow others to use it. The failure of consolidation on any scale may well be due as much to the lack of readiness and ability of professions to 'share' as to any other barrier.

National Policy and Legislation

These issues have been part of the discussion about health and welfare for many years. Government policy of the 1970s and 1980s promoted joint strategy, planning and working together, culminating in major policy and legislation such as the *NHS and Community Care Act 1990* (Department of Health 1990b), *Working Together Under the Children Act 1989* (Home Office 1991), the *Care Programme Approach* for people with mental health problems (Department of Health 1990) and the *Looking After Children* initiative (Ward 1995). To facilitate the new collaborative approaches, a number of government policy statements to promote joint training were issued (DoH/SSI 1991; Home Office 1989; NHSE 1996). Early research indicated that funding, complex bureaucracy and professional demarcations prevented the proposed framework from achieving any significant impact (Challis *et al.* 1988). These same barriers continued to undermine subsequent initiatives.

In May 1997 Tony Blair's Labour government inherited an NHS whose funding and framework were still based on competition and an internal market. While the previous administration had urged the development of a 'seamless service', its philosophy and systems had mitigated against achieving this end. Under New Labour, partnership would replace competition and lead to 'the third way'. The White Paper *The New NHS* (Department of Health 1997) introduced a statutory 'duty of partnership' on NHS bodies to be facilitated by the pooling of budgets, seats for the chief executives of local authorities on primary care groups and guidance about working together. The Green Paper *Our Healthier Nation* (Department of Health 1998) reinforced this partnership approach with the introduction of health action zones established by health authorities co-operatively with local public and private agencies.

Many of the Labour government's key social policies – on social exclusion, on working with young offenders and on supporting parents and children who may be at risk – all require agencies to collaborate on 'joined up thinking', 'joined up working' and 'joined up planning'.

Service Delivery

A number of high profile breakdowns in communication between health and care professionals resulting in serious consequences for service users proved a key driver for these significant policy developments. It became clear that working across professional and agency boundaries is essential to prevent further tragedies and to improve consumer satisfaction with care.

The changing focus to a 'primary care led NHS' (Department of Health and Social Security 1981; Hughes 1994), the development of the mixed economy of care and emphasis on user-led services all contributed to the demand for interprofessional and multi-agency working. Anyone who has been involved in trying to effect the change will recognize its many challenges. These were described by the Audit Commission (1986, paras 117–30) as 'reluctance to relinquish control over boundaries, different funding systems, suspicions about the motives behind initiatives to collaborate, professional barriers, perceived inequalities in status, different philosophies and conflicting priorities.' Many of these factors are still relevant today.

Nevertheless, progress has been made on a number of fronts and for a range of reasons. Barr (1997) described three key movements that overlap to a greater or lesser degree and which have given rise to both shared and conflicting agendas for those promoting multi-professional education.

The *collective* movement characterizes the process whereby groups have come together both within their profession and with other professions with a shared purpose. Examples include: social workers, nurses and occupational therapists becoming generic 'care managers'; Project 2000 programmes bringing together previously separate nursing disciplines; or the review of the Professions Allied to Medicine (PAMs), pulling them more firmly under one governing body. Government and employers have seized the opportunity to establish cost-effective measures such as streamlined approaches to quality assurance, validation, regulation and curricula. Some professions have welcomed the developments as strengthening their position; others have seen them as a threat.

The *comprehensive* movement describes the consensus between divergent groups, such as service managers, education managers in universities and government officials, to promote multi-professional education – each with their own agenda. Universities have been motivated by the need for economies and employers by the introduction of skill mix and the need for a more flexible workforce.

The *collaborative* movement is more directly related to practice on the ground and is exemplified by the developments in primary health care, community care, shared initiatives in child protection, mental health and health promotion. The motivating factor has been the cultivation of better collaboration to improve patient/client care. The most successful ventures involve service users in planning, delivery and evaluation and lead to less prejudice, increased knowledge about other professionals' skills and greater mutual respect.

Delivery of Professional Education

Changes in higher education (HE) such as the move of nursing, midwifery and health visiting education into universities, often in the same or neighbouring departments with social work, have facilitated the development of shared learning opportunities. Some NHS education and training purchasing consortia, established in 1996, encourage an interprofessional approach as part of their contracts with HE providers.

The continuing pressure to reduce expenditure in HE has led to a reduction in staff–student ratios. This 'mass production' policy with the opening up of access to HE has made the sharing of learning between different student groups seem attractive. Credit accumulation and transfer, open and distance learning, modularization, work-based and portfolio assessment have all facilitated progress, offering greater flexibility and increased student choice.

Studies have shown that there are large areas of commonality in the curriculum content of a range of health and social work qualifying/ pre-registration/undergraduate programmes (Tope 1994). Many universities have developed shared learning in these common areas. However, where the motive is purely to cut costs and there is no interactive professional learning, students can feel cheated and the positive impact – to foster a culture of co-operation and collaboration – is lost.

Interprofessional Competences

The identification of shared competences and competences for inter-professional working was significantly facilitated by functional mapping – a process which helped to reconceptualize the changing roles and tasks of care professionals. The functional map of the care sector describes the intended outcomes or results of work – not job titles, activities tasks or skills (Mitchell and Coats 1997). It was developed between 1993 and 1994 by the Care Sector Consortium (replaced in 1998 by national training organizations) and used as the basis for national vocational qualifications (NVQs) in Health and Care. Professionals involved in detailed consultation about the map could not help but be aware of the considerable commonality in their roles and tasks.

Amid great debates, the Health and Care Professions Education Forum (H&CPEF), which represents eleven health care professions, agreed to initiate the development of National Occupational Standards for Professional Activity in Health Promotion and Care (Care Sector Consortium 1997). These standards are used to develop shared learning programmes at post-registration level. The methodology of building a shared programme of learning and/or assessment using common standards can be less cumbersome than trying to combine traditional uni-professional curricula.

Some of the resistance to NVQs and the 'competence movement' was a fear that the exposure of overlaps between roles might lead to the erosion of individual professions and therefore to a dilution of the quality of care offered (Barr 1994; Webb 1992). In spite of opposition to the extension of the framework to higher levels (Weinstein 1998a), it became clear that standards or specified learning outcomes, however they are expressed, would become the tools used by purchasers and education providers to develop and evaluate education and training (Mathias and Thompson 1998). This was undoubtedly a significant spur to the expansion of interprofessional education.

Nature and Extent of Interprofessional Education

Once the principle of interprofessional education had been accepted, discussions moved on to consider the best way to deliver it and the most appropriate stage at which it should be introduced. From a fixed position that shared learning should not even be considered prior to qualification, the consensus is now in favour of incorporating some shared learning at all stages, including initial qualification training.

Many of the debates leading to this consensus occurred at workshops or conferences organized collaboratively by professional and statutory bodies representing social work, nursing, medicine or professions allied to medicine. While the talking was useful, fundamental change remains illusive and each professional group continues to train separately, with suspicion or stereotypes of each other built into their socialization. Interprofessional education in the new century will still be contending with these problems and with the continued reluctance of all the professional and statutory bodies to share their gatekeeping role.

Nevertheless, a gradual rise up the policy agenda for interprofessional education can be traced partly through the establishment of a number of key organizations. These included a joint CCETSW and ENB umbrella group (1993), the European Network for Multi Professional Education, (EMPE) (1987), the Council for the Advancement of Interprofessional Education,

CAIPE (1987), the Marylebone Centre Trust, MCT (1988), the Primary Care Alliance, and the Commission on Primary Care (1993).

While these organizations aim to foster collaboration from above, several grass-roots developments have begun to lay foundations from below. The joint DipSW/Registered Nurse programmes (Learning Disability) are now well established, although at the time of writing no systematic evaluation of these unique dual qualification initiatives had been undertaken. Anecdotal evidence and some research into the predecessor Certificate in Social Services/Registered Mental Handicap (CSS/RNMH) courses (Brown 1994; Walton 1989), indicate that, while dual qualified graduates are highly valued in the field, they tend to move rapidly up the management ladder rather than remaining in practice. Within the 'tribal' system, students from these programmes may experience identity problems and can find themselves at the sharp end of the nursing and social work culture clash.

It is anticipated that programmes on a similar model may be developed for people working in the mental health field. In the light of a perceived breakdown in community care for people with mental health problems (Ritchie, Dick and Lingham 1994), controversy centres on whether to create a new generic mental health professional (Sainsbury Centre 1997). Although the professions have successfully kept this proposal at bay, it is likely to be revived unless collaboration improves.

In 1992 the Joint Practice Teaching Initiative (JPTI) promoted collaboration in practice as well as in educational institutions and demonstrated several different models of shared learning which were adaptable according to their context (Bartholomew, Davis and Weinstein 1996). The different modes of delivery all used a core curriculum, expressed in terms of learning outcomes, which had been approved by the three statutory bodies for nursing, social work and occupational therapy education (Weinstein 1997). JPTI showed how interprofessional programmes could be integrated into different professional frameworks for continuing education, with credits counting towards academic awards

Building on the model developed by JPTI, a comparison was undertaken of the pre-registration training requirements for occupational therapists and social workers (Alsop and Vigars 1998). This led to the establishment of two shared learning projects for social work and occupational therapy students at the universities of Derby and Wales. Although there were few problems identifying common areas for learning, the organizers reported struggles with practical problems such as timetables and dual sites; cultural differences such as age, gender and values; and conflicting teaching and learning styles – didactic or experiential. Nevertheless, the value was thought by students and tutors to outweigh the problems that were eventually overcome by careful preplanning and investment in training the trainers.

The full extent of interprofessional shared learning is unclear, although it undoubtedly increased significantly during the 1990s. A survey of shared learning in primary health in 1987–88 identified 400 initiatives in England, Scotland and Wales (Horder 1992). A subsequent survey carried out in 1996 identified 700 interprofessional learning initiatives for primary and secondary health care provision (Barr and Waterton 1996). The majority of these initiatives were at post-qualifying level using flexible, modularized pathways with some open learning.

Shared Learning in the Workplace

Only a minority of professionals will take part in university-based continuing education programmes. The majority of shared learning is more difficult to quantify because it happens within the workplace and often takes the form of one- or two-day workshops which may be ad hoc or possibly run as a 'rolling programme'. Most highly valued by participants, whatever their views about the content, is the opportunity to meet and talk together and to get to know each other. Building relationships and trust, more than anything, facilitates good communication about clients, patients and service issues. User involvement in such programmes ensures that the focus remains on service delivery rather than on professional differences.

Shared learning in child care

A common example of this kind of multi-disciplinary, work-based training is child protection. Interestingly, although the ENB and CCETSW produced guidelines for jointly validated post-qualifying/post-registration, college-based courses, only three programmes materialized. An evaluation by Stanford and Yelloly (1994) indicated that, in spite of the positive outcome for students, lack of agency resources to release staff impeded recruitment.

Funded through the Training Support Programme (TSP) and organized under the auspices of Area Child Protection Committees, work-based training in child protection tends to be unevenly spread across professions (Birchall and Hallett 1995). Those in the wider network, such as teachers and GPs, who are most likely to detect early signs of abuse, need urgent access to training, although their working hours present practical difficulties. The key professionals – social workers and health visitors – need more training together to develop coherent and commonly understood approaches.

The success of joint training between the police and social workers on joint investigation of child abuse has demonstrated that it is possible to address both practical and cultural problems. Although these two professions in their stereotypical manifestations exemplify the most extreme clash of values, barriers can be overcome by 'the facilitative skills of the trainers, who need to be able to challenge entrenched attitudes in a positive way which really effects change and does not produce lip service to jargon or doctrine'. (Metropolitan Police and London Child Protection Co-ordination Group 1991, p.23).

Shared learning in primary care

With the establishment of primary care groups or trusts, successful interprofessional collaboration is essential. The research on primary health care teams, summarized by West and Poulton (1997), indicates that, while the benefits of effective teamwork are universally recognized, the problems of achieving it abound. Field and West (1995) point out the failure of primary health care teams to set aside time for communication and shared decision-making. Barriers of status, gender, race, class and professional accountability are exacerbated by the inability of many GPs to provide democratic rather than autocratic leadership. If these dynamics are not addressed, they could inhibit successful collaboration in the primary care groups where GPs have won a battle to hold the majority of seats on the governing bodies.

Interprofessional work-based learning in primary care has consisted to a large extent of team building. Since the 1980s, health authorities have supported members of practice teams to attend residential workshops. The lack of enthusiasm for spending time on process rather than task has led to this approach being discredited by some health professionals. 'Learning Opportunities Through Teams' known as LOTUS (Billingham 1999) provides a more flexible approach whereby primary health care teams are encouraged to identify their own training needs and preferred means of meeting them. The focus must be clinical or client centred, ideally with service user involvement; team building will be a by-product. Learning methods may include shadowing, case discussion, open learning or customized courses.

If these positive developments are to continue, it is important to be aware of the barriers that continue to impede progress and the ways in which these can be overcome.

Barriers to Interprofessional Education

Factors which have impeded both interprofessional working and education initiatives have been well documented (Leathard 1994; Mahaolrunaigh, Clifford and Hicks 1995). Examples include professional socialization and culture (Bligh 1980; Spratley and Pietroni 1994), ideological differences, ineffective communications (Brown 1994), organizational difficulties and inadequate service support. Lack of equality and reciprocity, different education and social backgrounds and a range of structural barriers, such as different locations, timetabling and funding arrangements, have also been identified (National Health Service Executive 1997).

Different professional language and use of technical terminology can become barriers to shared learning, leading to misunderstandings. The use of jargon and language reflecting perceived professional hierarchy can inhibit collaborative approaches to working and education.

Professional roles and preparation for those roles often reinforce differences in professional values that underpin contrasting approaches to care. While each profession has to have its own sense of identity and values, these can become so entrenched that they create problems for working across professional boundaries. Much of the resistance to multi-professional education is due to the fear of dilution of professional role and loss of professional identity.

Separate professional education also gives rise to stereotyped ideas of other professions and the way they work. These images reinforce the perception of status and power (Blane 1991) held by one profession of another. Unless this is explicitly addressed, bringing different professional groups together for educational purposes does not, unfortunately, guarantee shared learning and may reinforce barriers that already exist.

Communication problems have consistently been identified as a significant factor in determining whether or not shared learning initiatives are successful. Ineffective communications may be due to poor organization, lack of agreed processes or a lack of commitment by those involved.

The structural barriers to planning and delivering shared learning can sometimes seem overwhelming to the most committed enthusiasts. Practical difficulties relating to different locations of education provision, funding arrangements for both teachers and students, different lengths of programmes, curricula issues and assessment processes, particularly in practice, cannot be ignored. Professional statutory bodies that have different requirements and are perceived to be rigid in their approach may be criticized as obstructive.

Overcoming the Barriers

While the barriers to shared learning have been well documented, the means of overcoming them (Bartholomew *et al.* 1996; ENB/CCETSW 1995; Spratley and Pietroni 1994; Thurgood, 1992; Weinstein 1994) are now emerging with more confidence.

Unspoken fears of role dilution have to be recognized. Professionals need and want to maintain their own professional identity. Atkins (1998) is of the view that 'tribalism' is a normal part of professional culture and perceived resistance to multi-professional education is often a legitimate expression of loss of culture. It is crucial that professionals who undertake shared learning are enabled to work through this 'bereavement' process. Those planning and delivering interprofessional education have to recognize and perhaps go through this process themselves in order to facilitate successful shared learning.

The importance of acknowledging professional differences in order to be able to address conflict openly has been highlighted by Weinstein (1994). Professionals must have a clear understanding both of the fundamental principles underpinning their own profession and a respect for those of other professions. Multi-professional working or education can only be successful if there is knowledge and understanding of each professional role, a commitment to a common goal and a willingness to work collaboratively in an equal partnership.

Key factors for success were suggested by ENB/CCETSW (1995) in relation to planning, organizing and delivering shared learning:

- clarity of purpose, communication, philosophy, values and expectations of all those involved
- user involvement at all stages
- clarity in relation to the resources needed, commitment, time, personnel, support and finances
- clarity of language, mutual respect and support.

With these in place, it is possible to determine where commonalties exist and where areas of difference remain and need to be accepted or resolved.

There is evidence to suggest that even when organizational and structural barriers have been overcome, the success of shared learning initiatives is dependent on the expertise of the facilitator (Council for the Advancement of Interprofessional Education 1996; National Health Service Executive 1997). Research commissioned by the ENB (Miller, Ross and Freeman 1999) into shared learning within programmes of preparation for nurse, midwife and health visitor teachers confirmed the need for preparation of teachers to facilitate shared learning. Experience has shown that the facilitation of interprofessional shared learning requires a wider range of knowledge and skills than are needed for single professional education.

The development of key individuals with enthusiasm and commitment is noted by a number of writers. Pietroni (1992) highlighted that in any collaborative venture, skilled leadership is vital. Enthusiasm and commitment is not sufficient for success. The complexity of interprofessional and interagency work requires that the gaps and conflicts between different professional perspectives and practices should not only be bridged but creatively exploited. For example, she stresses 'the ability to be able to tolerate and work with disparate or opposed views, and the radically different constructions of what the problems and potential solutions really are'. This requires a high level of expertise in mediation and diplomacy used with pragmatism and authority. Atkins (1998) suggests that teaching in the affective domain is essential in this respect. A consensus view has evolved that interactive learning is the significant element of shared learning and teachers need to be proactive to achieve this.

Key questions about what should be taught, when and how still remain unresolved. Weinstein (1998b) proposes a framework for interprofessional competencies comprising the knowledge, skills and values required to work collaboratively. The *knowledge* component covers the legal and policy context, purpose and values of other agencies and professions; theories of group and team processes; and change management. *Values* include a user-led approach; preparedness to challenge own values; and willingness to acknowledge and challenge prejudice or discrimination. The *skills* emphasize listening, communication, working as part of a team, anti-discriminatory practice and reflection. It is suggested that all professions should include the assessment of interprofessional competencies as part of their requirements for registration and qualification.

Perhaps more controversial is the suggestion that we should follow the Scandinavian model (Lãmsa, Hietanen and Lãmsa 1994) whereby all health professionals share a foundation year, prior to moving into their own training. They subsequently reconvene for shared learning events at regular points during their courses. This perhaps is a vision for the future.

Conclusion

In this chapter we have described the policy, education and service delivery context within which interprofessional education has developed and outlined its extent and history. We have offered a critical analysis of some key interprofessional education initiatives delivered in colleges, in the workplace or in primary care teams. We have argued that, in the past, while interprofessional education was recognized as important, structural, financial and cultural barriers often hampered any systematic integration within the mainstream. We hope that the Labour government will succeed in its aim to improve collaboration and partnership by addressing at last some of the structural and financial barriers which have so far impeded progress.

If interprofessional education is to be truly integrated, preparation of teachers will be essential to ensure that those involved in trying to implement interprofessional education understand the conflicting agendas of their stakeholders and become a cadre of interprofessional facilitators with the skills to address the less tangible barriers of professional protectionism. The professional and statutory bodies must also provide the necessary leadership, guidance and support. Rather than simply supporting individual projects, serious consideration should be given to the provision of an education and learning approach which enables professionals to collaborate effectively and to achieve competences in working across traditional lines of agencies, disciplines and professions. By this we do not mean the creation of a 'generic care professional' and the loss of specialist skills, which continue to be vital in the increasingly complex world of health and social care. We mean that part of the skill of any health or care professional must be the ability to work flexibly and collaboratively – looking outwardly across barriers rather than hiding behind them.

In our view, the most effective way forward is not to focus on interprofessional education as such, but rather on interprofessional learning for collaborative practice, with the clear understanding that interprofessional learning cannot ensure collaborative practice, but can enhance the skills needed to work collaboratively. Whatever the level or context, we commend an approach which emphasizes field and practice-based education as well as shared college-based learning; involves service users at all stages and provides students with specific competencies – knowledge skills and values – for collaborative practice. Above all, research or evaluation must be incorporated to assess the impact on the quality of services to users.

References

Alsop, A. and Vigars, C. (1998) 'Shared learning, joint training or dual qualification in occupational therapy and social work: a feasibility study'. *British Journal of Occupational Therapy 61*, 4, 146–152.

Atkins, J. (1998) 'Teaching in the Affective Domain'. Paper presented London, ENB.

Audit Commission (1986) *Making a Reality of Community Care*. London: HMSO.

Barr, H. (1994) *Perspectives in Shared Learning*. London: Council for the Advancement of Interprofessional Education in Primary Care.

Barr, H. (1997) 'Competing agendas in interprofessional education: the issues at stake'. Paper presented at a workshop Perspectives on Multiprofessional Education. Oxford.

Barr, H. and Waterton, C. (1996) *Interprofessional Education for Health and Social Care in the United Kingdom.* London: CAIPE.

Bartholomew, A., Davis, J. and Weinstein, J. (1996) *Interprofessional Education and Training – Developing New Models.* London: CCETSW.

Billingham, K. (1999) 'Developing new ways of learning together: LOTUS: "learning opportunities through teams"'. In K. Billingham, M. Flynn and J. Weinstein (eds) *Developing Primary Health Care: A World of Difference.* London: Royal College of General Practitioners.

Birchall, E. and Hallett, C. (1995) *Working Together in Child Protection.* London: HMSO.

Blane, D. (1991) 'Health professionals'. In G. Scrambler (ed) *Sociology as Applied to Medicine.* London: Balliere Tindall.

Bligh, D. (1980) *Education Principles in Interprofessional Learning: Education for Co-operation in Health and Social Work.* London: Royal College of General Practitioners, Occasional Paper 14.

Brown, J. (1994) *The Hybrid Worker – Lessons Based Upon a Study of Employers Involved in Two Pioneer Joint Qualifying Training Courses.* York: University of York.

Council for the Advancement of Interprofessional Education (1996) *Principles of Interprofessional Education.* London: CAIPE.

Care Sector Consortium (1997) *National Occupational Standards for Professional Activity in Health Promotion and Care.* Luton: Local Government Management Board.

Challis, L., Fuller, S., Henwood, M., Plowden, W., Webb, A. and Wistow, G. (1988) *Joint Approaches to Social Policy, Rationality and Practice.* Cambridge: Cambridge University Press.

Department of Health (1990a) *The Care Programme Approach for People with a Mental Illness Referred to the Specialist Psychiatric Services.* London: HMSO.

Department of Health (1990b) *The NHS and Community Care Act.* London: HMSO.

Department of Health (1997) *The New NHS.* London: HMSO.

Department of Health (1998) *Our Healthier Nation.* London: HMSO.

Department of Health and Social Security (1981) *The Primary Health Care Team: Report of a Joint Working Group of the Standing Medical Advisory Committee and the Standing Nursing and Midwifery Advisory Committee (The Harding Report).* London: HMSO.

DOH/SSI (1991) *Training for Community Care: A Joint Approach.* London: HMSO.

ENB/CCETSW (1995) *Shared Learning: A Good Practice Guide.* London: ENB/CCETSW.

Field, R. and West, M.A. (1995) 'Teamwork in primary health care 2: perspectives from practices'. *Journal of Interprofessional Care 9,* 2, 23–130.

Gyarmati, G. (1986) 'The teaching of the professions: an interdisciplinary approach'. *Higher Education Review 18,* 2, 33–34.

Home Office, DOH, DES and Welsh Office (1991) *Working Together Under the Children Act 1989.* London: HMSO.

Horder, J. (1992) 'A national survey that needs to be repeated'. *Journal of Interprofessional Care 6*, 1, 65–71.

Hughes, J. (1994) 'Primary Care 2000, a shape of things to come'. *Primary Care Management 4*, 3–5.

Lāmsa, A., Hietanen, I. and Lāmsa, J. (1994) 'Education for holistic care: a pilot programme in Finland'. *Journal of Interprofessional Care 8*, 1, 31–43.

Leathard, A. (ed) (1994) *Going Interprofessional: Working Together for Health and Welfare.* London: Routledge.

Mahaolrunaigh, S., Clifford, C. and Hicks, C. (1995) *An Evaluation of Shared Learning in Educational Programmes of Preparation for Nurse, Midwife and Health Visitor Teachers.* London: ENB.

Mathias, P. and Thompson, T. (1998) 'Trends in education and training for health and social care'. In P. Mathias and T. Thompson (eds) *Standards and Learning Disability,* 2nd edn. London: Baillière Tindall.

Metropolitan Police and London Child Protection Co-ordination Group (1991) 'The joint investigation of child abuse by police and social services. Review of joint training courses and proposals'. Unpublished.

Miller, C., Ross, N. and Freeman, M. (1999) *The Role of Collaborative/Shared Learning in Pre and Post Registration Education in Nursing, Midwifery and Health Visiting.* London: ENB

Mitchell, C. and Coats, M. (1997) 'The functional map of health and social care'. In J. vretvit, P. Mathias and T. Thompson (eds) *Interprofessional Working for Health and Social Care.* Basingstoke: Macmillan.

National Health Service Executive (1996) *Primary Care: the Future.* London: Department of Health.

National Health Service Executive (1997) *Learning Together: Professional Education for Maternity Care.* London: Department of Health.

OUP (1995) *The Concise Oxford English Dictionary,* 9th edn. Oxford: Oxford University Press.

Pietroni, P.C. (1992) 'Towards reflective practice – the language of health and social care'. *Journal of Interprofessional Care 6*, 1, 7–16.

Ritchie, J., Dick, D. and Lingham, R. (1994) *The Report of the Inquiry into the Care and Treatment of Christopher Clunis.* London: HMSO.

Sainsbury Centre for Mental Health (1997) *Pulling Together: The Future Roles and Training of Mental Health Staff.* London: Sainsbury Centre for Mental Health.

Spratley, J. and Pietroni, M. (1994) *Creative Collaboration: Interprofessional Learning Priorities in Primary Health and Community Care.* London: Marylebone Centre Trust.

Stanford, R. and Yelloly, M. (1994) *Shared Learning in Child Protection.* London: ENB/CCETSW.

Thurgood, G. (1992) 'Let's work together, let's learn together'. *Journal of Advances in Health and Nursing Care 1*, 5, 13–40.

Tope, R. (1994) 'Integrated inter-disciplinary learning between health and social care professionals: a feasibility study'. Unpublished PhD thesis, University of Wales.

Walton, I. (1989) 'Workforce needs and training resources. The development of the first ENB/CCETSW validated joint training courses in mental handicap'. Unpublished, University of York.

Ward, H. (ed) (1995) *Looking After Children: Research into Practice.* London: HMSO.

Webb, D. (1992) 'Competencies, contracts and cadres: common themes in the social control of nurse and social work education'. *Journal of Interprofessional Care 6*, 3, 223–230.

Weinstein, J. (1994) *Sewing the Seams for a Seamless Service: A Review of the Developments in Interprofessional Education and Training.* London: CCETSW.

Weinstein, J. (1997) 'The development of shared learning: conspiracy or constructive development?' In J. Vretvit, P. Mathias and T. Thompson (eds) *Interprofessional Working for Health and Social Care.* Basingstoke: Macmillan.

Weinstein, J. (1998a) 'The use of national occupational standards in professional education'. *Journal of Interprofessional Care 12*, 2, 169–179.

Weinstein, J. (1998b) 'The professions and their interrelationships'. In T. Thompson and P. Mathias (eds) *Standards and Learning Disability*, 2nd edn. London: Ballière Tindall.

West, M.A. and Poulton, B.C. (1997) 'A failure of function: teamwork in primary health care'. *Journal of Interprofessional Care 11*, 2, 203–216.

CHAPTER 14

Lifelong Learning for Care Professionals

Elaine Ennis and Norma Baldwin

Lifelong Learning: Origins

Lifelong learning is now an established part of the vocabulary of educators and trainers across many disciplines. It is a phrase imbued with positive connotations: of openness to new learning opportunities; of continuity and renewal; of tangible benefits to individuals, employers, communities and the economic well-being of the nation (DfEE 1998; Scottish office 1998a). While lifelong learning and the associated notion of a learning society is a key concept currently, it is not a new idea. Cooke has traced its roots to the early part of the twentieth century:

> Immediately after the First World War, a government committee on adult education demanded that 'adult education should not be regarded as a luxury for a few exceptional persons here and there ... adult education is a permanent national necessity, an inseparable aspect of citizenship and therefore should be universal and lifelong' (Ministry of Reconstruction Report 1919). The term came into more general use internationally through the work of UNESCO in the 1970s. (Cooke 1998, p.1)

Contemporary strategies in education to improve standards in schools, to widen access to further and higher education and to encourage lifelong learning are some of the responses to the growing pressures of globalization. While a better trained, more highly skilled and flexible workforce is one major objective of lifelong learning policies, others are still associated with the promotion of good citizenship (DfEE 1998) and, more recently, as a means of combatting social exclusion (Scottish Office 1998a).

Optimistic and upbeat messages predominate in the lifelong learning discourse but some commentators are more sceptical. Rinne (1998, p.109) notices that much of the literature shows 'an impressive range of imagination' where 'flights of fancy in the committee reports and memoranda all too often remain merely ink on paper'.

In this final chapter we explore the meaning that lifelong learning may have for care professionals and consider the part it plays in their rapidly changing landscape. Although lifelong learning is often broadly defined and may encompass liberal adult education, community education and Third Age initiatives, we focus here on learning relevant to continuing professional development in social care.

We consider the origins and context of lifelong learning in the UK and its relationship with continuing professional development. We explore ways in which bridges can be built between the vision and the reality of lifelong learning, between education and training frameworks and the everyday demands of practice.

Lifelong learning holds the promise of rich rewards; of care professionals more confident and knowledgeable in their practice, of continually improving services and of responsive and supportive organizations. Good progress has already been made towards a framework of qualifications and standards of practice appropriate to care professionals in different settings and with differing roles and responsibilities. It is a complex enterprise and this chapter aims to explore some of the issues in developing its role – in constantly changing work environments – to support the most effective practices in social work and social care.

Pierce and Weinstein, in Chapter 1, have explored the changing nature of the professions and Croton (Chapter 12) has discussed key issues in the assessment of professional competence. These changes in professional education are associated with themes such as accountability, professional responsibility and competence. The period of specialized initial education and training – one of the traditional features of professional socialization (Etzioni 1967; Freidson 1973; Todd 1987) – is now regarded as insufficient for continuing professional practice over a working lifetime. As their environment changes ever more rapidly, professionals face demands to keep pace by updating both knowledge and skills. Watkins, Drury and Preddy (1992) have suggested an average currency or 'shelf life' of four years, although this may be even shorter for professionals in scientific and technical fields. A 'competence gap' may grow, when knowledge and skills acquired early in a career lose relevance to changing demands and challenges. Recognition of emerging social problems, the significance of demographic changes, the need to keep abreast of research outcomes, new legislation, regulations and policy reforms, the fiscal context and changing public expectations will all have a major impact on practice. Professional autonomy, responsibility and accountability for delivering high standards of service are essentially linked to continuing professional development.

The case for lifelong learning in the workplace is therefore compelling. Some professions, such as nursing and medicine, have already acknowledged this by making evidence of continuing professional development a mandatory requirement for continuing professional registration.

Who Needs to Learn?

Some international comparisons

Participation rates in education and training after the age of 16 years in the UK have not compared favourably with those of economic competitors and European partners. Hoggart *et al.* note bleakly that a 'front end model' has predominated with education seen as a 'finite (and compulsory) experience from which most of the population gratefully escape as soon as the minimum school-leaving age is reached and for the most part ... never return for formal education' (Hoggart *et al.* 1982, p.39).

Recent expansion of higher education means that the proportion of graduates in the workforce has almost doubled over a decade and participation rates and performance at degree and post-graduate levels now bear favourable comparison with other countries. The quality and outputs of UK research have continued to compare well internationally.

Fourteen million people have now achieved vocational qualifications (NVQ/SVQ) at level 2. However, as *The Learning Age* (DfEE 1998) points out:

> The [UK's] weakness lies in our performance in basic and intermediate skills. Almost 30% of young people fail to reach NVQ level 2 by the age of 19. Seven million adults have no formal qualifications at all: 21 million adults have not reached level 3 (equivalent to two A-levels) and more than one in five of all adults have poor literacy and numeracy skills ... we lag behind France, Germany, the USA and Singapore in the proportion of our workforce qualified to level 3. In the case of graduates, even though we have a high number, we need to encourage more of our highly qualified people to update their skills through continuing professional development. (DfEE 1998)

Participation rates are related to inequalities in access to resources and to class divisions. The Kennedy Report (Kennedy 1997, p.10) indicated that 'one fifth of households which have the highest incomes in our country receive more in educational subsidies than those forming either of the bottom two fifths'. Fundamental questions of social justice, realisation of potential, as well as economic competitiveness are involved.

A number of initiatives are now in train to promote participation and to create a culture where learning is ever more highly valued. These include:

further expansion of further and higher education; the development of qualification frameworks building on credit accumulation and transfer principles; in Scotland, a unified Credit and Qualifications Framework aligning vocational and academic awards; the University for Industry; new funding arrangements for part-time students; and the development of innovative methods of supporting learning and teaching.

These initiatives are of the highest relevance to care professionals across the education and training continuum. Recent data from CCETSW show that 1.25 million people are employed across the social care sector (local authorities, voluntary and private agencies) and of these, around 250, 000, or 20%, hold formal qualifications such as NVQs or further and higher education awards. Within this group 65, 000 staff hold DipSW, CQSW or recognized equivalent social work qualifications (CCETSW Information Service, personal communication 1999).

The most recent data on Scotland relate to local authorities only and indicate that of the 49, 963 full- or part-time staff in post in October 1996, 62% of staff were without any qualifications (Scottish Local Government Information Unit 1998). Although steady progress is being made, data such as these highlight starkly the task for employers, social care educators and trainers in the coming years.

Rowlings, in Chapter 3, explores the important contribution of higher education. Higher and further education have a central role in the agendas set by the Dearing and Garrick (1997) and Kennedy (1997) reports, as central government lifelong learning policies are implemented. An encouraging development is the recognition now afforded to professional bodies and societies for the valuable part they play in influencing curriculum design and assessment, and in promoting positive collaborative arrangements between institutions and employers (DfEE 1998; Scottish Office 1998b). The roles of professionals have changed radically, as have notions of professionalism (Bennet and Hokenstad 1973; Hoyle 1974; Scottish Office 1998b; Todd 1987; Watkins *et al.* 1992). Increased emphasis on public accountability, clearly defined standards for professional awards and subsequently, of professional practice, mean that the relationship between further and higher education institutions and professional activity should be nurtured for the benefit of service users and care professionals alike. The UK-wide initiatives on regulation of the social services workforce, occupational standards, codes of practice, national inspection and quality controls for services all support the emphasis on lifelong learning in social care, as a means to enhance the quality of life of vulnerable service users and communities with diverse problems (Scottish Office 1998b).

Lifelong Learning: Competing Interests

Lifelong learning is a nebulous term that can easily become over-used; it may also mean different things to different people. Consideration of the benefits to the individual learner in relation to personal development and to future career progression sits alongside consideration of specific, current work responsibilities and the benefits to the employing organization. Some commentators have remarked on tensions between the needs of employers and those of individuals (Ball 1990; Brennan and Little 1996; Hughes and Tight 1995). Financial considerations inevitably affect views of continuing professional training and development. To lose sight of individual staff members' needs and aspirations within workforce training and planning strategies is likely to lead to lowering of morale, paradoxically undermining the role of lifelong learning in improving services. A commitment to continually improving services is an aspiration likely to be shared by staff at all levels in an organization and is often the reason why a career in social care was chosen.

In relation to social care, agencies and individual staff members are seeking congruence between educational and professional principles and complex human situations. There are some technical aspects of the work, but fine judgements about competing interests and conflicting values and principles are characteristics of the work.

Continuing Professional Development

Continuing professional development and lifelong learning are closely connected. Over the second half of the twentieth century educators and trainers have increasingly recognized the need for coherent responses to meet workplace demands. A number of terms emerged to describe adult learning following mandatory schooling, higher education and initial professional training. Hoggart *et al.* (1982) cite 'recurrent education' (OECD), 'éducation permanente' (the Council of Europe), 'lifelong learning' (UNESCO), 'continuing education' and 'post-initial education'.

There is a range of definitions of continuing professional development, including 'the systematic maintenance, improvement and broadening of knowledge and skill, and the development of personal qualities necessary for the execution of professional, managerial and technical duties through the professional's working life' (Walsh and Woodward 1989, p.56).

Todd (1987) provides a helpful, additional dimension by emphasizing diversity within continuing professional development. He draws no distinction between people who use private study, those who are taught informally or those who learn by formal means. 'People can develop themselves; others can also help them develop; the important thing is that professional development occurs' (Todd 1987, p.5). Within these definitions some features are particularly noteworthy:

- systematic learning
- ownership of, and the assumption of some personal responsibility forlearning
- appropriate support for learning.

The work of other educationalists, for example Kolb (1984), emphasizes that learning may be incidental, but that in a work setting it is more likely to be associated with good practice and professional development if it is planned; if appropriate supervision or mentoring is provided; and if time is made available for reading, reflection and the evaluation of alternative interventions in the lives of service users.

It is recognized that conscientious professionals in the past took opportunities to update their knowledge either through private study or through more formalized programmes of study. The benefits of some of these programmes have been evaluated and disseminated (Ennis 1998; Rushton and Martyn 1990). What is strikingly different now, however, is the move towards more structured arrangements for continuing professional development linked to both academic and professional credit frameworks and, increasingly, to regulatory bodies.

Since 1990 qualified social workers have had their own continuing professional development system, the Post-Qualifying Framework with two awards, the Post-Qualifying Award at undergraduate level 3 and the Advanced Award at Master's level. A competence-led approach to assessment underpins both awards. Taylor (1998) identifies the flexible features of the Framework in that credits for assessed competence may be gained through presentation of individual portfolios, through accredited programmes or a mixture of the two, and experienced professionals may choose to use mechanisms for accreditation of prior learning. A number of authors in this book (Chapters 1, 2, 3, 10 and 12) explore the debate around definitions of competence in the workplace and how it is assessed. Work continues to develop methods of assessment which are both feasible and affordable and which address legitimate issues raised by Eraut (1994) and by Gonczi (1994). Eraut views the commonly used reflective reports as necessary indicators of *capability* but only partially indicative of competence; Gonczi states that competence can only be inferred from performance. In our view, professional competence in social work and social care – the integration of values, knowledge and skill – can only be assessed through the *outcomes* of work for service users.

Vocational frameworks based on national vocational qualifications (NVQ) and Scottish vocational qualifications (SVQ), which link with the qualifying and post-qualifying frameworks, have been explored in Chapter 1 by Pierce and Weinstein. They are accessible to a much wider range of social care staff with varying levels of previous education. While there is greater emphasis at foundation levels on the demonstration of competence relating to particular tasks, at more advanced levels there are similar debates about the definition of competence. Vocational qualifications play a major role in continuing professional development for the majority of workers in social care.

Building Bridges

From vision to reality in the workplace

Thus far, some of the contextual issues associated with lifelong learning have been identified. There are particular challenges within social care in linking the principles of lifelong learning to the everyday demands of practice. Initial education and training frameworks set in place over the last 10 to 15 years have responded to service needs, to employing organizations and to individual professionals, within available resources. Developments in the wider world of education and training have been incorporated, for example:

- systematic evaluation of training needs in the workplace
- qualifications based on the assessment of competence
- learner-centred programmes of training and development
- promotion of equality of access to qualifications (Taylor 1998 pp. 83–92).

The mechanisms, systems and resources which can build bridges between the vision of lifelong learning in social care, the qualification frameworks and the realities of working lives in diverse settings will need continuous development. Some of the priorities are explored in the rest of the chapter.

Accessible and comprehensive information and advice systems

Clear, well-written information is essential for informed decision-making and is an integral part of good professional practice. Care professionals need to know how to acquire information about learning opportunities, qualification frameworks and the assessment of competence. Education institutions are subject to quality inspection systems of funding councils and the Quality Assurance Agency for Higher Education and are required to produce comprehensive documentation including information on resources and sources of help. Similarly, some social care agencies demonstrate good practice in the production of good quality catalogues of in-house and purchased programmes of study and professional development. At Post-Qualifying levels, the regional consortia play important roles in updating and making available a range of materials, advice and information.

Beyond paper materials, innovative use is made of the Internet and examples include databases on the literature relating to competence and assessment and exemplars of practitioners' reflective and anonymized accounts of their practice (Scottish Network 1998).

Practitioners outside the sphere of education and training frequently comment on the complexity of qualification frameworks and the impenetrability of the language associated with them. Clear, uncomplicated language and the use of graphics or diagrams to accompany information and presentations are known to be helpful. The links between learning opportunities and the range of awards need to be transparent and direct.

Creating a culture for learning

The 'Readiness to Practise' research (Triseliotis and Marsh 1996) identified problems within agencies in the culture of learning, enquiry and research mindedness. Scant attention to theory and little systematic application of research findings is a common experience. Social workers have complained that to be seen reading in the workplace is to invite derogatory comment about too light a caseload or a possible lack of commitment. Programmed opportunities to read widely on accredited courses are enthusiastically welcomed, however, and comments from student evaluations confirm their value. Comments such as 'I didn't realize how out of touch I was with research' (or with the latest practice developments) recur frequently. Cheetham, in Chapter 4, shows how research can be used in a practical way to improve practice.

A cultural shift is required to achieve equal emphasis of theory and knowledge with practice activity (Triseliotis and Marsh 1996). Care professionals need to recognize that any aspect of practice may provide opportunities for continued learning – and the demonstration of practice competence. False divisions are sometimes made between in-service courses, research methods teaching in higher education, supervision, discussing a dilemma with a colleague and 'real work'. Seagraves et al. (1996) helpfully identify three types of work-based learning; learning for work, learning at work and learning through work. Learning for work can include vocationally relevant college courses, Open University broadcasts or TV documentaries. Learning at work might include in-service courses or IT instruction. While learning through work is likely to be integrated in daily practice and include supervision, a joint intervention with a more experienced or senior colleague or discussion within a team. All have the potential to be of immense value.

The importance of basing policies, services and practice on evidence available from research is finally being acknowledged in social work. It provides a further push to emphasize the importance of learning and knowledge for organizations and for all individuals within them. 'Top-down' approaches should meet 'bottom-up' initiatives, giving unequivocal messages that learning is valued and that the education and training continuum is relevant to everyone.

Careful planning and preparation are cost effective. In PQ programmes it is common for staff to meet with the line managers of prospective students prior to the start of an accredited programme. Meetings may have several functions. These might include: providing information; affirming line managers as an important source of competence evidence – because they have direct access to the student's professional practice; and demonstrating how supervising the post-qualifying work of a team member can be used to build up evidence for their own claims for professional credit, whether at PQ or Advanced Award level.

Supervision and support for staff

The Midas elements – the factors that are critical in transmuting learning opportunities into improved practice outcomes – link with the attitudes, knowledge, experience and values of individual staff members and of staff in the organization charged with responsibility for helping learning to take place. A major task for everyone is to develop strategies to encourage all line managers to address the supervisory and mentoring aspects of their practice in hard-pressed teams who are often the first casualties. Yet the team environment has the potential to be one of the most powerful forces for change and for learning (Larson and LaFasto 1989). Both professional awards in social work – PQ and Advanced Award – include competencies for team working. Initiatives to develop these skills are emerging nationwide. It may be that the development of professional awards has been too much the province of specialist educators and trainers and that line managers need to be brought on board. Unless they are, there is a possibility that cynicism, fed by pressure of work and anxiety about a new generation of social workers equipped with the language of competence-led assessment, will stifle their professional development in the workplace. All professionals need to be aware of the principles underpinning lifelong learning and continuing professional development, whether or not they are formally involved as supervisors, mentors or assessors.

Many different models of mentoring, supervision and support can be effective; some where all staff have a role, some where there is specialization, others where independence is seen as essential. All involved need to be aware of issues of power. Roles should be clearly delineated, responsibilities and expectations agreed. For example, where professional values, knowledge and skills are essential to the delivery of a sensitive and effective service, there needs to be a clear differentiation between *management* and *supervision*. Where they are exercised by the same person, it must be recognized that the knowledge and skills needed to manage resources and oversee procedures differ from the knowledge and skills required to exercise leadership, offer supervision and assess competence in complex professional interventions. Effective professional supervision, drawing on the most up-to-date research and models of practice, for example, in the care of someone with dementia, or in the investigation of a child abuse allegation, is a key support in continuing professional development. By modelling relationships which value critical enquiry, research evidence, links between theory and practice, reflective developmental thinking and practice, supervisors and mentors have the potential to make a major contribution to the changing cultures of agencies.

Public and private lives

Care professionals work in a context of constrained, if not diminishing, resources: financial, material and human. Combining a busy professional life with competing demands of families and homes and study requires commitment and a measure of self-discipline. The experience of educational institutions and agencies each year is that large numbers of care professionals achieve awards, or credits towards awards, often demonstrating practice of the highest calibre.

There are, however, times when exceptional stresses coincide and make the demands of study impossible on practical and humanitarian grounds. Recognition from further and higher education institutions, agencies and mentors of these situations and applying strategies to deal with them are essential. There is a fine balance to be struck between support for learners which is aided by clearly defined targets and agreed deadlines for assessed work and the flexibility needed to respond to an individual in distress. Effective strategies include:

1. The development of regulations which allow for a period of time to be discounted so that a member of staff can address personal issues free from additional stress.

2. The establishment of good communication systems between the learner, the supervisor/mentor and the course provider. Good

practice dictates that learners are informed about this pattern of communication at the beginning of a programme and have written information available about processes involved. This avoids situations where work-related stresses are discussed with course providers but mentors are unaware of them or, conversely, where work or personal issues disrupt a learner's studies and the course provider is unaware of them.

3. Participation by agency staff in the design, delivery and assessment of vocationally and professionally accredited programmes is now an established feature. Discussion linked to annual evaluation and monitoring of courses and students' progress provides a valuable opportunity to review agency and course provider relationships and systems with a view to continuous improvement.

Multiple and changing motivations

Learners' motivations are likely to be multiple and to change over time (Drummond and Croll 1983; McCombs 1991; Marton 1982; Reeve 1989; Rogers 1989). Attention needs to be paid to complementary and competing objectives. Although the social care and social work education and training continuum presents the possibility of moving across the range of awards, not all individuals will wish to do so. The metaphor for progression used to be that of climbing a ladder, implying progress from a lower to a higher award. With the advent of national qualifications frameworks, the metaphor of a climbing frame seems more apt, suggesting the options of sideways as well as upwards movement.

Workforce training plans, still underdeveloped in social work and care (Kent 1998; Peryer and Peryer 1997; Utting 1997) need to take account of the appropriate knowledge, skills and occupational standards for staff in different roles and work settings and the numbers required to achieve service objectives. Individual development plans will take account of this context, but continuing professional development should also be seen in relation to a highly skilled and flexible workforce. If plans relate solely to the wider commitment to improve training, to advancement through the organizational hierarchy, or movement to a new post, morale will suffer. For some, affirming commitment to lifelong learning will mean promotion or transfer into a particularly specialized area of practice, but others will look for different forms of recognition. Studies of post-qualifying courses (Ennis 1998; Rushton and Martyn 1990) found that graduates of accredited post-qualifying programmes valued their qualifications and new learning and realized new levels of confidence in their practice. However, a clear message emerged that organizations did not always recognize and make full use of enhanced expertise. Despite this, a study by Ennis (1998) of a child care course found impressively high levels of commitment to continuing practice in the same field, with a majority expressing a wish to develop practice skills yet further.

Exemplars and role models

In the developing culture of lifelong learning, continuing professional development and assessment of competence there is a need to provide guidance through illustration and to celebrate individuals' successes. Libraries of materials developed by former students can be a source of guidance and support, along with clear information about the best ways to provide evidence of competence (O'Hagan 1996; Baldwin forthcoming). Educators and trainers, not only those associated with accredited courses, are steadily compiling exemplars of good practice, with the permission of the care professionals involved. As a central issue in professional competence discourse, confidentiality needs to be addressed by the practitioner and supervisor/mentor prior to submission of any work.

Effective partnerships and working relationships

Effective working relationships are fundamental to successful education and training of care professionals. Consortium arrangements throughout the country provide opportunities for staff from higher and further education institutions and agencies to develop a shared understanding of systems, models of assessment, service needs and emerging professional issues.

Universities have worked in collaboration with local authorities, nationally based voluntary organizations and other agencies concerned with a wide range of services in health and social care – some with central government support, others with charitable funding – to set up national programmes in child protection, child care, community care and criminal justice. There are many more local examples where colleges and universities have collaborated with local agencies to gain academic and professional credits for established Mental Health/Approved Social Worker programmes and Practice Teaching Awards. Existing in-service programmes have been extended and developed to meet the requirements of the CCETSW post-qualifying framework and academic requirements in higher education institutions. Colleges of further education have developed training strategies, or individual and specialist programmes of study, to meet the developing needs of local agencies from statutory and voluntary sectors.

There are many in-built problems because of the instability and uncertainties of funding streams, but many high quality, practice focused, imaginative projects have been developed. Continuing analysis of need and co-ordinated national support and funding may become more effective following the establishment of the national training organisations and regulatory bodies. An example from the east of Scotland illustrates how links can be made between research outcomes, likely new demands following regulation of the workforce and expectations of professional registration and continuing professional development of staff. The findings of Marsh and Triseliotis (1997, p.207), when they evaluated the transition from qualification to work, that DipSW students were generally 'ready to practise ... but ... not fully competent to practise', led to a range of recommendations designed to achieve a 'seamless approach' to the qualifying course and the first year of work. Particular attention was drawn to differentiation between induction and in-service training and the need for supervision of work at a suitable level and complexity.

In the east of Scotland local authorities, voluntary organizations and higher education social work training institutions are planning to establish a joint programme, accredited both academically and professionally, to enable newly qualified social workers to work to post-qualifying (PQ) awards at stage 1 following induction. In response to a survey of existing induction, in-service courses and supervision arrangements, open learning materials and assessment guidelines are being prepared, before a joint submission to relevant validating bodies.

This example and many others throughout the country are based on concepts of continuing professional development responsive to the changing social care context. Existing firm foundations can be built on through the following measures:

- Earlier participation on DipSW and PQ projects leading to a common understanding of contemporary educational issues and links between all levels of social care training.

- Existing partnership arrangements in place for DipSW and PQ programmes, where agency staff have a voice in quality assurance issues within institutions and in curriculum development while staff from education are aware of emerging policy and practice in agencies.

- Collaboration about workforce planning and resource issues which often determine the pace at which agencies are able to promote continuing professional development initiatives in the face of competing demands from other parts of the training continuum and elsewhere.

Links between academic and vocational award structures, access – APL/APEL

Work is taking place throughout the UK to articulate academic and vocational award structures and to put in place unified Credit and Qualification Frameworks. If the ideals of flexible learning and progression are to become realities, nationally agreed pathways for individuals to move on from success in vocational awards to academic awards will be needed. Not all care professionals will wish to make use of these facilities but for those who do, for example, holders of NVQ/SVQ awards at levels 3 and 4 who wish to become qualified social workers, bridging schemes are required. These should take account of the different learning and assessment modes underpinning the respective systems. In summary, priorities for moving from vision to reality are:

- accessible and comprehensive information and advice systems
- support for learning from a variety of sources and specific strategies to promote the training, improve the status and support those who help other staff to develop professionally (workplace assessors, supervisors and mentors)
- strategies to create a culture conducive to learning which is inclusive of all staff, from the most junior to the most senior
- recognition of the relationship between the public and private lives of staff
- recognition of multiple and changing motivations – of complementarity and possible conflicts
- the value of exemplars and role models
- effective partnerships and working relationships
- links between vocational and academic award structures, the development of access, APL and APEL routes.

Conclusion

Experience of continuing change in social care links closely to the need for continuing professional development, highlighting the need to underpin improvements in the quality of services and care through lifelong learning. Previous chapters have provided examples of changes in policy and thinking which promote lifelong learning for care professionals and the emerging systems that can ensure coherence and convergence. They have also noted challenges that remain to be addressed. Professionals in social care show enormous commitment, energy and creativity in meeting these challenges – to the potential benefit to their own sense of worth and success, to good working relationships across sectors and disciplines, to public confidence in services and above all to the outcomes for service users.

References

Baldwin, N. (ed) (forthcoming) *Protecting Children: Promoting their Rights? A reader in theory and practice.* London: Whiting & Birch.

Ball, C. (1990) *More Means Different: Widening Access to Higher Education.* London: RSA.

Bennet, W.S. Jr. and Hokenstad, M.C. Jr. (1973) 'Full time people workers and conceptions of the professional'. In P. Halmos (ed) *Professionalisation and Social Change.* Keele: Keele University, The Sociological Review Monograph.

Brennan, J. and Little, B. (1996) *A Review of Work Based Learning in Higher Education.* London: Quality Support Centre/DfEE.

Cooke, A. (1998) 'Lifelong learning policy in Scotland' in R. Taylor and D. Watson (eds) *Lifelong Learning Policy in the UK.* Universities Association for Continuing Education, Occasional Paper 23, 38–45.

Dearing, R. (1997) *National Committee of Inquiry into Higher Education, Higher Education in the Learning Society: Summary Report.* London: HMSO.

Dearing, R. and Garrick, R. (1997) *Higher Education in the Learning Society: Report of the Scottish Committee to the National Committee of Inquiry into Higher Education.* London: HMSO.

DfEE, The Scottish Office, The Welsh Office (1995) *Lifelong Learning: A Consultation Document.* Sheffield: DfEE.

DfEE (1998) *The Learning Age: A Renaissance for a New Britain.* London: The Stationery Office.

Drummond, R.J. and Croll, J. C. (1983) 'Intrinsic and extrinsic motivation and attitudes towards professional continuing education: implications for the counselors'. *Journal of Employment Counseling 20,* 88–96.

Ennis, E. (1998) 'Doing a PQ programme: what happens next?' *Scottish PQ Network Bulletin 5,* 2–3.

Eraut, M. (1994) *Developing Professional Knowledge and Competence.* Brighton: Falmer Press.

Etzioni, A. (1967) *The Semi-Professions and their Organization.* London: Collier Macmillan.

Freidson, E. (1973) *The Professions and their Prospects.* London: Sage.

Gonczi, A. (1994) 'Competence based assessment in the professions in Australia'. *Assessment in Education 1,* 1, 27–44.

Hoggart, R., Stephens, M., Taylor, J. and Smethurst, R. (1982) 'Continuing education within universities and polytechnics'. In D. Bligh (ed) *Professionalism and Flexibility in Learning.* Guildford: SRHE.

Hoyle, E. (1974) 'Professionability, professionalism and control in teaching'. *London Educational Review 3,* 2, 13–19.

Hughes, C. and Tight, M. (1995) 'The myth of the learning society'. *British Journal of Educational Studies 43,* 3, 290–304.

Kennedy, H. (1997) *Learning Works: Widening Participation in Further Education.* Coventry: Further Education Funding Council.

Kent, R. (1997) *Children's Safeguards Review*. Edinburgh: Social Work Services Inspectorate for Scotland.

Kolb, D. (1984) *Experiential Learning: Experience as the Source of Learning and Development*. Englewood Cliffs, NJ: Prentice Hall.

Larson, C.E. and LaFasto, F.M. (1989) *Teamwork: What Must Go Right/What Can Go Wrong*. London: Sage.

O'Hagan, K. (ed) (1996) *Competence in Social Work Practice. A Practical Guide for Professionals*. London: Jessica Kingsley Publishers.

McCombs, B.L. (1991) 'Unraveling motivation'. *Journal of Experimental Education 60*, 3–88.

Marton, F. (1982) *Towards a Phenomenology of Learning III: Experience and Conceptualisation, Vol 2*. Molndal: Goteborg University, Department of Education.

Marsh, P. and Triseliotis, J. (1996) *Ready to Practise? Social Workers and Probation Officers: Their Training and First Year in Work*. Aldershot: Avebury.

Peryer, A. and Peryer, D. (1997) *Human Resources for Personal Social Services*. London: CCETSW/Local Government Management Board.

Reeve, J. (1989) 'Intrinsic motivation and the acquisition and maintenance of four experiential states'. *Journal of Social Psychology 129*, 841–854.

Rinne, R. (1998) 'From labour to learn: the limits of labour society and the possibilities of learning society'. *International Journal of Lifelong Learning 17*, 2, 108–120.

Rogers, J. (1989) *Adults Learning*, 3rd edn. Milton Keynes: Open University Press.

Rushton, A. and Martyn, H. (1990) 'Two post-qualifying courses in social work: the views of course members and their employers'. *British Journal of Social Work 20*, 445–468.

Scottish Local Government Information Unit (1998) 'Bulletin'. May.

Scottish Network for Post Qualifying Social Work (1998) *Reflecting Competence; Examples of Submissions for the Post-Qualifying Award in Social Work (PQSW)*. Glasgow: Scottish Network for Post-Qualifying Social Work.

Scottish Office (1998a) *Opportunity Scotland: A Paper on Lifelong Learning*. Edinburgh: The Stationery Office.

Scottish Office (1998b) *Modernising Social Work Services. A Consultation Paper on Workforce Regulation and Education*. Edinburgh: Social Work Services Inspectorate

Seagraves, L., Osborne, M., Neal, P., Dockrell, R., Hartshorn, C. and Boyd, A. (1996) *Learning in Small Companies (LISC) Final Report*. Stirling: University of Stirling, Educational Policy and Development.

Taylor, B.J. (1998) 'Service needs and individual qualifications – training social workers for the community care policy initiative and post-qualifying credits'. *Social Work Education 17*, 1, 77–93.

Todd, F. (ed) (1987) *Planning Continuing Professional Development*. London: Croom Helm.

Utting, W.B. (1997) *People Like Us: The Report of the Review of Safeguards for Children Living Away from Home*. London: The Stationery Office.

Walsh, L. and Woodward, P. (1989) *Continuing Professional Development; towards a National Strategy. (The Pickup Report.)* London: HMSO.

Watkins, J., Drury, L. and Preddy, D., (1992) *From Evolution to Revolution: the Pressures on Professional Life in the 1990s*. Bristol: University of Bristol.

Contributors

Cathy Aymer is Director of Professional Studies in the department of social work at the University of Brunel. She has been involved in anti-racist and anti-discriminatory practice teaching for many years, both on social work courses and in organizations. Her particular research interests are in the experiences of black students in higher education and black professionals in white welfare organizations.

Norma Baldwin is Professor of Child Care and Protection at the University of Dundee. She has been involved in the development of continuing education in social work and social care from the time of the first proposals in CCETSW for a Post-Qualifying Framework and was formerly the Director of Post-Qualifying Studies in Social Work at the University of Warwick.

Juliet Cheetham was a probation officer before becoming a lecturer in applied social studies at the University of Oxford. In 1986 she became the first director of the Social Work Research Centre at the University of Stirling. She was the vice chair of the Social Policy and Social Work panel for the Higher Education Funding Council 1996 Research Assessment Exercise. She is now the Social Work Commissioner for the Mental Welfare Commission for Scotland and Professor Emeritus at the University of Stirling.

Judith Croton is a Principal Advisor to CCETSW for post-qualifying education and training. Her responsibilities are the development of regulations and guidance relating all aspects of social work qualifications at PQ level. Her research interest is in the integration of higher education and work-based learning, development routes for continuing professional development for all social workers. She is a qualified social worker and worked for twenty years in local government in London before joining CCETSW. The positions she held include social work manager, mental health trainer and head of social services training. Mental health remains a main interest.

Mark Doel is Professor of Social Work and Head of the School of Social Work and RNIB Rehabilitation Studies at the University of Central England in Birmingham. His experiences in social work practice, teaching, training and research have provided a wide variety of opportunities to learn about the teaching and learning of practice. His research and writing interests also include task-centred practice and groupwork. Recent publications include *The Essential Groupworker*.

Lena Dominelli is Professor of Social and Community Development and Director of the Centre for International Social and Community Development at the University of Southampton. She has been a practitioner, researcher and educator in the field of social work for over two decades. She has published extensively, including 17 books, her most recent of which are *Anti-Racist Social Work* (Second Edition, 1997) and *Social Work: Current Issues, Themes and Dilemmas* (1998) (with Adams and Payne) and *Community Approaches to Child Welfare: International Perspectives* (1999). Lena is also the current President of the International Association of Schools of Social Work.

Elaine Ennis is academic development officer in the Department of Social Work, University of Dundee and is also a teacher in the Child Care and Protection Studies Programme which delivers post-qualifying and advanced award level courses throughout Scotland.

Miriam Hastings is a writer and researcher. She has a doctorate in representation theory in literature and women's studies. She also works as an independent consultant and trainer in mental health, and as a part-time lecturer at Birkbeck College, University of London. She is a published novelist.

Elizabeth Kemp qualified as a social worker in 1978 at York University and practised in Yorkshire and East Sussex until 1989. She is now a senior lecturer at University College Chichester and programme co-ordinator for the West Sussex Diploma in Social Work. Her other roles include that of a CCETSW approved external assessor for DipSW. Correspondence would be welcome at e.kemp@chihe.ac.uk.

Helena Low has been an education officer with the English National Board for Nursing, Midwifery and Health Visiting since 1991, with a specialist remit for community/primary healthcare nurse education. As a practitioner, manager and teacher she has always been committed to interprofessional and interagency working in order to enhance patient care. In her present role she takes a lead in the Board's collaborative work within other statutory and professional bodies. This has included a number of successful joint initiatives and publications with CCETSW.

Rachel Pierce was a child care officer and social researcher before moving into social work education and training. She spent 15 years at the North London Polytechnic, latterly as principal lecturer and course tutor of a four year Hons. Applied Social Studies Degree, with options in social work and social research and planning. In 1987 she became CCETSW Assistant Director (Education and Training). On her retirement in 1995 she was made a fellow of the Joint University Council and an honorary doctor of the University of Central England at Birmingham.

Michael Preston-Shoot is Professor of Social Work and Social Care at Liverpool John Moores University. He has written widely in the area of social work law. His most recent books are a second edition (with Suzy Braye) of *Practising Social Work Law* (Macmillan 1997) and *Acting Fairly* (CCETSW 1998). He has undertaken research and curriculum development work on teaching and assessing social work law, and is a member of the Social Work Law Research Group. His other major research interest is how community care law, policy and practice are experienced by service users and practitioners.

Cherry Rowlings is Professor of Social Work at the University of Stirling, having formerly worked at the University of Oxford, Keele and Bristol. A council member of CCETSW and vice chair of its Scottish Committee, her long-standing involvement in what might be termed the politics of social work education in the UK and internationally forms the basis of the chapter in this volume. She currently teaches on undergraduate and postgraduate routes to the DipSW and on MSc/Advanced Award programmes and has additional research interests in services to older people and community care. Recent publications include 'Social work and elder abuse: practitioner perspectives from Scotland' in J. Pritchard (ed) *Elder Abuse Work*.

Jenny Weinstein spent eighteen years as a social worker, trainer and manager in four local authorities. She joined CCETSW in 1989 where she took a lead role on the DipSW and the Practice Teaching Award. She became actively involved in promoting interprofessional education through research, development and publications – the most recent of which is *Making a World of Difference: Developing Primary Care* edited with Kate Billingham and Margaret Flynn. Her interest in partnership working with service users took her into the voluntary sector in 1998, where she works as the Quality Assurance Manager for Jewish Care.

Jeremy Weinstein is course director for the MSc in Social Work and the MSc in Psychotherapy at South Bank University. He has a part-time private practice as a Gestalt psychotherapist working with individuals and organizations. His research and publishing interests are in counselling and bereavement.

Julie Wilkes leads a team of advisers responsible for the regulation of qualifying social work training in England. An experienced trainer, she has also taught systemic management at Kensington Consultation Centre. She is a member of the Discourse and Rhetoric Group at Loughborough University, where she is completing a PhD on the subject of fairness at work. Her previous publications include 'The social construction of a caring career' (1994) in C. Burck and B. Speed (eds) *Gender, Power and Relationships*.

Subject Index

Author Index